P6-CEJ-467

D0015479

Also by Howard Gardner

The Quest for Mind
The Arts and Human Development
The Shattered Mind
Developmental Psychology
Artful Scribbles
Art, Mind, and Brain
Frames of Mind
The Mind's New Science
To Open Minds
The Unschooled Mind
Multiple Intelligences: The Theory in Practice
Creating Minds
Leading Minds
Intelligence: Multiple Perspectives
(with Mindy Kornhaber and Warren Wake)
Extraordinary Minds

The Disciplined Mind

What All Students Should Understand

HOWARD GARDNER

Simon & Schuster

SIMON & SCHUSTER
Rockefeller Center
1230 Avenue of the Americas
New York, NY 10020

Copyright © 1999 by Howard Gardner
All rights reserved, including the right of
reproduction in whole or in part in any form.

SIMON & SCHUSTER and colophon are registered
trademarks of Simon & Schuster Inc.

Designed by DEIRDRE C. AMTHOR

Manufactured in the United States of America

3 5 7 9 10 8 6 4 2

Library of Congress Cataloging-in-Publication Data
Gardner, Howard.
The disciplined mind / Howard Gardner.
p. cm.
Includes bibliographical references (p .) and index.
1. Education—Philosophy.   2. Learning, Psychology of.
3. Comprehension.   4. Multiple intelligences.   I. Title.
LB885.G37W45   1999
370'.1—dc21   98-43544
CIP

ISBN 0-684-84324-2

The "Trio" from *The Marriage of Figaro* is reprinted
with permission from Dover Publications, Inc.

Acknowledgments

In *The Disciplined Mind,* I seek to synthesize over thirty years of research in the cognitive and biological sciences, and over fifteen years of involvement in precollegiate education. A great many individuals have contributed to my thinking, and several institutions have generously supported my research; there is, alas, no way in which I can single each out for the thanks that are due.

I do want to express my appreciation to the several colleagues and friends who have read and commented substantively on earlier drafts of this manuscript: Thomas Armstrong, Veronica Boix-Mansilla, Patricia Bolanos, Mihaly Csikszentmihalyi, William Damon, Patricia Graham, Thomas Hatch, Fred Hills, Thomas Hoerr, George Klein, Mindy Kornhaber, Mara Krechevsky, Tanya Luhrmann, Joanna Martin, Arthur Powell, Barbara Powell, Carlina Rinaldi, Eric Schaps, Theodore Sizer, Margot Strom, Frank Sulloway, Ike Williams, Ellen Winner. I am also indebted to my two hardworking and dedicated assistants, Lisa Bromer and Alex Chisholm (Alex skillfully prepared the Mozart score reproduced as an appendix). Thanks to Jolanta Benal, the talented copy editor at Simon & Schuster. I want to thank, as well, the members of the Pew Forum on Educational Reform. Finally, I want to express appreciation to the many colleagues who have worked with me in the ATLAS Communities Project and the ATLAS Seminar; and to the New American Schools organization and the MacArthur, Rockefeller, and Spencer Foundations, which have supported the ATLAS enterprise. Without our seven years of work and discussion, I could not have written this book.

Cambridge, Massachusetts
January, 1999

To my parents, Hilde and Ralph Gardner

my wife, Ellen Winner

my children, Kerith, Jay, Andrew, and Benjamin

and the generations to come

Contents

The Disciplined Mind

CHAPTER 1
A Personal Introduction: An Education for All Human Beings

From the Parochial to the Universal

As a psychologist with a deep interest in education, I have been gratified by the growing concern about educational issues throughout the world. Whether I am traveling in the United States or visiting Europe, Latin America, or the Far East, I find a surprising consensus: the belief that the quality of a nation's educational system will be a chief—perhaps *the* chief—determinant of its success during the next century and beyond.

Yet I often feel frustrated as well. Everywhere, much discussion about education remains mired in the parochial. Frankly, I am tired of writings by educators that focus on the instrumental or the momentary: Should we distribute vouchers so that youngsters can attend private schools? What are the advantages of charter schools? Are teacher unions the problem? The solution? Should teaching degrees be granted at the college level, only in graduate school, or only for those trained "on site"? How much education should take place at the computer or over the Internet? Should we have local control, national standards, international comparisons? And I am equally weary of debates that array one educational philosophy against another—traditionalists versus progressives, proponents of phonics versus advocates of "whole language."

These discussions, while not unimportant, skirt the most fundamental question. They avoid consideration of the purposes of education—the reasons why every society should devote monetary and human resources to the education of its young persons. During my years of studying education, writing about education, and visiting hundreds of schools throughout the world, I have come to my own conclusions about this question. These conclusions are personal; in a sense, I am addressing this book to my own four children and their descendants. At the same time, however, I intend this book to be universal, to speak to individuals all over the world who care about education: indeed, as the title of this chapter states, my concern is the education of all human beings. Not that I think there is only one ideal education; that idea is naive. Still, I've come to believe that certain features ought to characterize good education—or, more properly, good *educations*—everywhere in the world.

An Uncluttered Perspective:
The True, the Beautiful, and the Good

I want everyone to focus on the content of an education—the meat and potatoes: on how that content should be presented, mastered, put to use, and passed along to others. Specifically, I believe that three very important concerns should animate education; these concerns have names and histories that extend far back into the past. There is the realm of *truth*—and its underside, what is false or indeterminable. There is the realm of *beauty*—and its absence in experiences or objects that are ugly or kitschy. And there is the realm of *morality*—what we consider to be good, and what we consider to be evil.

To make clearer what I include in these realms, let me mention three topics that I would like individuals to understand in their fullness. My example in the realm of truth is the theory of evolution, as first articulated by Charles Darwin and as elaborated upon by other scientists over the last one hundred and fifty years. This is an important area of science, with particular significance for a developmental psychologist like me. Unless one has some understanding of the key notions of species, variation, natural selection, adaptation, and the like (and how these have been discovered), unless one appreciates the perennial struggle among individuals (and populations) for survival in a particular ecological niche, one cannot understand the living world of which we are a part.

The processes of evolution are fascinating in their own right, as countless budding scientists have discovered. But such understanding has also become necessary if one is to participate meaningfully in contemporary society. Absent a grasp of evolution, we cannot think systematically about a whole range of topics that affect human beings today: the merits and perils of cloning; the advisability of genetic counseling, gene therapy, and various forms of eugenics; assertions that "lifelike entities" have been created computationally and that these entities evolve in a manner similar to organic matter; claims that human behavior is best explained by sociobiology or evolutionary psychology.*

As my example in the realm of beauty, I select the music of Mozart: to be specific, his opera *The Marriage of Figaro*. This choice begins in the personal. I love classical music, and in particular the works of Mozart; for me, at least, they represent the pinnacle of beauty fashioned by human beings. I believe that everyone ought to gain an understanding of rich works like *Figaro*—their intricate artistic languages, their portrayals of credible characters with deeply felt human emotions, their evocation of the sweep of an era.

Again, such understanding is its own reward; millions of people all over the globe have been enriched by listening to Mozart or immersing themselves in other artistic masterpieces from diverse cultures. Moreover, a sophisticated grasp of Mozart's achievement can be brought to bear on unfamiliar works of art and craft and perhaps also inspire beautiful new creations. And such understanding also proves relevant to the decisions that we make as citizens: which arts, artists, and other creative individuals to support; how to support them; how best to encourage new works; whether there are artistic creations that ought to be censored or regulated, and, if so, by whom; whether the arts should be taught in school, after school, or not at all.

Finally, as my example in the realm of morality, I would like individuals to understand the sequence of events known as the Holocaust: the systematic killing of the Jews and certain other groups by the Nazis and others, before and especially during the Second World War. This event has personal significance, since my family came from Germany and several of its members were victims of the Holocaust. But every human being needs to understand what it is that human beings are capable of doing, sometimes in secret, sometimes with pride. And if the Holocaust is mostly an account of unprecedented human evil, there are scattered incidents of goodness and heroism even in that grim chapter.

*Specific references are found at the end of this book.

Like the study of science and art, accounts of historical events can be intrinsically fascinating. But they have a wider significance. I believe that people are better able to chart their life course and make life decisions when they know how others have dealt with pressures and dilemmas—historically, contemporaneously, and in works of art. And only equipped with such understanding can we participate knowledgeably in contemporary discussions (and decisions) about the culpability of various individuals and countries in the Second World War. Only with such understanding can we ponder the responsibility of human beings everywhere to counter current efforts at genocide in Rwanda and the former Yugoslavia and to bring the perpetrators to justice.

The understanding of striking examples of truth, beauty, and goodness is sufficiently meaningful for human beings that it can be justified in its own right. At the same time, however, such an understanding is also necessary for productive citizenship. The ways of thinking—the disciplines—that have developed over the centuries represent our best approach to almost any topic. Without such understanding, people cannot participate fully in the world in which they—*we*—live.

One might think that at least some understanding of these well-known topics is widespread. It is therefore sobering to discover that the theory of evolution is considered to be false by one out of every two Americans, and even by 20 percent of science educators. According to the noted scientist Carl Sagan, only 9 percent of Americans accept that humans have evolved slowly from more ancient beings without any divine intervention. As for the Holocaust, about one-third of all Swedish high school students believe that the Holocaust did not take place. Comparable skepticism (if not outright denial) is expressed by various American groups; 20 percent of Americans admit that they do not know what happened in the Holocaust and 70 percent wish that they were better informed about it. Robert Simon, who teaches philosophy at Hamilton College, reports that anywhere from 10 to 20 percent of his American students cannot bring themselves to say that the Nazi attempt at genocide was wrong.

It is not difficult to anticipate a response to this trio of topics: How can one call this an education for all human beings? It is time-bound (the modern era); it is place-bound (Western Europe and places influenced by it); and it is even linked to the author's personal concerns.

"Right and not right," as they say. I would indeed be pleased if all human beings became deeply immersed in the themes of evolution, Mozart, and the Holocaust. There are worse ways to enlarge one's universe. *But—note well—these choices are not privileged, and certainly not uniquely so.* Within the West, there are numerous other scientific theories of importance (Newtonian mechanics and plate tectonics, to name just two examples); other singular artistic achievements (the works of Michelangelo or Rembrandt, Shakespeare or George Eliot); other morally tinged historical events (the French and Soviet revolutions; the American struggle over slavery). And within other cultural traditions, there are abundant examples of the true (these would include folk theories about healing or traditional Chinese medicine); the beautiful (Japanese ink and brush painting; African drum music); and good and evil (the precepts of Jainism, the stories of Pol Pot and Mao's Cultural Revolution; the generosity of bodhisattvas).

I am not contending, then, that everyone needs to be able to explain what constitutes a species or to discern the development of melodies and the intermingling romances in a work like *Figaro,* or to analyze the reasons why so many Germans were complicitous in the Holocaust. Rather, what I claim is that "an education for all human beings" needs to explore in some depth a set of key human achievements captured in the venerable phrase "the true, the beautiful, and the good."

Another possible objection. Aren't the categories "true," "beautiful," and "good" themselves time- and culture-bound? Again, this is a valid point, but not a decisive one. The articulated concepts of "truth," "beauty," and "goodness" reflect a philosophically oriented culture; indeed, our first records of explicit discussion of these virtues are the dialogues recorded by Plato in Greece nearly 2500 years ago. Other cultures have developed similar notions, although how they parse the three domains may well differ. However, the beliefs and practices of cultures—the beliefs and practices that they value, transmit, punish, or prohibit—reveal that each culture harbors specific views of how the world is and how it should (and should not) be. And these views embody implicit senses of truth, beauty, and morality.

There is another, more important reason for my endeavor. In the end, education has to do with fashioning certain kinds of individuals—the kinds of persons I (and others) desire the young of the world to become. I crave human beings who understand the world, who gain sustenance from such understanding, and who want—ardently, perennially—to alter it for the better. Such citizens can only come into existence if students learn to understand the world as it has been portrayed by those who have studied it most carefully and lived in it most thoughtfully; if they become familiar with the range—the summits, the valleys, the straight and meandering paths—of what other humans have achieved; and if they learn always to monitor their own lives in terms of human possibilities, including ones that have not been anticipated before. No doubt there are various routes to this wisdom; in this book, I lay out my preferred path.

I've selected my three textbook examples because they are familiar to me, and because they will be familiar to many readers. But I must repeat: there is nothing sacrosanct about this trio. Another book, on another day, could focus upon relativity, revolutions, and the ragas of southern India. And I would devour such a book.

About This Book

Though this is a personal book, I would like to think that it is not an idiosyncratic one. It is based on my analyses of educational efforts in the past, and, equally, on what the sciences have learned about the human mind and human culture. In the next two chapters, I survey that past and identify new pressures on education today. Indeed, never has the world changed more quickly. We need an education that is deeply rooted in two apparently contrasting but actually complementary considerations: what is known about the human condition, in its timeless aspects; and what is known about the pressures, challenges, and opportunities of the contemporary (and the coming) scene. Without this double anchoring, we are doomed to an education that is dated, partial, naive, and inadequate.

Following this look at the timeless and time-bound aspects of education, I move to an account of what we now know (from recent scientific and humanistic research) about the human mind, the human brain, and human cultures. Each of these vantage points is crucial and irreducible. Studies of the mind/brain (reviewed in chapter 4) tell us about how human beings come to know and understand. For example, they reveal the different ways in which individuals acquire knowledge and represent that knowledge mentally; and such researches indicate the difficulties of changing early understandings of the world, even as they suggest possible approaches for effecting needed transformations. Studies of human cultures (reviewed in chapter 5) convey the array of educational routes that human beings have followed. In some societies, education is prescribed in the finest detail, while in others, students are encouraged to "construct" knowledge for themselves or in tandem with a group of peers.

Jointly considered, the mind/brain and the spectrum of human cultures define both the possibilities for education and the constraints on it. Alone, the topic of education refutes the naive opposition between nature and nurture. An education for all human beings needs to be constructed upon these foundations, even as it must incorporate the remarkable knowledge that has been achieved in this century.

In the latter half of the book, I turn directly to issues of education in and outside of classrooms. Much has been established about the difficulty of achieving deep understanding in the classroom; and much has been learned recently about which educational practices are likely to succeed in cultivating such understanding. It is timely to review these findings and to craft an education that builds upon the most powerful insights.

Yet it is often frustrating to read about effective education in the abstract. Examples are at a premium. As my primary illustrations, I revisit the three areas of study that I've already introduced. I show how, building upon new insights, one might craft an education that yields deep understanding of questions and issues as important as evolution, Mozart, and the Holocaust: an understanding that is worth achieving in its own right, and that permits meaningful participation in today's (and tomorrow's) world.

My survey of these three topics represents a sustained effort to bring together the two most powerful ideas with which I have worked. Specifically, I draw on findings about *the attainment of understanding* and findings about the *multiple intelligences* of human beings. I contend that educators can reach many more students, and affect them much more deeply, by activating the multiple intelligences of their students, in ways spelled out in chapters 7, 8, and 9.

In the final pages of this book, I confront the difficult question of how to achieve, on a large scale, the kind of education that I would like for all. I draw on certain promising educational experiments in which I and

others have been involved in recent years. Clearly, I have my own preferred educational approach; this book stands, in a sense, as a brief in
favor of that regimen, as well as a guide to how it might be realized.

At the same time, because of the huge differences in value systems
found across groups and cultures, I doubt that it will ever be possible to
develop one ideal form of education and to implement it throughout the
world. Perhaps that is just as well; a world with a single educational system—or, for that matter, a single culture—might be a dull place. It
seems far more feasible to design a limited number of powerful
approaches, each of which can meet the needs and desires of a significant
portion of the world's population. Accordingly, I describe how one
might develop six distinct educational pathways, including the one I prefer, each with its own set of standards. And finally, I return to the indispensable issue of values: which educational values we cherish, and how
to make sure that a good education is also a "humane education" for all
human beings.

Signposts

That, in short, is what this book is about. Let me now erect a few sign-
posts that signal my beliefs—or, to adopt an even more basic metaphor,
let me lay my educational cards on the table.

First, education consists of more than school. Much of what I write
about concerns what does—or should—occur in classrooms. But education took place long before there were formal institutions called
schools; and today, other institutions—for example, the media—vie
with schools in their educational scope and power.

Relatedly, discussion of education has often been restricted to the
cognitive realm, even to specific disciplines. My own scholarly and
applied work has often been viewed as being restricted in this way. Yet I
see education as a far broader endeavor, involving motivation, emotions,
and social and moral practices and values. Unless these facets of the person are incorporated into daily practice, education is likely to be ineffective—or, worse, to yield individuals who clash with our notions of
humanity.

Much of education occurs implicitly rather than explicitly. One can
certainly mount specific courses in how to think, how to act, how to

behave morally. Some didactic lessons are appropriate. Yet we humans are the kinds of animals who learn chiefly by observing others—what they value, what they spurn, how they conduct themselves from day to day, and, especially, what they do when they believe that no one is looking. Continually, I will call for schools—more properly, school *communities*—that embody certain values, and for teachers who exhibit certain virtues. Ditto with respect to the media, the family, and other influential educational institutions.

I turn next to labels. Much of what I write about can be identified with the educational tradition of John Dewey—with what has been called progressive or neo-progressive education. I reject the baggage that has (inappropriately, I believe) come to be associated with this label. One can be progressive while also espousing traditional educational goals and calling for the highest standards of work, achievement, and behavior. In the words of Dewey himself: "The organized subject matter of the adult and the specialist . . . represents the goal toward which education should continuously move."

What about the canon? Given my examples of evolution, Mozart, and the Holocaust, it may seem as if I have taken up the cause of Western thought, or even championed the controversial legacy of the Dead White Male. I am indeed dedicated to in-depth study of the most important human achievements, topics, and dilemmas. I think that everybody should have heroes and that we can learn even from those figures who, like all heroes, are flawed. But unlike those who define an a priori canon, I believe that decisions about what is important are best left to a specific educational community; that all such decisions are tentative at best; and that they should be subject to constant negotiation and reconsideration.

To put it in the terms of my endeavor, I do not believe in *singular or incontrovertible* truth, beauty, or morality. Every time period, every culture will have its own provisional favorites and tentative lists. We should begin with an exploration of the ideals of our own community, and we should also become acquainted with the ideals of other communities. We may not endorse the aesthetics of postmodernism or the morality of fundamentalist Islam or the truths of the Vatican Council. But we live in a world where these preferences exist, and it is necessary and proper for us to learn to live with them—and for them to learn to live with us.

It should be evident that I believe even less in "core knowledge" or "cultural literacy"; not only is this an idle pursuit, but it conveys a view of learning that is at best superficial and at worst anti-intellectual. If this book is a sustained dialectic—read "disagreement"—with any contemporary educational thinker, that thinker is the noted literary analyst and educator E. D. Hirsch. Hirsch calls for a sequenced K–12 curriculum in which students cover a large number of specified topics and concepts for each year of school. To be sure, I cherish individuals who are familiar with their own and other cultures, but such literacy should come as a result of probing important issues and learning how to think about them in a disciplined way—not as a consequence of mastering fifty or five hundred predetermined topics each year.

NO

On my educational landscape, questions are more important than answers; knowledge and, more important, understanding should evolve from the constant probing of such questions. It's not because I know for certain what the true and the beautiful and the good are that I call for their study. In fact, I distrust people who claim that they *know* what is true, beautiful, or good. I organize my presentation around these topics because they motivate individuals to learn about and understand their world, and because, frankly, I reject a world in which individuals cease to pursue these essential questions just because they do not permit unequivocal resolution.

No one likes jargon, especially other people's jargon, and few bodies of professional lingo are less beloved than the argot of educators. I try to keep "ed talk" to a minimum and to introduce and illustrate terms when I use them. Still, the study of education is itself a discipline; it would be foolish to ignore its insights, disingenuous to censor its vocabulary. And so, with a tinge of regret, I will on occasion speak about educational goals (why we want/need to educate); curriculum (the topics and contents that one chooses to emphasize); disciplines (which subjects and, more critically, which ways of thinking are important to inculcate); pedagogy (the strategies, tactics, and "moves" made by those formally charged with responsibility for education); and assessment (the means, formal and informal, by which educators and the wider community establish what has and has not been mastered by the "student body").

A final concern. If readers know my work at all, they are likely to be familiar with my claim that human beings have at least eight separate forms of intelligence, and that we differ from one another in our "profiles of intelligence." Others, as well as my own associates, have devoted a great deal of effort to investigating the educational implications of this theory, and I'll touch on some of that work later on.

My psychological work on multiple intelligences has had an unanticipated consequence. This is the assumption on the part of some critics that I am unsympathetic to a rigorous education, and that I eschew high standards. I suppose that is because the idea of multiple intelligences is rightly seen as a critique of the notion of a single intelligence, and of a school curriculum targeted exclusively to linguistic and logical capacities and concerns. Also, my critique of traditional standardized testing, with its almost total emphasis on linguistic and logical skills, has also led some to conclude that I am uncomfortable with assessment more generally.

A belief in multiple intelligences, however, is in no sense a statement about standards, rigor, or expectations, and it is certainly not a rejection of these desiderata. On the contrary: I am a demon for high standards and demanding expectations. I do not always succeed in my own life and work, but it is not for lack of trying. It pains me to see my work aligned (I could have written "maligned") with that of individuals who are apologists for low standards, low expectations, "anything goes."

Perhaps there is little that I can do to correct such a misrepresentation. But I can state, as emphatically as I know how, that an education for all human beings is an education that demands much from all of us—teachers as well as students, societies as well as individuals, and (if I may) readers as well as writers. Moreover, an education for all human beings cannot succeed unless we have ways of ascertaining what has been understood and what has been mildly or fatally misconstrued. I envision a world citizenry that is highly literate, disciplined, capable of thinking critically and creatively, knowledgeable about a range of cultures, able to participate actively in discussions about new discoveries and choices, willing to take risks for what it believes in.

This statement of values may confound both friends and foes. "Progressives" may fear that, in my talk about truth and standards, I have left their fold. "Traditionalists" may welcome these "confessions of middle age" but will continue to quarrel with my focus on individualized education and my resistance to a fixed canon. I hope that this book will stimulate partisans of both stripes to examine and reexamine their unexamined assumptions.

So far as I know (this is a surmise about truth), we only come to this planet once (at least in a precloning era). Let us make as much of our brief appearance as we can. I hope that most of us will use this opportunity positively, building on what has been established in our culture about the true, the beautiful, and the good. I believe that the educations for understanding described here can yield rewards for the individual as well as for the communities in which we must live together.

CHAPTER 2
Educational Constants

An Educational Montage:
The Transmission of Roles and Values

Let's say that, as a television director, you were asked to prepare a montage of education over the course of human history. You would need to consider a stunning variety of settings and an astonishing array of "subjects" and "practices," some still available for filming, others in need of re-creation or dramatization. You might begin with early humans as they proceed on a hunt across the savannah; the young boys (perhaps strapped across their fathers' backs) are watching closely as their fathers hunt. Then these boys help carry, divide, and share the game, while the young girls watch from afar and then aid their mothers in cleaning, cooking, and serving the meat. Perhaps that evening, the children gather around a fire as their elders relate heroic stories about the gods, or cautionary tales about perilous fires, pernicious villains, and predatory neighbors. You might then pan to an agricultural setting. There, youngsters awake at the crack of dawn to help their elders tend to the animals and plant, till, and harvest the main foodstuffs; later in the day (or the year) individuals of different ages participate in rituals or carve amulets designed to ensure favorable weather, abundant crops, or long lives for their relatives and allies.

Initially, one may think of these examples as remote, exotic. But one can discern reverberations of such long-standing practices in the lives of children today. Our televised survey might include children playing hunting games with elders or peers; accompanying a parent to work; helping with repairs, cooking a family meal, or shopping with a parent; watching a movie or a live performance in the company of their family;

assuming roles in a religious ceremony or collaborating in the creation of works of art. While little may be said overtly on these occasions, the practices of the adults often signal clear beliefs about how the world is and how it should be. And these beliefs include notions about truth, beauty, and goodness.

Indeed, the two major goals of education across time and space could be called the modeling of adult roles and the transmission of cultural values. Every society must ensure that the most important adult roles—leader, teacher, parent, priest—are properly filled by members of the next generation. Whether the culture depends upon hunters, preparers of food, sailors, weavers, priests, lawyers, merchants, or computer programmers, it is important that a certain proportion of youngsters be able to perform these roles skillfully and, eventually, transmit their key features to succeeding generations. By the same token, every society must ensure that its most central values—valor or peacefulness; kindness or toughness; pluralism or uniformity—are passed on successfully to those who will themselves one day transmit them.

In the past, both roles and values have evolved very slowly. In many societies, means of transmission scarcely changed over the centuries. Nowadays, values change more rapidly, but still at a measured pace. Roles, on the other hand, are changing considerably from one generation (or even decade) to the next, placing considerable pressure on the institutions of education.

Formal Schooling:
Mastering Notations and Disciplines
in a Remote Setting

Of course, nowadays we associate education primarily with formal school settings rather than with informal observation or work at home, in the fields, or at the fireside. Formal instruction comes about chiefly under specific circumstances. A procedure—such as sailing a craft over long distances in turbulent waters—may be too complex to be apprehended simply by observing. A notational system—such as those that convey verbal propositions, numerical relations, or geographical loci—may require careful study over sustained periods of time. A body of lore—often religious or legal lore—may need to be studied, committed to memory, drawn upon when appropriate, and transmitted eventually to the next generation. And finally, there are likely to be formal academic disciplines that reflect the culture's procedures for confronting questions about the physical, biological, and personal worlds.

Around the world, schools have gradually evolved to serve such functions. There are "bush schools" in Africa, where children learn about the past of their tribe. There are informal compounds in the South Seas where youngsters memorize information about the craft of sailing, as well as the names and locations of the hundreds of islands around which they will have to navigate. In communities with a written religious text, whether in Greek, Hebrew, Latin, Arabic, or Sanskrit—schools spring up so that students can learn to decode the sacred text, write out portions, and, perhaps, adapt the written language for secular purposes. And in societies where formal academic disciplines have evolved, schools transmit at least the rudiments to those who will need to use those disciplines at work or in their roles as citizens.

These institutions differ from informal educational settings in one crucial feature: they transmit material in a setting that is typically remote from where it will ultimately be used (for example, sailing in the South Seas, or arguing in the law courts, or handling commerce in the marketplace). To use the current jargon, school is largely a "decontextualized" setting. Indeed, as our hypothetical television show might document, schoolrooms around the world resemble one another. For while education all over the world has long featured the transmission of roles and values in appropriate settings, "decontextualized schools" have been devised primarily for two more specific goals: the *acquisition of literacy with notations* and *the mastery of disciplines.*

Humans have used notation to record numerical, calendrical, and religious events for tens of thousands of years. But it is only in the last few thousand years that more sophisticated notational systems have come into widespread use. If individuals are to be able to read, write, and carry out calculations of any complexity, they must spend several years mastering the elements of these literate systems and learning how to use them fluently and flexibly.

While some individuals in each society may experience particular difficulty in mastering the literacies, most societies have devised pedagogical systems that can effectively transmit "the three Rs" to their young people. Continuing illiteracy in the world is due not to ignorance about how to teach reading, 'riting, and 'rithmetic, but rather to the failure to devote adequate resources to these tasks. In China and Cuba, where (as it happens, under Communist regimes) literacy has become a high priority, it has proved possible to raise the entire population's level of literacy within a few decades.

The use of schools to inculcate the disciplines entails more complex considerations. It is important that the history of the group, its religious and moral precepts, and its technical knowledge (about hunting or cooking, weaving or sailing, selling wares or settling disputes) be passed on to succeeding generations. Sometimes such transmission can be done informally, through demonstrations and casual talk "on the scene"; sometimes, as in the case of cultures that have lengthy oral epics in verse, a more formal network of lore must be committed to memory; and, in more recent times, disciplines have arisen in which formal knowledge is preserved in written and illustrated texts. Within religious settings, these texts are often committed to memory and recited ritualistically; in secular settings, it is only necessary that the student be able to read the text, derive meanings therefrom, and draw on this knowledge when needed (at least, for the test; ideally, for life beyond school, as well).

Single texts can be memorized; a single discipline can, perhaps, be learned through an informal apprenticeship. But where familiarity with a family of literacies and disciplines is at a premium, the formal school comes into its full glory. Mere "literacy in decoding" does not suffice. The capacities to read a variety of texts fluently, to be able to write down one's own summary and reactions, to calculate rapidly and accurately, and to use numerical systems for measurement or experiment— all of these require more than a year or two of informal study. (To be sure, a few talented individuals have managed to master these pursuits without much formal guidance; and in milieus where education was available chiefly to boys, girls have traditionally had to learn to read and write surreptitiously or with help from a caring relative.)

Our conception of school has been closely linked to the existence of formal written systems, whose mastery was deemed necessary for religious, economic, and social purposes. And as schooling has extended beyond the "basic" primary years, formal education has become equally associated with the mastery of scholarly disciplines ranging from history to theology to science. We have come to assume that mature adults must be versed in several disciplines—able not only to pass written examinations but also to use these disciplines' ways of thinking in their vocations and as citizens.

It would be misleading, however, to think of traditional educational institutions as merely, or even primarily, instrumental in a narrow sense. To do so would be to commit the sin of presentism—reading back into earlier institutions our current beliefs (or concerns). Rather, such institutions have traditionally foregrounded clear notions of what one should believe, what one should value, and how one should live.

Consider, for example, the apprenticeship. An individual enters into a formalized relationship with a specific master and is required to pass through a set of stages before he himself achieves the status of master. In contrast to school, apprenticeship does not merely consist of spending a few hours each day with the master; rather, the apprentice commits himself fully to a single dominant authority figure, signing a contract with the master and even living in his home. He is drawn fully into the hour-to-hour life of the master and his family. Through these contacts, he comes to absorb an entire worldview—what the master believes to be true about the world, what standards a work must meet if the master is to consider it acceptable, and what behaviors are desired, tolerated, and strictly proscribed in and outside the workplace.

Or consider the traditional religious school. Typically, the master of the school is a man, often unmarried, who has been selected by the community in part on the basis of his presumed moral virtues, and who is given considerable intellectual and ethical authority over the students. He is expected not only to pass on the culture's beliefs and traditions but also to embody them in his own being. Even as he has the power to discipline the students, he will be held accountable if his own behavior does not conform to communal standards.

The special nature of school is well conveyed by the rituals that accompany it. In Jewish tradition, for example, the boy's first day at the *cheder* is a joyous occasion. The whole family dresses up and accompanies the lad to school. He is served bread in the shape of letters that have been dipped into honey; the sweetness of learning is coded deeply into the youngster's limbic system.

Let me hasten to add that I am here discussing ideal situations. We know that some masters ruthlessly beat their charges, and some teachers blithely ignore their students' moral failings—and their own, for that matter. Such less-than-perfect realizations have not, however, challenged the fundamental, broad educational vision: a featuring of the true, the beautiful, and the good. This vision, like its intriguing variations, should be captured in my hypothetical educational montage.

A Virtue-Filled Education in the Disciplines

The delineation of these three virtues, and the extent to which they are distinguished from one another, differ significantly across cultures. Traditionally, the most important truths have been religious ones—the culture's beliefs about what human beings are, what place they occupy in the cosmos, how they relate to deities and other spiritual figures, and which divine forces determine one's fate. Even truths that may seem mundane—for example, the names and identities of particular individuals or species—are often tinged with totemic significance.

Gradually, as empirical discoveries are made, the number of truths increases, and their relation to religious orthodoxy may prove problematic. Divine theories of conception and birth, for example, may comport with daily experience and common sense; but then again, they may not. (What does one conclude, for example, when a child looks suspiciously like the farmer or the warrior in the next village?) Sometimes, religious and empirical truths exist side by side with little tension. Sometimes, however, one side in this struggle must make concessions.

The rise of the scholarly disciplines represents a long-standing effort to add to our knowledge of the world. The biological sciences tell us about the nature and processes of the living world; the physical sciences describe the material world and forces governing physical objects; the more recently initiated social sciences inform us about human nature, actions, motives, and possibilities. And—if less decisively than the scientific disciplines—the humanistic and artistic disciplines also furnish information and knowledge. They add significantly to our understandings of the varieties of beauty and morality; they familiarize us with the multifarious ways in which individuals over time and space have conceived of themselves, their worlds, their options, their fates.

There is also a convenient division of labor between these spheres. The sciences strive to discover patterns that obtain across objects, species, people; the arts and humanities dwell on the particularities of individual persons, works, and experiences. Clearly, as a scientist, Darwin wanted to understand the laws that govern all species; in contrast, those who immerse themselves in a single scene in a Mozart opera are reveling in the specifics of a character, a situation, a melody, a phrase, a pause. Historians of the Holocaust can be divided, informally, into those with a scientific cast of mind, who look for parallels with other genocides; and those of a humanistic persuasion, who explore the particular events that marked the Nazi Holocaust.

The relationship between the virtue of truth, on the one hand, and the virtues of beauty and goodness, on the other, is a vexed one. In modern secular society, we tend to see these as separate domains—loosely speaking, as science, art, and morality. Enlightenment and post-Enlightenment thinking has designated a separate, autonomous realm comprising reason, science, knowledge, and truth; aesthetics and morality are cleaved off or minimized as emotional, subjective, or particularistic; and the relationship between "goodness" and "beauty" is seen as problematic at best. Many (including those of contrasting political persuasions) see morality as the concern of the home and/or the church and seek to dissociate it altogether from the school. Religion, once seen as the final arbiter of truth, now cedes ascertainment of truth to the sciences, and takes the moral sphere as its central concern. And of course, some postmodern thinkers challenge whether such historically tainted terms as "true," "beautiful," or "good" are useful at all.

In times past, the links among these realms were not seen as complex. The ancient Greeks evolved a sense of the virtuous person, the individual who was fully developed. Such individuals cultivated knowledge; were courageous, loyal, just, physically strong and supple; and evinced a developed sense of beauty in matters of body and spirit. The purpose of education (*paideia*) was to ensure that as many individuals as possible achieved such rounded excellence.

In the Confucian view, which evolved around the same time, it was important that the youth become a gentleman: skilled in the arts—graphic, musical, military; loyal to the family and the state; humble, gracious, kind, just, and courteous in all company. Again, this ensemble of qualities could only come about through an ideal education, one that endured through life and that fostered continuing self-transformation. In Confucian society, beauty and goodness were seen as fused: the notion that an object or person might be beautiful and yet morally corrupt could not be countenanced.

To aid people in the process of becoming virtuous human beings, classical cultures looked to certain figures in literature, in history, and in contemporary life who embodied desirable features: the Homeric heroes, for example, or the person of Confucius himself. There were also negative examples—individuals notorious for their weakness, cowardness, arrogance, selfishness, or for a "tragic flaw." One could judge oneself with reference to these human (or superhuman) landmarks, and teachers could help students see how they approached these ideals, and how they fell short.

Classical cultures also looked to certain disciplines as particularly important in the formation of the whole person: thorough knowledge of certain key texts; the mastery of music and poetry; the training of the body (through gymnastics or riding or marksmanship, for example); and at least the rudiments of rhetoric, measuring, medicine, music, and astronomy. The curriculum, so to speak, may have differed across region and era; but the virtues embedded in its mastery remained remarkably constant through the Middle Ages in the West and the feudal era in China.

In attempting to understand these classical views of virtue, we must grasp one point. The ancients did not see the individual as a set of virtues that might or might not be connected. Rather, they took a determinedly *holistic* view of the person. One attempted to achieve excellence in all things, continued to strive throughout life, and sought, as well, to be an integrated and balanced human being. Either a person represented an integration of these intellectual, physical, ethical, and aesthetic features, or a person did not. The acquisition of knowledge and skill was seen as the necessary handmaiden for the attainment of moral virtue—the highest good—in the service of one's society.

Many of us today find it difficult to see the true, the good, and the beautiful as integral parts of the same ensemble. The spheres have become separate. Yet we can still be moved by the concluding lines of John Keats's "Ode on a Grecian Urn":

> *"Beauty is truth, truth beauty"—that is all*
> *Ye know on earth, and all ye need to know.*

Over time, then, educational institutions have had the primary task of conveying to a culture's young its current take on what is true (and not true); what is beautiful (and what lacks beauty); what is good (and what is evil). More controversial, nowadays, is the proper compass of education. Few would deny to the school the primary role in the inculcation of knowledge and truth. However, whether schools should be the principal communicators of beauty and goodness is much less certain. In cultures where considerable agreement can be found on these issues, their transmission is often ceded to the school; thus, in those European countries with relatively homogeneous populations, students study religion in school and also master formal curricula in the arts.

In American society, however, there are both constitutional and cultural reasons to bifurcate or trifurcate the educational obligation. Many individuals who readily send their children to community schools balk at the notion that those schools might impart religious or moral instruction; that, they contend, is the task of the home, the church, or the relevant institution elsewhere in the community. Organizations like the Boy and Girl Scouts, after-school clubs, and summer camps often step into this breach. And a growing number of Americans are so intent on transmitting their own *personal* value system that they spurn the public schools altogether, preferring religious or home schooling. These customized forms of education may include a direct rejection of the community's notions of truth. For example, some parents would challenge generally agreed-upon views about evolution (that it is the best explanation of human origins) in favor of the fundamentalist biblical version of human creation.

I perceive the situation this way. Once, it was relatively unproblematic to inculcate truth, beauty, and goodness through scholastic institutions. The consensus that made a "virtue-oriented" education possible has frayed throughout the world, and is especially tenuous in modern and postmodern societies like the United States. Some would conclude that the mission was forlorn anyway and that we are better off not looking to schools to transmit these ancient virtues. Here I undertake a sustained meditation on the opposite alternative: education must *continue* to confront truth (falsity), beauty (ugliness), and goodness (evil), in full awareness of the problematic facets of these categories and the disagreements across cultures and subcultures. The concerns may be ancient, but they must be perennially revisited and refashioned. And the academic disciplines remain the best way to pursue this mission.

Perennial Choices

So far, I have stressed the quartet of purposes that spans educational time and space: to transmit roles; to convey cultural values; to inculcate literacies; and to communicate certain disciplinary content and ways of

thinking. And I have emphasized the trio of virtues that have long animated education: a search within one's culture for what is true, what is
beautiful, and what is good. It is important to recognize, however, that
educational institutions have implemented these in various ways. Over
time, the pendulum has oscillated between a number of polarities:

• Between breadth and depth. In general, the push has been toward
covering as much information, conveying as many truths, as possible.
However, the advantage of pursuing a smaller number of topics in far
greater depth has also been recognized intermittently. The British-
American philosopher Alfred North Whitehead maintained: "Let the
main ideas which are introduced into a child's education be few and
important, and let them be thrown into every combination possible."
Today, in the United States we see the tension between educators like
Theodore Sizer, who argue that "less is more," and those like E. D.
Hirsch, who specify the considerable quantity of core knowledge
needed to be culturally literate. Everywhere from Italy to Singapore,
the same debate rages.

• Between accumulation and construction of knowledge. The majority
of schools over time have stressed the importance of accumulating a
great amount of knowledge that is prized by the society. The teacher lectures, the textbook is read, knowledge is absorbed, retained, spat back.
Indeed, medieval texts often devoted considerable attention to how to
memorize the material faithfully—how best to fill the mental vessel.

However, a rival "constructive" or "transformative" stance toward
knowledge dates back to classical times; it is exemplified in the collo-
quies of Socrates. Some educators call for the tackling of enigmatic
questions, and place a premium on struggling with alternative
responses, and on the student's effort to construct a personal conclusion
as the result of sober reconsiderations of the question.

• Between utilitarian outcomes and intellectual growth for its own
sake. There have long been pressures on educators to communicate the
utility of their teaching—if not for making more money, or "staying
ahead of the Japanese," at least for smoothing one's entry to heaven. But
an alternative tradition, associated particularly with English educators
like John Cardinal Newman and, anciently, with Cicero and Confucius,
argues for the importance of knowledge in its own right. In this view,
exploration of the world and development of the spirit are important
virtues, whether or not they lead to greater material goods. And, in a

perhaps surprising corollary, some (including some American corporate executives) maintain that the best preparation for a rapidly changing world remains a classical liberal education.

• Between uniform and individualized education. Most schools have been uniform, in the sense that they have taught and assessed all individuals in essentially the same way. This approach is embraced by East Asian societies, but also by centralized ones elsewhere, such as France and other Francophone communities. One argument in favor of uniform education is that it appears to be the most equitable variety.

Standing in opposition is an individualized perspective that highlights the vast differences among individuals' strengths, needs, goals. It makes sense to construct an education that takes into account these differences among persons. Perhaps, indeed, such an education is fairer; it does not valorize a certain kind of mind but rather meets each student where he or she is. Nor does such an education mandate that each person should come to resemble others in the community. In contrast to a Lockean view, that the individual should be shaped according to the designs of the community, this "Rousseauian" view would allow the natural inclinations of the human individual to unfold and endure.

• Between education by many private parties and education as a public responsibility. Historically, education was largely a private affair; the American common school, the first public school in the world, was conceived only in the middle of the nineteenth century. Mass public schooling is a distinctly twentieth-century phenomenon. Nowadays, public education is under attack from many quarters, both by those who favor independent nonprofit secular or sectarian schools and those who would like private enterprises (like corporations) to run schools. The alternative Jeffersonian perspective argues that education should be a public responsibility—paid for by the community, open to the community, and dedicated to the preservation and transmission of communal ideas and values. While this point of view seems to have originated in America, it is now accepted in most nations of the world, where, indeed, it often extends to the university level.

• Between an education that ignores or fuses disciplines and an education that stresses disciplinary mastery. Today, in many places, the disciplines are under fire. They are seen as old-fashioned, controlling, out of step with problem-based or theme-based learning, the province of "pale, stale males." Better to ignore or cordon off the disciplines, at least until students enter the university, and to allow students to follow their curiosity wherever it leads.

The contrasting point of view stresses that the disciplines represent human achievements of significance; in an evocative phrase, they "separate us from the barbarians." Much of what is crucial about truth, beauty, and morality has been encoded in one or more scholarly disciplines—particularly in how they frame and approach questions. Students should master the disciplines and crafts of their time even if, in the end, they detect the disciplines' shortcomings and succeed in surpassing or circumventing them.

• Between an education that minimizes or critiques assessment and one that is rooted in assessment and evaluation. Few students, teachers, or school administrators like tests; the general public, too, generally regards them as a necessary evil. Nowadays, there is considerable controversy about testing within and beyond the academy. Some feel that assessment is necessarily invidious; it should be done as little as possible, as carefully as possible, and as individually as possible.

A sharply contrasting perspective construes assessment as an essential and positive aspect of all learning. All skilled practitioners (including teachers) are involved perennially in assessment, and such experts find that assessment can often be a rewarding experience. For instance, they discover problems and are able to invent solutions on their own, and over time they can observe their own increasing skills. On this perspective, students ought from the first to be introduced to assessments; assessment ought to be a regular part of education; and as soon as possible, students should themselves join in the processes of (self-)assessment.

• Between relative, nuanced standards and high universal standards. Nowadays, no one dares oppose standards altogether—and perhaps that unanimity is a good thing. Politicians, businesspeople, parents, and educators vie to see who can invoke standards (and utter the words) most frequently and enthusiastically. But disparate strands exist within the standards camp. Those who worry about invidious standards or crippling loss of self-esteem ask that standards be spoken of softly, or that they be constantly adjusted in light of students' abilities and goals; or that "opportunities to learn" be equalized across schools and communities before any consequences (for teachers or students) are attached to the failure to meet standards.

A less flexible, more universalist approach stresses the need to enunciate clear, high standards for all students; to maintain focus on those standards; to make strenuous efforts to help students to master them; and to establish clear consequences when those standards have not been met. (There may, however, remain different views on how students should be prepared for and judged by these standards.)

• Between an education that showcases technology and an education that highlights the human dimension. Especially among businesspeople and politicians, technologies are often seen as saviors—as instrumentations that are finally going to professionalize education and make all our students eager—or, at least, effective—learners.

Many humanists fear technology. Already, they say, society is being dehumanized, and computers will simply hasten the demise of the human dimension. Education must build upon and preserve the precious bonds between human beings and the unique properties of the human spirit. Technology, say these present-day Luddites, must be kept firmly in its place.

With reference to each of these antinomies, I have a perspective or bias. To put it crisply, I favor depth over breadth, construction over accumulation, the pursuit of knowledge for its own sake over the obeisance to utility, an individualized over a uniform education, and an education that is public in character. I favor student-centered education over teacher-centered education, and I support an education attentive to developmental and individual differences. In all these dimensions, I might be seen as on the liberal or progressive side of the educational playing field.

At the same time, however, I also favor education that is rooted in the disciplines, that employs regular assessment, and that applies high standards to student work. In that sense, I align myself with the traditional or conservative camp.

Finally, with respect to technology, I find myself squarely in the middle: the new technologies hold tremendous promise, but they must be seen as means rather than ends. A pencil can be used to write Spencerian sonnets or to poke out someone's eye. A computer can deliver drill-and-kill curricula or stimulating scientific puzzles; it can educate, enlighten, entertain, and instruct, or it can dull perceptions, stimulate consumerism, and reinforce ethnic stereotypes. The Internet can help create vigorous and constructive communities; it can isolate

and desensitize individuals to their fellow human beings; it can even fo-
ment hatred.

On my better days, I hope that this modulated position will allow me
to make common cause with a wide range of educators and parents; at
hotter moments, I fear that the wrath of all may fall upon me. So be it.

•   •   •

Looking backward across time, and looking, with 360-degree perspective, across wide spaces, we can discern important universal aims of
education: transmission of values, modeling of roles, mastery of notations and disciplines. The identification of these aims is important; it is
foolish to disregard them as we look ahead to new times and new
worlds. However, it is equally myopic to ignore the many enormous
changes that are already patent in the world and that will unquestionably
affect education and schooling in the years to come.

CHAPTER 3
Education in the Future

An Understandably Conservative Institution

"Manners are always declining," quipped the Roman playwright Plautus. He could have added, "and the world is always changing . . . faster and faster." The vast changes under way in today's world are familiar to all. In every realm—the professions, business, other places of work, agriculture, transportation, the media of communication, the family, and the home—conditions are palpably different from those of a century or even a quarter-century ago. Downsizing, restructuring, reengineering are fixtures of today's commercial world; tomorrow's world will presumably feature these and other as yet unknown innovations.

It would be an exaggeration to maintain that schools have not changed in a hundred years. Both in the United States and abroad, there are new topics (such as ecology), new tools (personal computers, VCRs), and at least some new practices—universal kindergarten, special education for those with learning problems, efforts to "mainstream" students who have physical or emotional problems. Still, apart from a few relatively superficial changes, human beings miraculously transported from 1900 would recognize much of what goes on in today's classrooms—the prevalent lecturing, the emphasis on drill, the decontextualized materials and activities ranging from basal readers to weekly spelling tests. With the possible exception of the Church, few institutions have changed as little in fundamental ways as those charged with the formal education of the next generation.

Contrast this continuity with children's experiences outside the school walls. In modern society children have access to a range of media that would have seemed miraculous in an earlier era (and that still astonishes members of less industrialized societies): televisions, cellular phones, personal computers with CD-ROMs, fax machines, videodiscs, personal stereos, and still and video cameras, to name just a few. Youngsters can get in touch instantly with friends, families, and even kind or malevolent strangers all over the world. Youngsters' habits, attitudes, and knowledge are influenced not only—and perhaps not primarily—by those in their immediate surroundings, but also by the heroes and heroines presented in the media, particularly those larger-than-life figures who populate the worlds of entertainment and athletics. The visitor from the past who would readily recognize today's classroom would have trouble relating to the out-of-school world of a ten-year-old today. I confess that I often experience such difficulties myself.

Schools—if not education generally—are inherently conservative institutions. In large measure, I would defend this conservatism. Methods of instruction that have evolved over long periods of time have much to recommend them; and all too many trendy practices prove vapid if not useless or damaging. Educational experimentation has never been wholly absent, but it has occurred chiefly on the margins. In roughly the last century, important experiments have been launched by such charismatic educators as Maria Montessori, Rudolf Steiner, Shinichi Suzuki, John Dewey, and A. S. Neill. These approaches have enjoyed considerable success; indeed, they might impress our hypothetical visitor from 1900. Yet they have had relatively little impact on the mainstream of education throughout the contemporary world.

Six Forces That Will Remake Schools

It may be risky to say so, but I believe that the present situation is different. Changes in our world are so rapid and so decisive that it will not be possible for schools to remain as they were or simply to introduce a few superficial adjustments. Indeed, if schools do not change quite rapidly and quite radically, they are likely to be replaced by other, more responsive (though perhaps less comfortable and less legitimate) institutions.

There is precedent for such sweeping change. Three hundred years ago, schools served only an elite and were primarily religious in character; but over the next two centuries, they came to serve the wider population and to take on a primarily secular coloration. These changes came about because urbanization and industrialization required a reliable, functionally literate workforce; concomitantly, there emerged centralized educational ministries with explicit educational plans and powers.

Demands have once again shifted dramatically. One hundred years ago, it sufficed to have a highly educated elite and a general population with basic literacy skills. Nowadays, however, almost any function that can be executed through the application of regular procedures will sooner or later be computerized. To be attractive to employers, an individual must be highly literate, flexible, capable of troubleshooting and problem-finding, and, not incidentally, able to shift roles or even vocations should his current position become outmoded. Nor will societies be able to neglect large portions of their population. To remain competitive in a fast-changing world, they will have to deliver a good education to a sizable majority of their future citizens. And they will have to be responsive to at least six sets of trends.

Technological and Scientific Breakthroughs. The most important technological event of our time is the ascendancy of the computer. Computers already play a prominent role in many aspects of our lives, from transportation and communication to personal bookkeeping and entertainment. Scarcely oblivious to these trends, many schools now have computers with networking capabilities. To some extent, these technological appurtenances have been absorbed into the life of the school, though often they simply deliver the old lessons in a more convenient and efficient format.

In the future, however, education will be organized largely around the computer. Not only will much of instruction and assessment be delivered by computer, but the habits of mind fostered by computer interactions will be highlighted, while those that fall through the computational cracks may be lost. For example, precise, explicit step-by-step thinking is likely to be enhanced, while fine-grained aesthetic or ethical judgments may be marginalized. At the same time (if somewhat paradoxically), computers will permit a degree of individualization—personalized coaching or tutoring—which in the past was available only to the richest.

All students may receive a curriculum tailored to their needs, learning style, pace and profile of mastery, and record of success with earlier materials and lessons. Indeed, computer technology permits us to realize, for the first time, progressive educational ideas of "personalization" and "active, hands-on learning" for students all over the world.

Computer technology puts all the information in the world at one's fingertips, quite literally. This is both a blessing and a curse. No longer do we have to spend long periods of time hunting down a source or a person—these can be reached essentially instantaneously. (Indeed, soon we will not even have to type in an instruction in order to learn the capital of Montana, the population of Korea, or Ohm's law; we will just be able to ask out loud and the computer will print out or speak the answer. Thus people will achieve instant "cultural literacy.")

Less happily, the Internet has no means of quality control; "anyone can play." Information and disinformation commingle comfortably and, as of yet, there are no reliable ways to distinguish sense from distortions and downright nonsense on the Net. Ethnographer Sherry Turkle tells about the young child who insists that "there are always riots when taxes go up" because that is the common wisdom embedded in the widely available game program Sim City. Identifying the true, the beautiful, and the good—and which of these truths, beauties, or goods are worth knowing—constitutes a formidable challenge.

It might be said, in response, that the world has always been filled with misinformation. True enough, but in the past educational authorities could at least choose their favorite texts (and proscribe others). Today's situation, with everyone having instant access to millions of sources, is unprecedented.

Artificial intelligence and virtual reality are two computer-related technologies that may cast a large shadow on education. Much of school planning may be done not by human agents but by programs created by human agents; and much of what was once accomplished by textbooks and occasional field trips will now be performed in virtual reality. One can ask: What is the truth value of materials prepared entirely by nonhuman entities?

In a turnabout from previous trends, the acquisition of credentials from accredited institutions may become less important. Individuals will be able to educate themselves (largely if not wholly) and to exhibit their mastery in a simulated setting. Why pay $120,000 to go to law school, if one can "read law" as in earlier times and then demonstrate one's legal skills via computer simulation? Or learn to fly a plane or conduct neurosurgery by similar means, for that matter?

Much of education in the past was calibrated to make sure that individuals could carry out a regular job, reliably, throughout their productive adult years. Nowadays, this assumption is doubly flawed. First, almost everything that can be handled algorithmically will be carried out by automata. Second, few people will remain in the same occupational niche for their whole lives; and many will move frequently (either voluntarily or by necessity) from one niche, company, and sector of the economy to another.

The explosion of new and rapidly changing roles in the workplace complicates education in unprecedented ways. Most adult teachers and parents will not have experiences on which they can draw to prepare youngsters for a world in which they can expect to change jobs regularly. In the absence of precedent, youths will have to prepare themselves for rapidly changing "career paths" and life situations.

While computer-based teaching and curricula figure to be the dominant technological influence on education, other innovations will have impact as well. Imaging technologies will permit study of students' brain activity and blood flow as they engage in various kinds of problem-solving or creative activities. No longer restricted to research, these findings about a student's "mental life" are likely to influence pedagogical approaches as well as her placement in special or mainstream educational settings.

Enhanced understanding of the genetic basis of learning and of various talents is also likely to intrude on the classroom. It may be possible to determine which youngsters are likely to advance quickly and which ones seem doomed to "uphill" school experiences; some authorities will insist that these findings be applied in specific cases, while others will strenuously object to any decisions made on the basis of genetic information. Drugs that purport to improve learning, memory, or motivation will become readily available. Teachers and parents may face ethical dilemmas that would in earlier times have been restricted to science fiction.

Finally, recent breakthroughs in biology and medicine may change education in the most radical ways. If individuals seek to "design" offspring through genetic engineering, or to alter the genetic endowment

of an already existing person, or if human cloning becomes a reality as
well as a possibility, then our definitions of what it means to be a human
being, and to be a part of a human society, will be changed forever. Even
the laws of evolution may have to be reconceived.

Science and technology do not merely alter our conceptions of what
is true. New roles are spawned and traditional values are challenged.
Our array of moral possibilities is altered, and our aesthetic sensibilities
may be affected as well.

Political Trends. With the end of the Cold War, the constitutive assumptions of twentieth-century international relations have been under-
mined. Constant struggle against a powerful military foe no longer
provides a motive for education or training; democratic forms of government are on the rise; and with readier communication among individuals and nations, certain patterns of human interaction (such as a free
press and ready migration) become more attractive, while others (such
as censorship or violations of human rights) prove less easy to advocate.

Even those of us who cheer these developments recognize their vexed
character. There are degrees and types of democracy. The external
forms of democracy are more easily imitated than its underlying values.
Democratic principles are often honored more in the breach than in the
observance, both in the United States and abroad. Indeed, without
knowing their sources, many Americans cannot distinguish passages
from the Declaration of Independence from quotations drawn from the
writings of Marx and Engels. (One wonders how Eastern Europeans
would fare on the same test.)

The collapse of Communism and the weakening of socialism have not
been without their costs. Safety nets on which individuals were counting
disappear or become attenuated, and various criminal forces have often
inserted themselves into the political vacuum. Ethnic and tribal funda-
mentalisms that were hidden or suppressed under totalitarian regimes
have returned with unanticipated force. There may be fewer large-scale
wars, but there are endless local skirmishes, virulent forms of torture,
and even attempts at genocide.

Since education is concerned significantly with systems of values,
these rapid changes in the political ecology cause strains. Texts, lesson
plans, even worldviews have to be altered. Instructors must steer a
course among the various isms, racial and ethnic groups, past and

present political and social values. Consider what it has been like to be a teacher in an Eastern European country over the last fifty years. What was considered true, beautiful, and good in 1950 or even 1990 may not be today; and yet individuals trained in earlier eras—parents no less than teachers—cannot simply shrug off beliefs long since internalized. In the words of the British poet and educator Matthew Arnold, they may be "Wandering between two worlds—one dead, / The other powerless to be born."

Nor is this feeling of anomie restricted to the former Communist world. As we gain distance from the events of this century, many Western European and American citizens have had to rethink our nation's roles in major conflicts, such as the Second World War. Many dubious practices—for example, collusion with the Nazis by so-called neutral governments—were denied in years past; now, fifty years later, it is very painful for citizens of a country to come to terms with what they (or their parents or grandparents) did (or failed to do). And paradoxically, those who think of themselves as the most patriotic—for example, members of the right-wing militias in America—end up embracing aesthetic standards and moral values that are discrepant from the democratic values they are ostensibly committed to defend.

Economic Forces. Even those parts of the world that have little sympathy with democratic institutions and values now recognize the ascendancy of markets and market forces. Everywhere, once "Third World" regions—China and Russia, Iraq and Iran, Africa and Latin America, members of ASEAN and Mercosur—now are ineluctably involved with the new technologies, the buildup of powerful corporations, the pursuit of productivity, in sum, with a sustained, ceaseless competition involving goods and services in an ever more global marketplace.

Students must be educated so that they can participate and survive in this unrelentingly Darwinian environment. Such education is easier where capitalism has long been ascendant, either in the official policies of the society or at least "on the street." But in those societies where cooperation has been stressed over competition, where individuals are encouraged to subdue their own personal passions, and where the state has provided a safety net (often in exchange for political cooperation or silence), adjustment to a dog-eat-dog milieu proves difficult—and perhaps distasteful.

An inescapable part of the new environment—political as well as economic—is globalization. Whereas, earlier, much of the economy operated comfortably at a local level, the period of isolated economic systems is long since past. Multinational corporations, regional trading associations and pathways, international investments and financing are the new realities. Countries must find and press their competitive advantages; they must remain ever vigilant as they alternate between offense and defense in a rapidly shifting economic landscape over which they can never exert sufficient control. Each day financial institutions circulate one trillion dollars; a sudden drop in the stock market in one nation can trigger billions of dollars of losses worldwide within hours. When George Soros speaks, markets quake.

Globalization has ecological as well as economic ramifications. Pollution does not observe political boundaries, and efforts to clear up or protect air, water, and outer space require international cooperation. The market economy works against such endeavors, since the market responds to short-term pressures and profits rather than to longer-term strategic policies and needs. Also, developing countries often perceive ecological initiatives as veiled efforts to maintain an uneven playing field. But unless one assumes that these matters will somehow take care of themselves, it becomes an imperative to include ecological as well as economic awareness in any curriculum.

Though not necessary concomitants, other phenomena tend to accompany the market economy. There is the rush to produce numerous products, which often differ from one another only minimally; the need then to describe and advertise these products *as if* they were actually distinct from one another; planned obsolescence; a focus on consumption, commercialism, and consumerism. Alas, people do not seem to need "disciplinary training" to enter this world; it seems all too well adapted to deep human proclivities. Indeed, "defensive education" may be necessary if one is to resist the seductions of the market—the tastiest chocolate, the most stylish sneaker, the fastest motorcycle.

Finally, with economic growth comes the shift to the information society, the knowledge society, the learning society. More and more people work in the sectors of human services and human resources, and, especially, in the creation, transformation, and communication of knowledge. Workers may well be hired and fired on the basis of what they know, how well they can learn, and what they have contributed recently to relevant knowledge bases. No one will be able to rest on past school or educational laurels. Only those who can demonstrate their continued utility in a knowledge-suffused society can expect to reap the rewards of that society indefinitely.

In portraying these economic forces, I do not mean to endorse them—I have mixed feelings about them at best—or to indicate that they will be dominant forever. There are many ways to run a society, or a world—even as there are many ways to ruin it! The capitalism of Adam Smith and Milton Friedman—or of Singapore's Lee Kuan Yew or China's Deng Xiaoping—does not exhaust the options. But at least for the foreseeable future, viable alternatives do not exist on the international scene. Citizens (and especially future citizens) must be primed (or inoculated, if you prefer that metaphor) to participate in the market economy as needed, while perhaps being able to resist its less palatable facets.

Perhaps it should not be the job of schools to prepare students for life in a market-dominated world. Certainly other agencies and institutions are more than willing to step into the breach. However, schools cannot be cordoned off from the process either. Decisions about which skills to inculcate are one consideration; policies about placement, advancement, school leaving and school-to-work transition are other places where education meets the economy. How the curriculum highlights or marginalizes economic considerations proves an important variable. Equally telling are the implicit messages of the school community: is the school environment competitive, cooperative, or some amalgam? If it's competitive, does a zero-sum or a win-win mentality prevail? Schools can embody the marketplace or offer an alternative model of how life might be pursued; they can teach for the market or teach against the market. Indeed, the decision about which of these courses to pursue is itself a moral one, reflecting educators' and policymakers' sense of "the good."

Social, Cultural, and Personal Trends in the Modern Era. While the economic writing on the wall is unambiguous, it proves more challenging to discern the social, cultural, and personal trends of the coming years. One can envision a utopia, where individuals will be personally comfortable and secure, able to follow their own desires, to mix with whom they like, and to partake of a wider range of leisure and cultural opportunities than ever before. It is equally easy, alas, to envision a dystopia, where individuals are manipulated by unseen advertisers and spin doctors, where group conflicts are exacerbated, where our seemingly unlimited options are actually constrained by the cynical owners of the media, where privacy and personal space are perennially violated, and where the already sizable gap between affluent and indigent grows ever wider. Or one may be persuaded by the scenario developed by political scientist Samuel Huntington, who foresees a struggle between the authoritarian but economically powerful Asian Confucian societies and the democratic but less coherently organized West.

It is safe to make one prediction: The media of communication will be a dominating (if sometimes unintentional) agency of education throughout the world. Radio, television, movies, magazines, advertising materials will continue to proliferate and to convey powerful messages about roles and values around the world. (Just consider the global media messages of the past few years—those associated with names like "O.J.," "Diana," "Dolly," and "Deep Blue.")*

It will be extremely difficult—if not impossible—to isolate a particular culture. Individuals all over the world will have full-color access to the beliefs, attitudes, and styles of living of millions (indeed, billions!) of other individuals. In our terms, they will be exposed to, and challenged by, the truths, beauties, and moral visions of fellow human beings, including people whose assumptions and backgrounds differ considerably from their own. Islamic fundamentalists in Iran, Jewish fundamentalists in Israel, Christian fundamentalists in the Americas may adhere to their beliefs, but they will have to do so amid considerable "noisy" knowledge of the lives of those who belong to other sects, as well as of those millions for whom religion is no longer a potent force.

Some people will feel threatened (perhaps appropriately so) by exposure to alien lifestyles, and will be tempted to entrench themselves, to reject and dismiss these foreign infectants. But others—particularly the younger, the more courageous, the more adventurous—will enlarge their sense of options. And as knowledge of options (and how to act on them) becomes universal, it should prove more difficult to marginalize

---

*Fame can be fleeting in Andy Warhol's "fifteen minutes" world. In order: a former football star accused of two murders; a princess who died young; the first cloned sheep; the first computer to defeat the world's human chess champion.

large sectors of humanity on the basis of skin color, ethnic membership, gender, or sexual orientation.

Briefly, this is what cultural modernism has been about. In some Western civilizations, particularly those in Europe and North America, modernist practices, norms, and values have evolved gradually. More recently, people living in other parts of the world have been exposed via the media to ways of life in which individuals choose their own work, their mates, their places of residence, and even their systems of values. In such a modernist context, issues of personal expression, sports, entertainment, fashion become more important; political, religious, and ideological concerns wane to some extent.

Initially such exposure was shocking. In some countries, for example Iran and China, strong negative reactions ensued with respect to "modern society," "the West," "secular society," and other bogeymen. Yet, at the same time, there has been a fascination with what humans can be like when they are largely shorn of those "ligatures"—both comforting and confining—that have characterized most of human life in most of the world throughout most of human history. Notions of truth, beauty, and morality are irrevocably challenged and, perhaps, forever altered.

Whether the Western brand of modernism will survive and prevail remains an open question. Islamic societies (Indonesia, Malaysia) and Confucian societies (Singapore, China) have succeeded in assimilating much of the technological and economic expertise of the West without acquiring as well its liberal political beliefs and permissive social practices. Yet, whether formal education embraces such controversial Western features or inoculates against them, the increasing intimacy of our planet ensures a constant preoccupation with these issues.

Personal factors have typically influenced choices about partners, residence, work, and style of life; these "social considerations" remain important to people the world over. However, another dimension of personal life, potentially of equally great importance, has not yet been much remarked upon. I refer here to a greater understanding of human emotions, personality, and cognition. In our time, psychological insights have accrued and popular fascination with the mind's workings shows no sign of abating, whether in China, Brazil, or Denmark. But understanding of one's own mind has not yet been linked with personal responsibility for one's education.

So far, education has been largely seen as the responsibility of exter-

nal forces; individual minds have been treated like sealed black boxes.
However, people can now secure far greater insights into the operation
of minds, in general, and into the operation of their own minds, in particular. Personal knowledge about the mind might furnish people with a
sense of agency with respect to their cognitive lives that would have
seemed utopian in an earlier era. Metacognition, self-consciousness,
intrapersonal intelligence, second-order thinking, planning (and revising and reflecting), systemic thinking, and their interrelations need not
just be psychological jargon or "self-help" buzzwords; to put it plainly,
individuals can play a far more active role in determining the truth,
beauty, and goodness that will suffuse their own lives.

Education has traditionally been thought of as an imperative for the
young; people did not live that long, and adult lives did not change that
much. Now, however, adult lives change rapidly, and the longevity of
human beings pushes steadily upward, having reached at least the biblical seventy in most countries and approaching eighty in several.
Lifelong learning is becoming a necessity, not just a mellifluous phrase.
Again, for some this is a welcome development; certain ethnic and religious groups have long stressed the importance of bettering one's mind
perennially. But for those raised in less scholastically oriented environments, and for those who never much liked school, the prospect of a
life during which one must continue to study, to master, to practice—
above all, to improve one's mental skills and powers—proves less appealing.

Youngsters ought to be reared so that they enjoy learning, develop
wide-ranging interests, and want to nourish their minds for the remainder of their lives. Plato put it memorably: "The purpose of education is
to make the individual want to do what he has to do." Such virtue seems
lacking even in countries that excel in international comparisons of educational achievement; and the flocking of most individuals to the most
mindless forms of entertainment—and away from those that smack
even slightly of formal education—indicates that lifelong learning, however necessary it seems to policymakers (including me), may not be an
easy sell.

The Shifting Cartography of Knowledge. Knowledge has always expanded
but in the past that expansion has been gradual and seemingly control-
lable. It has been said, only partly in jest, that Matthew Arnold, who

died in 1888, was the last man (*sic*) in the world to know everything. Be that as it may, there is hardly a scholarly discipline now whose knowledge base does not grow at essentially geometric rates. By conservative estimates, the amount of information available doubles every few years; I recently heard a claim that the amount of information in the world doubles every eighty days! And even if those figures are largely meaningless (Does disinformation count as information? What counts as information, anyway?), the reality that they are attempting to quantify makes it more difficult to determine what "truth" is worth studying and what is worth living by.

In the future, the individual (or "intelligent agent") who can examine these bodies of knowledge and determine what is worth knowing will be at a tremendous premium. Even more estimable will be the person (or browser) who (or that) can synthesize the exponentially expanding domains of knowledge so that vital information can be made available in useful form to the average citizen and the average policymaker.

The conservatism of educational systems proves especially problematic here. Work at the frontiers of knowledge changes from decade to decade; indeed, friends in the world of molecular biology tell me that they cannot afford to stop reading professional journals and on-line services for more than three months! Even in the humanities, perspectives on art and literature are quite different from those of a generation ago. And yet, the world over, individuals in schools study the same "subjects," pretty much in the same way, that their parents and grandparents did. When such students discover—at the university, through their own reading or surfing, or in an apprenticeship—what cutting-edge work in the disciplines is really like, they are often astonished, sometimes pleasantly, sometimes rudely so.

The question of interdisciplinary study proves timely. At the beachheads, most problems do not readily fit into neat disciplinary niches. Teams of interdisciplinary workers are the norm, and the most effective investigators are those who are able judiciously to combine the insights and techniques of two or more disciplines—no easy task when the disciplines themselves are rapidly changing. And yet, interdisciplinary work proves challenging, as it requires the wedding of often disparate methods and ways of thinking.

In my view, it is appropriate to continue to teach disciplinary thinking in high school and perhaps even in college. The disciplines represent our

best efforts to think systematically about the world, and they are prereq-
uisite to competent interdisciplinary work. At the same time, such a
practice produces an unwelcome disjunction between the discipline-
based training of future practitioners and the interdisciplinary reality of
cutting-edge scholarship.

Changes in the cartography of knowledge can boggle the mind. While
individuals used to wait for long periods to read the results of research,
important discoveries are now known all over the world within days,
courtesy of the Internet. Print publication has increasingly become a
formality and is even bypassed altogether in certain breakthrough fields.
New fields and subfields are founded each year, even as once-dominant
fields recede in importance. The availability of large databases makes it
possible for individuals without formal training to master topics and to
make contributions to the scholarly world. Distance learning makes it
possible to pursue even advanced coursework without moving to a college or university setting. And, as I've already mentioned, virtual environments may allow talented or determined individuals to demonstrate
proficiency without lengthy and costly certification processes.

Given these disciplinary tensions, the very notion of literacy is
altered. To the classic three Rs, one must certainly add various comput-
ing and programming languages. A different mix among the literacies is
also coming to the fore. To function in hypermedia, to read and design
Web pages and embark on computer-based projects, one must orchestrate a fresh amalgam of graphic, linguistic, and even auditory literacies.
There is every reason to believe that these literacies will continue to
proliferate, even as their possible interrelations are explored (perhaps
especially by younger persons who are busily designing their own Web
sites).

Changes in the cartography of knowledge exert their chief effects on
a culture's sense of what is true. However, their impact does not stop
there. One can never anticipate the implications of a discovery. For
example, the Internet grew initially out of efforts to help government-
funded scientists and military personnel communicate efficiently.
However, it now transmits new forms of art and many varieties of sexual
material, including pornography. And the Internet enables people to
design their own portrayal of themselves—indeed, to change it at will.
Not only do these new forms of communication and art represent possible contributions to our evolving senses of beauty (or ugliness) and

goodness (or evil); but whether, and to what extent, such transmission should be regulated raises fundamental political and moral issues.

Beyond Modernism: A Postmodern Jag. New perspectives on knowledge, largely unknown to the general public, have developed in the West (especially in France) during the last generation. Called variously post-modernism, relativism, structuralism, post-structuralism, and decon-structionism (and, to be sure, these are not all the same thing!), these approaches collectively challenge the certainties assumed during earlier epochs.

In milder variants, this "postmodern perspective" cautions against privileging specific points of view; calls for a recognition of different (often previously suppressed) "voices"; and stresses the "constructed nature" of all knowledge. In its more radical variants, it questions even the possibility of advances in knowledge and truth. Postmodern "purists" claim that knowledge is essentially about power, and that those in power determine what is true and what is not, such determinations changing when "hegemony" (controlling political authority) changes. Texts cannot contain truths because they are inherently self-contradic-tory; all readings are necessarily misreadings; and the scholar's task is to uncover—through "deconstruction" of these texts—these rampant self-indictments and internal contradictions.

Postmodernist thought has broken through to public consciousness in a number of ways: Through ridicule, as when a traditionally oriented scholar seizes upon a particularly ludicrous passage and highlights it in a text that documents the current sins of academe. Through trickery—as when the physicist Allan Sokal succeeded in publishing an article on sci-ence in *Social Text,* a "postmodern" journal. Sokal then revealed that the article was actually a collage of largely nonsensical statements, designed to spoof the prototypical deconstructionist texts. And through scan-dal—as when a leading deconstructionist, Paul de Man, was revealed (posthumously) to have been a Nazi sympathizer during his youth.

Despite my effort to be descriptive, I must admit that I have little or no tolerance for the "pure" version of postmodernist thought. I believe that, rather than revealing the contradictions in the writings of others, this position is itself riddled with self-contradictions. If the only stan-dards are those of power, why should one pay any attention to the writ-ings of deconstructionists? If one should pay attention to *some* writings (as opposed to the impossible task of spending an equal amount of time on all writings), then there must be some standards at work—in which case the postmodern position does not cohere. One cannot take a position that stresses the relativity of all knowledge and yet at the same time claim the right to be listened to and taken seriously. I am reminded of the teacher who declared to a class of relativistically oriented students that he intended to grade them by whim. Instantly "cured" of their relativism, the students became converts to objective standards.

This book is not, however, the occasion to be fair, or unfair, to (my version of) postmodern scholarship and criticism. I mention this school of thought here for one reason. Taken at face value, the postmodern stance invalidates my enterprise of creating an education that focuses on the true, the beautiful, and the good. Indeed, from a postmodern perspective, my mission would be an impossibility. Since these virtues are themselves fictions, riddled with internal contradictions, how could one legitimately try to convey them? Even the effort to heighten sensitivity to *others'* versions of truth would be futile, though perhaps more politically correct.

I'd like to propose a truce, however. I am willing to cede a lot of running room to the postmodernists at the college and university level (particularly in elective courses!), as long as they will allow me to fashion curricula for kindergarten through secondary school. Whatever merits postmodern perspectives may have for the mature student or scholar, I think that they will stir up nothing but trouble for all but the most subtle-minded precollegiate students. As I see it, there may be validity in challenging easy assumptions about truth or beauty or goodness—once these have consolidated; but to try to undermine the very endeavor to move toward truth (or beauty or goodness) before it has had a chance to take hold seems to me unfair, even deeply disturbing, to the growing mind. I can add that efforts to terminate these discussions of the traditional virtues are doomed to fail: even the study of beauty has recently been resurrected in the academy.

Let me offer an analogy. Many psychology students have told me that Freud or Piaget has been disproved. I then ask whether the students have read their work and am assured that it is no longer necessary to do so! I am content to hear arguments against a major and still influential thinker from someone who has grappled with the work, but not from someone who transmits the conclusion secondhand or from someone who questions the very validity of a given form of inquiry. In this ecumenical context, let me say that in many ways I respect the scholarship undertaken by postmodern scholars like Jacques Derrida (with respect to Kant and Descartes) or Jean-François Lyotard (with respect to Freud and Marx) or Richard Rorty (with respect to the classical epistemological thinkers). It is a pity that their own students so often project their attitudes and their conclusions, rather than emulating their careful study of critical texts. *before disregarding them!*

A final point: in one sense, the postmodernists may well be right. Even in science, ultimate truth may be an impossible goal; and certainly conceptions of beauty and morality change, and will continue to change indefinitely, if slowly. A curriculum grounded in the traditional verities should not claim to be definitive. Instead, it should seek to elucidate current cultural conceptions of the true, beautiful, and the good; and it can certainly include a review of opposing claims and contentions as well as a recognition of the contingent status of all knowledge. More important, it should legitimate the continuing search for examples to admire, to condemn, to puzzle over. I reveal my traditionalist roots—and my most enduring struggle with "pure" postmodernism—in my assertion that these perennial concerns continue to be the proper ones for human beings. And I reveal my Enlightenment allegiance in my conviction that, over time, humanity has made some progress in the three realms I cherish.

The View from Multiculturalism. Postmodernism is sometimes confused with multiculturalism, perhaps because both are promoted in humanities departments, sometimes by the same individuals. Indeed, missionaries from both camps begin with a critique of standard Western humanistic scholarship. But then they diverge. Postmodernists focus on the epistemology of the canon, while multiculturalists attack the constitution of the canon—as they see it, an excessive focus on the ideas and works of "Dead White Males."

My view of multiculturalism is more nuanced than my critique of postmodernism. I agree that the insistence on a single canon is misguided; far more works and ideas are worthy of study than could conceivably be included in any canon. (Historians tell us that canons have always been loosely constituted.) Moreover, there is virtue in a pluralistic canon, one that deliberately draws on different historical, cultural, and ideological sources. Indeed, in a nation whose population is itself diverse, such eclecticism is both needed and desirable. Finally, what counts as a canon can legitimately change, depending on the educational community in question.

For me, the issues to consider are standards and accuracy. Here a possibly surprised Matthew Arnold makes his third appearance in this chapter. Borrowing his phrase, I call for educators "to learn and propagate the best that is known and thought in the world." I also want students to have information that is as accurate as possible. So long as these two criteria are met, I believe that multicultural curricula and approaches are beneficent. When, however, multiculturalists abandon high standards in their selections of work, or favor inferior work just because of its appealing provenance, I part company with them. By the same token, I have no sympathy for those who choose to rewrite history, so that credit for discoveries is given, without convincing evidence, to individuals or groups that happen to have a certain accent, cultural background, or political attitude.

Let me phrase my point positively. I want all students to develop a sense of high standards; I want all students to strive for accuracy and to use evidence properly; I want all students to respect a range of groups and cultures, but not to do so uncritically.

It is possible to have a precollegiate education that is multicultural and that meets these criteria, though that is not a necessary outcome of multicultural education. It is *not* possible to have a postmodern curriculum that meets these criteria—indeed, the criteria themselves have no legitimacy in the eyes of postmodernists.

An Educational Crossroad

My survey has touched on the constants that have characterized education over the centuries, as well as on the variables that figure to dominate the landscape in the coming years. Taken together, these factors constitute a sizable challenge for any educator. On the one hand, he or she must determine how best to convey desired roles, values, literacies, and disciplines, and a nuanced sense of the true, the beautiful, and the good. At the same time, the educator must be mindful of the world's scientific, technological, political, economic, social, cultural, and personal changes, and must respond to them. Finally, alert to the signals sent from the academy, the educator needs to situate his or her own work within the discourses of postmodernism and multiculturalism; for even if (as is claimed) all discourses contradict themselves, educators cannot avoid the fallout from the most vocal proponents of these provocative worldviews.

I have noted that education is conservative, and that this conservatism is not necessarily an evil. Indeed, with respect to the transmission of values and the mastery of certain notational systems and disciplines, a conservative approach may well be called for. Yet the explosion of knowledge and the ever-shifting cartography of disciplines call for close and fresh attention to curricular matters. And new and imaginative approaches will have to be developed if youths are to be prepared for the rapidly changing roles they can expect to assume.

With most other observers, I am convinced that education stands at a crossroad. The shifts in the world are so cataclysmic, their implications at such variance with past practices, that the status quo cannot endure in most parts of the world. Indeed, if somewhat paradoxically, the nations that are deemed most successful by current standards seem most concerned about the unsuitability of their current schools for future needs. East Asian societies call for more creativity and individuality; European and American leaders lament the failure of the schools to reach (let alone excite!) large segments of the population; and observers the world over note that centuries-old assumptions about the creation and transmission of knowledge no longer hold. We cannot anticipate what future schools and education will be like, but we can expect that they will differ substantially from what we and our forebears have taken for granted. Past and future provide one set of lenses; our expanding knowledge of human beings provides another.

Fortunately, in this quest for new educational visions, there is dry land. Indeed, there are several areas of shelter—provided by what we can learn from studies of the mind (psychology), studies of the brain (neurology and biology), and studies of cultures (anthropology). As it happens, part of what has changed in the recent past is our understanding of these several domains. We are now in a position to draw on this knowledge *as warranted* in our reshaping of the educational landscape to achieve an understanding of the true, the beautiful, and the good.

CHAPTER 4
Perspectives of Mind and Brain

Scientific Knowledge and Value Judgments

At conferences, I try to avoid unpleasant exchanges. But the speaker—a prominent neuroscientist—had managed to raise my hackles. In front of an audience of influential policymakers, he had made a bald assertion: "This is the decade of the brain. We are going to know what every region of the brain does and how the various parts of the brain work together. And once we have attained that knowledge, we will know exactly how to educate every person."

Extreme statements beget extreme responses. Standing up in the audience at the conclusion of the talk, I retorted, "I disagree totally. We could know what every neuron does and we would not be one step closer to knowing how to educate our children."

After the session, I engaged the speaker in discussion. I began by asking for an example of what he had been claiming. He immediately cited the teaching of language: "We know now that children easily absorb patterns, and particularly the patterns of language, when they are young. Therefore we should be teaching foreign languages to children during the early years of life."

"I am not convinced," I replied. "In the first place, everyone (and everyone's grandmother) has always known that young children pick up languages—and particularly accents—with ease. We did not need brain study to tell us that. Second, some research suggests that the military knows how to teach languages far more effectively than do parents and grandparents."

I went on: "But that is not my principal point. I'm arguing that decisions about what to teach, when to teach, and even how to teach entail value judgments. Such decisions can never be dictated by knowledge of the brain. After all, if children learn patterns well when they are young, that constitutes equal reason for teaching them math, music, chess, biology, morality, civility, and a hundred other things. Why should foreign languages get priority? You can never go directly from knowledge about brain function to what to do in first grade on Monday morning. And the decisions one makes about teaching languages might well differ, and properly so, depending on whether you live in Switzerland, Singapore, Iceland, or Ireland."

And so our discussion terminated. I don't think I convinced the speaker, and I admit, in retrospect, that I overstated my case. I find brain study—and its first cousin, "mind study"—fascinating; I would be the last person to question their importance for society as a whole, and for those of us interested in the education of future generations. But my central point stands. Education is too important to be left to the classroom teacher, the school board, the central ministry, the neuroscientific community, or any other single person or group. Decisions about education are, in the final analysis, decisions about goals and values; those are properly made by the larger, informed community and not by any privileged sector, even one fortunate enough to be unraveling some of the mysteries of the human mind.

We want to educate youngsters so that they can cope successfully with a world that has already changed dramatically and that is changing more rapidly still. If the community is to make informed decisions, we must determine what has been learned about human beings by psychology (the study of the mind), biology (the study of the brain and the genes), and anthropology (the study of different cultures). Indeed, in an age of continuing scientific advances, it would be delinquent not to attend to these sources of information, equally delinquent to attend to one while excluding the others.

In Olden Days:
Inborn Traits and Well-Shaped Behaviors

Long before there was a discrete field called psychology, education proceeded on the basis of what we might call lay or folk psychology. All sorts of assumptions are built into traditional educational systems; some seem so self-evident that they hardly bear discussion. It has been widely assumed that older people know more than younger people; that older persons should speak and demonstrate, while younger ones should be silent and observe; that rewards should be given to those who learn well, and punishments to those who seem slow or lazy; that teachers should not only be knowledgeable about their topic, their profession, and the norms of their community but should also serve as moral and ethical exemplars.

Perhaps surprisingly, one can invoke counterarguments—even "folk counterarguments"—against these widely held assumptions. Some have pointed out the wisdom and knowledge of the innocent (and the blinders often worn by the aging); the importance of children's questions and their active participation; the dangers of an educational economy based on the carrot and the stick; the benefits of hectoring the talented and soothing the less able; the irrelevance of an adult's private life or breadth of knowledge, so long as he or she has an area of specific expertise and knows how to convey it to the untutored. Nevertheless, the former perspectives have generally carried the day, which suggests that they tap deep intuitions shared by most human beings. It is an uphill struggle to argue against such apparently plausible insights.

The field of psychology has often been said to have a long past but a short history. That history began formally in the latter decades of the nineteenth century, when university courses and degrees in psychology were first offered, experimental laboratories were opened, psychological journals and organizations arose, and individuals like William James in America, Ivan Pavlov in Russia, and Alfred Binet in France came to be known as psychologists (rather than, respectively—and alliteratively—as philosophers, physiologists, and pedagogues).

Psychology was not fashioned to illuminate educational issues, but major figures in psychology almost invariably came to address (and sometimes affect) educational practices. And a few influential psychologists, like Teachers College's Edward L. Thorndike, focused their attention specifically on education. Writing in 1910, in the lead article of the new *Journal of Educational Psychology,* he declared:

> To an understanding of the material of education, psychology is the chief contributor. . . . A complete science of psychology would tell every fact about everyone's intellect and character and behavior,

would tell the cause of every change in human nature, would tell the result which every educational force . . . would have . . . every advance in the sciences of human nature will contribute to our success in controlling human nature and changing it to the advantage of the common weal. . . . Psychology helps here by requiring us to put our notions of the aims of education into terms of the exact changes that education is to make, and by describing for us the changes which do actually occur in human beings.

Two dominant strands characterized academic psychology during the first half of the twentieth century. (Psychoanalysis had considerable influence in the wider culture but little within the academy.) Interestingly, these two strands were not consistent with each other, in an intellectual sense; yet both exerted important and often synergistic effects. Recent "cognitive" trends in psychology can be seen as reactions to this pair of notions—which, while they hold less sway than they did at the time of Thorndike, are still potent in many corners of the world—and will be so in the minds of many readers of this book.

First and foremost, there were the ideas of the behaviorists (sometimes called the learning theorists). Influential especially in the United States and the former Soviet Union, these scholars lived up to their name: they were interested in behavior, in overt action, in endeavors that could be observed objectively and measured reliably. The psychologist could properly concern himself only with behaviors that were actually observed, not with hidden or subjective reactions, if any. As far as behaviorists were concerned, it was diversionary, misleading, dead wrong, to speak about the individual as having a mental life, complete with thoughts, ideas, dreams, consciousness, images, and the like. All that mattered—at least from the psychologist's perspective—was the *observable* pattern of actions that individuals "emitted" in different environments. If one wanted more of a certain action, one would reward or reinforce it; if one wanted to eliminate it, one would punish it or, if one were more sophisticated, simply stop rewarding it. Eventually the behavior would cease.

The basic epistemological premise of behaviorism can be conveyed by a joke: Two behaviorists have sex. Afterward, the first says to the second: "Well, it was obviously great for you. But tell me, how was it for me?"

How did behaviorism manifest itself in education? First of all, educators were discouraged from speculating on the mental life of their charges. What might go on between the two ears simply did not matter. Important was a delineation of the behavioral objectives. One thus had the task of teaching and rewarding in such a way that those objectives were achieved, while rival ones were skirted or eliminated. If, for example, one wanted youngsters to write and spell in a certain way, one would model that behavior; youngsters would try to imitate the model and would be rewarded whenever their actions approximated it, punished or ignored when they deviated from its particulars. In the behaviorist's view, how people thought about spelling, the tricks they used or the strategies they favored, how they felt about their performance—these were illegitimate considerations.

What about more difficult problems, which could not easily be modeled in front of students' eyes? The same line of analysis applied. One broke down these complex behaviors into simpler parts that *could* be modeled, and one "shaped" behavior until the individual parts were perfected. (Examples of such parts might be the different segments that went into the writing of an essay or the solution of a set of equations.) Next, one would patiently shape tentative, imperfect efforts at "assembling" the parts until the desired performance had been produced.

The epitome of this way of thinking is represented by the teaching machine. Without the need for human intervention (except, of course, to program the machine), the student sits at a terminal, emits behaviors, and is continually shaped through positive (or negative) reinforcement until the correct stream of actions emerges. Nowadays, when the machine is likely to be a computer, some have dubbed such programs "drill-and-kill."

Even extreme behaviorists recognized that some youngsters would learn more readily than others. But the behaviorists emphasized discipline and effort (though they might not have been able to give satisfactory definitions of these mentalistically tinged concepts). They took their lead from the founding behaviorist, J. B. Watson, who famously declared that he could make any child into any kind of adult, if he were simply given "my own specified world." According to this Archimedean attitude, anything was possible so long as one had leverage: time, patience, and the proper arsenal of rewards and punishments.

Lest one think that behaviorist ideas are dead, consider such current practices as standardized national tests and outcome-based education. Proponents as well as opponents of both focus entirely on the test score achieved by a student or on the specific outcomes mandated by a jurisdiction. Rarely is attention paid to the means by which these behaviors are achieved, let alone to the specific or general patterns of thought that might give rise to, or thwart, the emission of the desired behaviors. Which standard tests, after all, ever reveal the thinking that underlies the response? Not considered

So much for behaviorism. Differences in performances among youngsters lead us to the second strand of the psychologist's creed, circa 1950. It had to do with the nature and distribution of intelligence. I call it the trait view.

It is well known that the first intelligence tests were devised by Alfred Binet in Paris, almost a century ago, as a means of predicting which children would experience difficulties in school and which would prosper. Binet, as it happens, felt that the tests should be administered informally, and that any child's intelligence could be improved through sensitive training. Those sentiments did not affect how intelligence testing evolved in the ensuing century.

Once the instrumentation for assessing intelligence had migrated to America, a quite different worldview emerged. First of all, intelligence tests were standardized and "normed," so that any test-taker could be compared in mental age to any other. Then youngsters (as well as army recruits, immigrants arriving at Ellis Island, and others being "selected") were tested for their intelligence; decisions about their educability, and their proper track in school or life, were made on the basis of their recorded intelligence quotient, or IQ—the amount of the trait of intelligence that they exhibited on a particular linguistic or pictorial measure.

One could believe in the mutability of intelligence, but most psychologists chose not to. Instead, an orthodoxy developed. Intelligence is a largely genetic or innate trait; it features a single general capacity, often termed "g" for general intelligence; and there is not much that one can do about one's given intelligence. It followed that psychologists should determine a person's intelligence at an early age and base educational recommendations on the recorded IQ. This point of view has broken into public consciousness at regular intervals—for example, in the debate between psychologist Lewis Terman and essayist Walter

Lippmann in the pages of *The New Republic* in the 1920s; during the furor over Arthur Jensen's critique of early-intervention programs (like Head Start) in the late 1960s; and in the extended discussion of Richard Herrnstein and Charles Murray's controversial book *The Bell Curve* in the middle 1990s.

One can readily discern the tension between these two perspectives. The behaviorists suggest that almost anything is possible and that it is the job of educators to shape high levels of performance in all youngsters; the IQ testers believe that one's capacity and limits are largely set by nature. Yet, while these ideas are intellectually inconsistent, they can coexist quite comfortably in the actual classroom. Intelligence tests can define one's expectations, and perhaps mandate the groups or tracks into which one channels children. But then, whether one is dealing with the gifted or with the dull, one can teach on the basis of behaviorist principles and rewards. To put it succinctly, people act as if the genes determine the trait of intelligence; behaviorist methods allow optimal expression of each person's traits.

I must admit that the picture I have given is a bit of a caricature. Probably only zealots believed these views in as unmodulated a form as I have presented them. Moreover, few teachers (or parents) subscribed explicitly to the views of either behaviorist or the trait psychologists. They were much more pragmatic about what they believed and did. Yet their practices—from tracking youngsters on the basis of test scores, to holding frequent spelling bees and awarding gold stars—reflected the pervasive and often insidious power of these imports from laboratory psychology.

The Cognitive Revolution

One can criticize psychological and educational ideas until the cows come home, but the ideas rebound unscathed. Only a fundamentally different set of ideas has the potential to change conceptions and, ultimately, practices—or (as a reformed behaviorist might put it) behaviors and, ultimately, beliefs.

In the middle 1950s, a new set of ideas did indeed begin to circulate in the behavioral and human sciences. These ideas had many different sources and implications, but they had the cumulative effect of challenging the twin psychological orthodoxies I have just described. With the historian's benefit of hindsight, this ferment is usually called the cognitive revolution.

The key notion of the cognitive revolution is "mental representation." Cognitive psychologists believe that individuals have ideas, images, and various "languages" in their mind-brain; these representations are real and important, and are susceptible to study by scientists and to change by educators. Now, laypersons—not to mention an impressive array of philosophers including Plato and Aristotle, Descartes and Kant—have long believed that individuals traffic in such mental representations. But the behaviorist hegemony had ruled such ideas out of court in scientific psychology.

Paradoxically, the rise of representations was due primarily to the power of machines rather than to the examples of human beings. Computers were coming of age, so to speak; no longer simply speedy number-crunchers, they were capable of playing chess and of executing logical proofs. It made sense to speak of these computers as having representations (organized sequences of logical symbols or propositions) and as performing operations or transformations upon these representations. If it was valid to attribute representations to machines (so the argument went), it seemed churlish to deny them to human beings who, after all, had created and programmed the machines, and who interpreted their output.

Once the notion of representation had been readmitted into the pantheon of psychological concepts, all sorts of questions could be addressed. What kinds of representations do human beings have? Which ones are they born with? How do the representations change naturally? How, and to what extent, can they be changed deliberately? Are certain representations privileged? Do different individuals favor different mental representations? Much of cognitive science (the interdisciplinary field that arose in the wake of the cognitive revolution) constitutes an attempt to answer these questions.

The simple shift to representations brought about a revolution in thinking about the two earlier strands of psychology. No longer did one focus simply on behaviors. Indeed, one might almost think of behaviors as being epiphenomena (that is, as being the shadows of our determining mental representations). What was important was the (fixed or fluid) state of the individual's mental representations: those were the triggers of actions and nonactions as well as the interpreters of the meaning of such actions. Students still spelled or misspelled, to be sure; but cognitivists did not obsess over the number of items missed. Rather, these scientists searched for the rules that the students were following, the strategies they were employing, the ways in which they interpreted lessons, test scores, parental reactions, and their own performances in a bee.

By the same token, intelligence no longer needed to be seen as a "black box" entity, with which a person was born and which was (or, more likely, was not) subject to change. Rather, we could consider intelligence in terms of different kinds and combinations of mental representations. To be sure, people were probably born with certain mental representations—for example, the capacity to construe physical objects as discrete and enduring entities, and the ability to discriminate among the sounds of all languages spoken by human beings. However, just as the instructions in the program can be changed, so, too, these representations will change—as a function of maturation, as a consequence of experience, as a result of interactions with other representations. For example, one's initial, catholic arsenal of phonemic discriminations is gradually reduced and sharpened in ways shaped by the language sounds that one hears and does not hear. In this view, the old idea of intelligence becomes a sort of place-holder, invoked only until one can make far more specific statements about actual mental representations and how they might be altered.

Traditional and cognitive-revolutionary ideas can exist in various combinations. It is possible to believe in the primacy of traits (like a single intelligence), and yet believe that traits can be altered (for example, through a rigorous process of shaping, or through the creation of new and more powerful mental representations). It is possible to believe in the primacy of mental representations (language as a set of syntactic and phonological representations), and yet be skeptical about the influence of the environment upon these representations (which may just emerge lockstep, according to a biological clock). While a psychology text ought to draw clear lines between behaviorism and cognitivism, in practice many individuals subscribe to aspects of both orthodoxies.

A revolution in social science does not necessarily exert ready or clear effects upon the world of practice. Everywhere, most educators are only dimly aware of these changes in the thinking of psychological researchers; and even those who are—perhaps because they read publications like *Scientific American*—may not translate these new understandings into innovative educational practices. Yet the cognitive revolution ushered in a set of new ideas—ideas that, I believe, have powerful educational implications. Let me now mention six of the most prominent.

1. The Developmental Perspective. Thanks to the pioneering work of the Swiss psychologist Jean Piaget, we no longer believe that young children are just miniature or ignorant adults. Rather, children are credited with their own characteristic ways of representing the world. The infant's world is one of sensory perceptions and actions; the toddler's world features various kinds of symbols (such as words and pictures) for the first time; the young schoolchild is able to deal with concepts (such as amount and time) as long as these concepts are encountered in concrete, tangible form; the adolescent is able to reason abstractly about the same concepts in words or through the manipulation of logical symbols, without needing to refer constantly to tangible objects or displays.

An important point about development is that it is not strongly tied to age. In a group of seven-year-olds, some may not be capable of "concrete mental operations"; many will be on the cusp of this stage; and a few precocious types will have begun to think in the more abstract formal ways that we associate with adolescents.

Much research since Piaget has refined these stages and revealed their irregularities and wrinkles. Yet the broad Piagetian picture endures, and its educational implications are clear. Armed with it, educators are likely to present content and ideas in ways that are developmentally appropriate; they will realize that different children—even children of the same size and age—may be at different developmental levels and hence will benefit from different kinds of examples and lessons. And they will be skeptical of curricula or measures that purport to be suitable for all learners.

The developmental perspective is usually thought of with reference to children's understanding of truths, be they physical, biological, or historical. This reflects, in part, Piaget's own fascination with the changing contours of children's cognition—for example, the difficulties young children have in appreciating conservation of quantity or number, despite changes in the physical configuration of a display, or their tendency to confuse issues of time and speed. But developmental differences are equally relevant to the other educational virtues. Young children have distinctive moral outlooks; for example, they focus on the amount of damage an act results in, rather than on the intention of the actor. And their artistic views are similarly constrained: in their early school years, they believe that pictures must be realistic to have merit; and, as they head toward middle childhood, they avoid metaphors and other forms of figurative language in favor of literally precise formulations.

2. *Universal Mental Representations.* Perhaps unexpectedly, the other redoubtable figure in thinking about children's cognition is not a psychologist but rather a pioneering linguist. For many years, Noam Chomsky has argued that language is a very special kind of cognitive system, one with its own psychological and (presumably) neurological representations. (In this respect, among others, Chomsky challenges Piaget's view that mental representations are very general schemas that cut across disparate contents, like language, number, and space.)

Chomsky's work is important because it suggests that children are born with certain quite specific kinds of mental representations, which develop along narrowly constrained lines. There are structures dedicated to language, and these unfold in a prescribed manner—much like a physical organ growing—during the first years of life. There seem, as well, to be mental structures dedicated to the appreciation of number, spatial relations, music, and the understanding of other persons. All normal humans have the same family of mental representations; absent gross abuse, these representations will unfold in predictable ways according to a predictable timetable. Thus, for instance, by the early years of school, all normal children will become able to talk, understand, calculate, and interpret the motivations of others.

In light of this innatist perspective, one might well ask what is the role of the educator. And, truth to tell, Chomsky and his associates have had little to say on this question—perhaps because what they would say would not be very comforting. After all, educators have little influence on the development of the eye or the liver, and Chomsky explicitly uses these organs as metaphors for the different faculties of the mind.

However, it is possible to draw out implications. First, if there are normative milestones in the development of different mental "organs" (like those that represent and process language or number), it is important to establish what they are. Only then can their normal course be observed and occasional absences or anomalies be identified and addressed. Second, many educational activities—reading, for example—require the interaction of these representations; such interactive processing involving, say, graphic and verbal representations cannot be left simply to chance. Third, how various symbolic capacities are used will vary. Not only do natural languages differ in phonology, syntax, and semantics, but the "pragmatic" circumstances in which one elects to speak (or remain silent) and the ways in which one addresses individuals of various statuses differ revealingly across and even within cultures. The mental representations themselves cannot be cognizant of these patterns of use; such identification is preeminently the task of educators within a given cultural setting.

So far, the universalist perspective has been applied chiefly to language and other cognitively oriented domains. Of late, however, there have been intriguing efforts to broaden the set of capacities under examination and to view them through a Darwinian lens. The argument from evolutionary psychology goes like this. Just as linguistic (and numerical and spatial) capacities have evolved to allow optimal adaptation to the environment, other human capacities may also have universal properties, and these, too, would be adaptive consequences of millennia of evolution. Specifically, there may be universals in the moral realm (e.g., the inclination to seek fairness in each transaction) and in the aesthetic realm (e.g., the attraction to visual or auditory patterns that are moderately discrepant from those typically encountered in one's surroundings). Educators take note: perhaps lessons need to be crafted in light of these universal mental representations of beauty and morality.

3. Different Patterns of Intelligence. In my own work, I have sought to unite the study of mental representations with a focus on differences among individuals. I believe that Chomsky and his associates are correct in delineating a set of realms, each of which features its own forms of representations and its own developmental (or maturational) history. However, it does not suffice simply to identify those realms and to observe them as they unfold.

According to my analysis, all human beings possess at least eight quite separate forms of intelligence. Each intelligence reflects the potential to solve problems or to fashion products that are valued in one or more cultural settings. Intelligences are identified by a set of criteria: these include representation in specific parts of the brain; susceptibility to encoding in a symbolic system; and the existence of special populations, such as prodigies and savants, that often exhibit intelligences in splendid isolation.

Intelligence tests typically tap linguistic and logical-mathematical intelligence—the intelligences of greatest moment in contemporary schools—perhaps sampling spatial intelligence as well. But as a species we also possess musical intelligence, bodily-kinesthetic intelligence, naturalistic intelligence, intelligence about ourselves (intrapersonal intelligence), and intelligence about other persons (interpersonal intelligence). And it is possible that human beings also exhibit a ninth, existential intelligence—the proclivity to pose (and ponder) questions about life, death, and ultimate realities. Each of these intelligences features its own distinctive form of mental representation; in fact, it is equally accurate to say that each intelligence *is* a form of mental representation.

This set of intelligences helps define our species; to this extent, it is consistent with the Chomskian view that there are universal forms of mental representation. But individuals also differ from one another in personality, in temperament, and in the peculiar array of their intelligences. While we all possess all of the intelligences, perhaps no two persons—not even identical twins—exhibit them in the same combination of strengths. Moreover, the configuration of intelligences, and relationships among them, will also shift over time, in response to people's experiences and the sense that they make (or fail to make) of them.

Should this picture be even approximately correct, it presents significant educational implications. In times past, schools have been uniform, in the sense that they taught the same materials in the same way to all students, and even assessed all students in the same ways. This procedure may have offered the illusion of fairness, but in my view it was not fair, except to those few blessed students strong in the linguistic and logical domains. If one seeks an education for all human beings, one that helps each achieve his or her potential, then the educational process needs to be conceived quite differently.

In short, school must be individualized and personalized. We need to understand the specific mental representations of each student in as much detail as possible. And then, insofar as is feasible, we ought to configure education to allow two outcomes: (1) students encounter materials in ways that allow them access to their content, and (2) students have the opportunity to show what they have learned, in ways that are comfortable for them yet also interpretable by the surrounding society. Such an individualized education for all moves to center stage when I address the specifics of an education centered on truth, beauty, and goodness.

4. The Pros and Cons of Early Representations. As everyone (echoing my sparring neuroscientist) now acknowledges, the early years of life are important for the development of health, cognition, personality—indeed, for the full growth of the child. During these early years, and without formal tutelage, youngsters develop quite powerful theories about how various worlds work—the physical world, the natural world, and the world of human beings.

Some of these ideas are useful. For example, youngsters come to appreciate that objects continue to exist even when they are out of sight, and that each class of objects allows certain actions but not others (compare a rubber band with a stone or a strand of taffy). They come to appreciate that some objects are propelled by their own power, while others require the intervention by humans or other external entities. And they come to appreciate that all human beings have minds, just as they themselves do, and that these minds come stocked with intentions, fears, and desires.

That is the good news: the existence of certain universally achieved representations that are accurate and adaptive. Alas, however, some ideas that develop in early childhood are much less well grounded. Youngsters come to believe, for example, that individuals who look like them are good, while those who look different are bad. They come to believe that something that moves is alive, while something that does not move is dead. They come to believe that objects are propelled by unseen magical forces. And so on. Much of children's literature and drama plays with these beliefs in ways that engage youngsters, even as these features may amuse oldsters standing in the wings.

Moreover, these early representations—misconceptions, as they have come to be called in the trade—do not simply disappear with age. On the contrary, they prove to be disconcertingly robust. Even students who have studied formally in school continue to hold on to a variety of misconceptions about topics ranging from evolution to opera to the Holocaust. The persistence of early misconceptions is due to a number of factors: the unexpected strength of early representations; the fact that educators have not appreciated that strength and so have ignored them; the tendency on the part of many adults to confuse the accumulation of factual information or cultural literacy with the alteration of robust mental representations; the pressure to cover too much material in a necessarily superficial manner. As a result of such ubiquitous factors, even the best students in the best schools often continue to harbor misconceptions. The durability of the "unschooled mind" has been all too well documented by ingenious cognitive researchers.

The educational relevance of these findings is all too patent, and it is discouraging. Many of the ideas that furnish the minds of students—even of good students—have little basis in reality. Evolution is not a continual march toward perfection; operas need not be relics from the past; the Holocaust happened, and something like it could happen again. Yet their inadequacy does not prevent these representations from enduring. Indeed, just how to excise fallacious ideas and replace them with more accurate ones might be seen as the central question of formal education.

5. *The Desirability of Higher Cognitive Functions.* We want all students to acquire basic facts and basic literacies. Current rhetoric notwithstanding, I have never met an educator who questions the importance of these basics. Yet many of us also want youngsters to go beyond these elementary capacities—not only because they can then grapple with more complex and subtle ideas but also because the world of work will increasingly require them to go beyond basic competencies.

Recently, psychologists have explored the so-called higher cognitive functions: problem-solving, problem-finding, planning, reflecting, creativity, deeper understanding. And they have also called attention to the emerging capacity to think about one's own mind—to reflect on one's own memory (metamnemonic capacities), one's own thinking (metacognitive capacities), and even one's own representations (metarepresentational capacities).

Thinking explicitly about one's own mind, about one's own thinking, may be a relatively new phenomenon, except among philosophers. Most of us, for most of history, have resembled Molière's Monsieur Jourdain, who only latterly discovered that he had been speaking prose all his life. It may well be that an individual can think well and deeply without taking a distanced view of his or her own thought processes. It has been said, of such great writers as Henry James and Dante, that their minds were so fine that they were never interrupted by thought.

For the rest of us, however, it may be valuable to be able to take stock of our own thinking—to evaluate the ways in which our minds work well, the ways in which they are inadequate, the kinds of strategies and prosthetics that can be of assistance as we attempt to master disciplinary contents in ways of thinking. (For all we know, Henry James, Dante, and even Shakespeare were acute practitioners of metacognition.)

Further, in the world of today, the opportunity to supplant our own inevitably limited cognitions with the rich representations furnished by technology is invaluable. In earlier times, if one could not manipulate shapes in one's mind, one might well be stymied in a geometry class; nowadays, however, it is possible to create an image on screen and manipulate it in a myriad of ways to one's heart's (or mind's) content. Similarly, aids to our memory, or vehicles that enhance our capacities to ponder our own representations, can be of singular help as we seek to master and keep up with expanding knowledge. For many of us, our computers' various lists, databases, and display and storage functions assume in almost profligate fashion the role played in the past by hand-written journals, penned notes on one's wrist, or one's own stretched mnemonic capacities.

With or without technological aids, the option to heighten awareness of one's thinking process is likely to be taken up in many educational settings. So long as one does not succumb to the centipede's dilemma—which foot should I move first?—this self-consciousness is likely to prove beneficent for both students and teachers. And in particular, it may stimulate them to seek connections among the various contents and disciplines that they are studying—including those that span the three virtues of truth, beauty, and goodness.

6. *Beyond Cognition: The Role of Personality, Motivation, and Emotion.* Whatever intelligence is, whatever intelligences may be, it is helpful to have been born with considerable intellectual potential. It helps as well to have excellent teachers and technologies available, for these can hone our intelligences and enrich our mental representations. Finally, aware-

ness of our own learning and knowledge structures can also be advantageous. Even as we can improve our own health by intimate knowledge of the body and regular monitoring of its structures and functions, so, too, we can improve our thinking by strategic monitoring of our mental representations and processes.

Educators' understandable focus on cognition has sometimes had the unfortunate consequence of minimizing awareness of other equally important factors. Probably the most crucial is motivation. If one is motivated to learn, one is likely to work hard, to be persistent, to be stimulated rather than discouraged by obstacles, and to continue to learn even when not pressed to do so, for the sheer pleasure of quenching curiosity or stretching one's faculties in unfamiliar directions.

But why are some people motivated to learn, while others are not? Flying in the face of the behaviorists, who tied motivation directly to the receipt of tangible rewards, researchers now believe that learners are best served when their motivation is intrinsic: when they pursue learning because it is fun or rewarding in itself, rather than because someone has promised them some material benefit. Indeed, Mihaly Csikszentmihalyi has documented the motivating power of the "flow state," in which an individual becomes so absorbed in a physical or mental activity that she temporarily loses track of space, time, worldly concerns, and even pain.

Darwin's testimony on the virtues of intrinsic motivation is worth quoting: "It may be more beneficial that a child should follow energetically some pursuit, of however trifling a nature, and thus acquire perseverance, than that he should be turned from it, because of no future advantage to him."

What enhances motivation? Early pleasurable experiences of play, in which the exploration of materials and situations leads to deeper understanding, are precious. Close identification with adults, who may accompany a youngster as he or she broaches a new domain, is also crucial; youngsters crave the approval of adults whom they love, and these adults can acclimate students to the world of discipline, the dialectic between fun and effort. Certain cultures have long featured a continuous cycle of practice, learning, and public performance as a pursuit that ultimately becomes its own reward; for educational purposes, it helps to be reared in such a milieu of continual improvement.

The theory of multiple intelligences suggests another factor: people may be most motivated to learn when they undertake activities for which they have some talent. In pursuing such activities they are likely to make progress and avoid undue frustration. It therefore behooves educators not simply to attempt to motivate students en masse but rather to identify activities that will rapidly become rewarding for a certain group of predisposed students.

The role of emotions in learning has also undergone renewed scrutiny. Emotions serve as an early warning system, signaling topics and experiences that students find pleasurable to engage in, as well as those that may be troubling, mystifying, or off-putting. Creating an educational environment in which pleasure, stimulation, and challenge flourish is an important mission. Also, students are more likely to learn, remember, and make subsequent use of those experiences with respect to which they had strong—and, one hopes, positive—emotional reactions.

The integration of the emotional realm into a cognitivist perspective remains an ongoing challenge. Initially, in part to simplify their work, cognitive scientists exhibited a distaste for dealing with affect—it was soft, wet, messy, more suited for the psychoanalyst's couch than for the experimentalist's laboratory. It has become evident, however, that any portrait of human nature that ignores motivation and emotion proves of limited use in facilitating human learning and pedagogy. At the end of the day, people are not computers. And so, in the last several years, cognitivists have proposed various models of how emotions can structure, guide, and influence mental representations. All point to a simple truth: if one wants something to be attended to, mastered, and subsequently used, one must be sure to wrap it in a context that engages the emotions. Conversely, experiences devoid of emotional impact are likely to be weakly engaging and soon forgotten, leaving nary a mental representation behind.

From the Study of the Mind to the Study of the Brain

So far, I have largely avoided mention of the brain. In this neglect, I am in part respecting my intellectual forebears. Neither the behaviorists nor the trait psychologists wanted anything to do with the brain; it was a black box. Deliberately eschewing mentalistic theory and physiological underpinnings, psychologists insisted that "intelligence is what the tests test." And even those psychologists who (like me) have long ago spurned the behaviorist and trait traditions are wary of a wholehearted endorsement of the brain. After all, if everything can be explained by the brain, then there is little reason for psychology and other human sciences—no doubt, one reason for my sharp reaction to the preening neuroscientist!

Of course, for most thinkers today, the divorce of mind from brain is simply a terminological tic. Certainly, I am a materialist. I believe that everything in the mind is the product of a brain—though I would be willing to add that the brain is situated in a human body and develops in an ever-changing human environment. I reject any ethereal spirit, any extrasensory communication, any ineffable angels or demons. As I sometimes remark to students who spend too much time wafting in a New Age milieu: "If you think that the mind is anything other than the brain, simply slice away the brain, part by part, and see what is left when the dissection has been completed."

How can I hold this position, while continuing to resist claims that the brain harbors all secrets of the mind, all keys to learning?

First, study of the brain in itself is simply the study of an organ. In order to be able to think of the brain psychologically, one has to invoke a psychology as well as a neurology. To be specific, let us say that one finds that a certain column of neurons responds to a certain stimulus. How can we describe that stimulus? Is it a face, an oval shape, a moving form, Johnny's grandmother, any gray-haired smiling woman? This question cannot be answered simply in neurological terms. It requires a theory of cognitive psychology: What are the actual entities to which organisms (or their neurons) respond? How can these entities be most accurately (and least misleadingly) described? And how are they represented in the mind-brain? Left to their own devices, neuroanatomists may resemble those self-styled car mechanics who understand nothing about the principles of physics. They might know where a part goes, but they are clueless about how the motor works, and they are helpless when a part breaks down in an unanticipated way.

Second, brains do not exist in isolation. They exist in bodies, which in turn exist in a culture. Brains have the potential to develop in a huge variety of cultures, but once neural development commences (and that is shortly after conception), the culture in which one happens to live becomes an important determinant of the brain's structure and organization. Perhaps there are brain sites wired to anticipate human faces or clusters of phonemes. But which faces and linguistic sounds are encountered—*and how sense is made of them*—is never determined by the brain. Sense-making is inherently a cultural phenomenon. And so one must always think of the brain as inside a mind that is developing in a particular culture, and that must necessarily take on the coloration of life in that (itself ever-changing) culture. Moreover, to the extent that the brain is exposed to a mix of cultures, their complementary and conflicting messages must also somehow be represented and reconciled.

Finally, and most important, education features—indeed, follows from—a set of values. One does not just teach and learn. One makes choices about what to teach, how to teach it, and why it should be taught and learned. These decisions are value judgments, ones with fateful consequences. All the wiring in the brain, known in detail down to the last synapse, can never account for values. However inviting to audacious explorers of mind or matter or metaphysics, the chasm between "is" and "ought" is unbridgeable.

But, you might protest, knowledge of the brain can tell you what is possible and what is not; how to achieve something and why other things cannot be achieved. "Not so fast," I respond. To be sure, knowledge of the brain's structure and functioning might well hold interesting implications for learning and pedagogy. But the only way to know for sure whether something is possible is to try it. And should one succeed despite the predictions of neuroscience, that success becomes the determining fact. Success will simply cause us to change the ways in which we think about the brain, rather than revising the ways in which we think about pedagogy.

An example. Let us suppose that two parts of the brain (we will call them the spatial cortex and the musical cortex) are remote from each other and have relatively few connections with each other. This might lead our Simplistic Neuroscientist to infer that mastering a skill that depends on the musical area should have no effect on one's skills in handling spatial information. But our Ignorant Pedagogue ignores this evidence and insists on teaching music to subjects and then testing those subjects' spatial skills. To many people's surprise, it turns out that the musically trained subjects surpass a control group on some measures of spatial skill.

The Neuroscientist has been disproved.

When we then go on to peer at the brains of the learners "in vivo," we might discover various states of affairs. Perhaps the subjects have strained neurological probability by having—or causing to form—new neural connections between these previously disconnected areas. Perhaps the domains of music and spatial perception share features that had not been anticipated by a consideration of the brain structures usually involved in musical and spatial thinking; for example, both activities may draw upon a previously unknown subcortical structure that maps orders of similar magnitude upon one another irrespective of sense modality. Or perhaps the musical experience turns out to be a general motivator, and ultimately produces superior performance on a gaggle of nonmusical tasks (in which case there is nothing special about the spatial materials). In each case, the fact is the same: existing brain knowledge alone could not have predicted the outcome of the study.

Education and the Brain

Lest I be mistaken for a neurological Luddite, let me reiterate that I believe that brain study is vital in its own right and most suggestive for social scientists and educators. I spent twenty years in neuropsychological research; I continue to devour all the popular science on the brain that I encounter and, when possible, I plunge into the more technical literature as well. I love biological truths!

Indeed, the cognitive topics mentioned above have direct implications for brain study. We know that different patterns of neurological structures underlie different developmental stages. The brain mechanisms underlying universal mental representations and individual intelligences are being elucidated. Much exciting research on neural networks documents the development of early schemas and representations, and the nature (and extent) of the experiences that are necessary if these representations are to be fundamentally altered. The connections and interactions among emotional sensitivities and cognitive capacities have now been documented with exquisite thoroughness. Only when it comes to the highest cognitive functions, like metamemory or creativity, has brain science yet to make its contributions.

Nor does brain science merely reinforce what is already known. Some of the most compelling insights about the mind have come from studies of the dissociations between capacities that were thought to be closely related, and, conversely, from the associations of capacities that were thought to be quite disparate. For example, brain science has made important contributions to the dissection of the once singular capacity called memory; we now acknowledge the existence of different kinds of memory: short-term versus long-term; semantic (generic) versus episodic (memory for specific events); and motor and linguistic forms of memory. By the same token, brain science has shown that linguistic symbols, whether presented in speech, in writing, or in sign, are processed in the same way, and quite differently from numerical symbols; that different numerical capacities are exhibited by the respective hemispheres; and that there exist curious ties, not intuitively obvious, between certain abilities, such as color naming and reading.

Recently, much public attention has focused on the new imaging techniques that allow us to look at brain activity as it is happening and to detect just which structures are involved; these techniques are sure to reveal new operations of the mind. Already such studies have allowed us to identify specific regions of the brain that are involved in different parts of complex processes like naming objects or remembering a musical passage; and other studies have shown that novices process information quite differently than do those expert in a domain.

Let me list some brain-and-mind findings that ought to be kept in mind by anyone concerned with education. I note that most of these findings are based primarily on animal work rather than on research with humans, but I have listed only those that I believe obtain as well with respect to human beings.

1. *The tremendous importance of early experience.* All experiences matter, but those in early life have particular importance for later life. Accordingly, education (in a general sense) should begin in the first months of life.

2. *The imperative "Use it or lose it."* The possession of brain tissue and potential connections is not enough. If that tissue is not stimulated by appropriate sensory perception, and then used actively, it will eventually atrophy or be appropriated to other functions.

3. *The flexibility (more technically, the plasticity) of the early nervous system.* Young children can survive and thrive even if they are missing large portions of the nervous system. But as we age, our brain becomes

far less flexible, and it becomes increasingly difficult to compensate for lost capacities and functions.

4. *The importance of action and activity.* The brain learns best and retains most when the organism is actively involved in exploring physical sites and materials and asking questions to which it actually craves answers. Merely passive experiences tend to attenuate and have little lasting impact.

5. *The specificity of human abilities and talents.* Far from being a generalized machine that works well or not so well, the human brain comprises numerous zones and neural networks, each geared to quite specific capacities. While nature is not entirely fair, and some individuals are blessed with more potentials and talents than others, abilities prove surprisingly independent of one another; a person can excel in one sphere while not faring well with others.

6. *The possible organizing role played in early childhood by music.* A number of intriguing studies suggest that learning a musical instrument in early life may yield positive consequences in other cognitive domains, including those valued in school. (My earlier example of musical and spatial processing draws on these studies.) This novel research still requires extensive replication. However, it suggests that certain activities may assume privileged roles in the organization of subsequent experiences.

7. *The crucial role played by emotional coding.* The formative role of emotions in learning is being increasingly recognized. Experiences that have emotional consequences (and are registered as such) are likely to be retained and utilized subsequently. Individuals whose brains are impaired in ways that make it difficult for them to code experiences emotionally may also find it difficult to retain and make subsequent use of these experiences.

This list could be expanded; it would undoubtedly read differently if I were writing it a decade or two from now. Of special importance are the new imaging techniques, which will allow us to establish the extent to which findings obtained primarily in research on other animals also apply to human beings.

So far, despite the biological bent of this chapter, I have said virtually nothing about genetics and heritability, probably the most hotly debated topic in the study of the mind. With most scientists, I acknowledge the surprisingly large role played by heredity in the performances achieved by human beings. Whether one is dealing with general (psychometric) intelligence, or with specific capacities like spatial or musical ability, it seems that half of the variation is due to genetic factors. That is, roughly half of the variability found within a given population proves to be a function of individual genetic history, while the remaining half, roughly, is due to (typically differing) individual experiences in the world.

Despite the fascination with this topic, particularly in Anglo-American circles, I feel that it holds little import for education. The reason is simple. Youngsters and their teachers are dealt a certain genetic hand and there is nothing—at least so far!—that can be done about that hand. Education has to focus on the approximately half of one's ultimate accomplishments that are due to nongenetic, environmental factors. And the same argument obtains whether future studies should document a heritability coefficient as high as .8 or as low as .2 (the latter indicating that most of the variation is due to environmental factors).

At least so far. I would be disingenuous if I did not note the possibility that in the future people may attempt to change their own genetic composition or make life-and-death decisions such as abortion on the basis of the fetus's ascertainable genetic profile. Such playing God would wreak havoc with all our cultural institutions, including education. I pray that it will not happen.

Less dramatically, and perhaps more likely, studies of the human brain in vivo will be undertaken to suggest specific lessons (for individual children) and policy recommendations (for groups). Suppose, for example, one can determine that areas ordinarily used for the processing of written language are not being activated in a particular brain; this information will certainly be important for diagnosis, and will in all probability be used in treatment as well. Sensitively employed, these measures could be quite helpful. However, the potential for abuse—in labeling; in premature decisions about the course of treatment or the range of outcomes—is real; keen vigilance and enduring humility should accompany any forays into this brave new world.

The Considerable Distance Between Science and Practice

For scientists of the mind, the brain, the genes, these are exciting times. A great deal of cognitive and neuroscientific knowledge has been accumulated in my lifetime; far more will be accumulated in the lifetimes of today's students. Ignorance of these findings is hard to justify; but at the same time, it is important not to be overwhelmed or intimidated by them.

Note well: there is never a direct route from scientific discovery to an educational practice. Every data point, every generalization, can lead to a variety of recommendations, some even contradicting one another. Take, for example, the claim in *The Bell Curve* that it is difficult to change intelligence. This claim led authors Richard Herrnstein and Charles Murray to conclude that there is little point in funding programs like Head Start, which attempt to enhance the intelligence of young children. However, shortly before his death, Herrnstein admitted to me that one could look at the same data and reach the opposite conclusion—that just *because* it is not easy to alter intelligence, we ought to devote enormous resources to that end. (I might add that perhaps we have been trying the wrong methods; new methods, or new technologies, might make it quite easy to raise intelligence significantly. In fact, simply going to school has steadily raised the IQs of children all over the world.)

Similarly, it is important to take the imperial claims of neuroscience or cognitive science with more than a pinch of salt. We are pelted nowadays with statements such as "To develop properly an infant brain requires almost nonstop stimulation from birth to age three." Certainly, stimulating infants is preferable to ignoring them (though excessive stimulation may well be counterproductive). It is crucial to remember that most of the research cited on behalf of these claims has been done on lower mammals, and mostly in the unnatural setting of the psychologist's laboratory. And it is equally crucial to realize that we cannot make statements about what is possible unless we have tried out a broad spectrum of environments; tomorrow's technological prosthetic could render irrelevant all previous claims about human potentials in a given domain.

Modern Westerners often think of the science of human beings as that enterprise which begins and ends within the skin of the individual. I do not believe this is true. What we learn about human beings from studies of the cultures in which our bodies dwell is at least as important as what we learn from psychology and biology; indeed, educational decisions should not be made without equally firm anchoring in both camps. And so, it is time to consider the insights gained from ethnographers, anthropologists, and other observers of cultures.

CHAPTER 5
How Cultures Educate

The Best Preschools in the World

In the rolling hills of northeastern Italy, nestled between Parma and Bologna, lies Reggio Emilia, a city of 130,000 inhabitants. The province of Emilia-Romagna is one of the most prosperous regions of Europe, with fertile fields, abundant agricultural products, extensive hydroelectric networks, and a smattering of light, technically oriented industries. It is also an area with an unequaled history of civic cooperation in economic and cultural activities, dating back to the later Middle Ages; its arts, crafts, and theater are admired all over Italy. Citizens belong to a multitude of associations, including hunting clubs, literary guilds, and cooperative agricultural enterprises; participation in the political process is among the highest in Italy. For most of the last fifty years, Reggio Emilia has had a left-wing government: even after the collapse of world communism, the inhabitants continue to embrace a political system that is democratic, socialistic, and communally oriented.

Shortly after the conclusion of the Second World War, a young journalist named Loris Malaguzzi, who was living in Reggio, happened to visit a small bombed village near the town and was deeply moved by the experience. Having studied pedagogy, he decided to remain in the Reggio area and to attempt to create good schools for young children. Over the next decades, he worked tirelessly and imaginatively with a growing cadre of committed young educators to launch and improve a group of schools for infants (from under a year old to three years old) and for preschoolers (three to six years old). In the early 1990s, *Newsweek* declared that the preschools of Reggio were the best in the world. In general I place little stock in such ratings, but here I concur. The twenty-two municipal preschools and thirteen infant-and-toddler day care centers and preschools in this charmed community are unique.

If you walk into one of the preschools on a given morning, you will first be struck by the beauty and spaciousness of the building. Reggio buildings are ample, open, streaming with light; potted plants and inviting chairs and couches are strategically placed, adding color and comfort to the surroundings. There are secluded alcoves to which youngsters can retreat; interior gardens; and common space where the teachers can meet. Most of the classrooms flow easily into one another and spill out into a large central piazza. Passage to the play areas outside the school is also convenient, and in good weather, one will see groups of children playing together on the grounds. On neat shelves are stored literally hundreds of materials—from colored geometric forms to grains of cereal to seashells to recyclable wooden sticks—with which the youngsters may become engaged at some point (or repeatedly) during the year. Everything seems in place; there is no clutter or mess; and yet, the spaces feel inviting and flexible.

So far, of course, this description does not differentiate the Reggio schools from hundreds of affluent, attractive, well-appointed schools for young children throughout the world. The Reggio schools stand out by virtue of the type and quality of the activities that the children carry out on a regular basis; the deeply caring and *respectful* ways in which teachers interact with the youngsters and with one another; the availability of the education free of charge throughout the municipality (about half the children attend them).

In each of the classes in a school, groups of children spend several months exploring a theme of interest. These themes are ones that attract young children, usually because they offer rich sensory stimulation and raise intriguing puzzles. Among the many dozens of motifs that have been investigated over the years (and sometimes on a number of separate occasions) are sunlight, rainbows, raindrops, shadows, the city, a city for ants, the town lions that preside over the central piazza of Reggio, poppy fields, an amusement park for birds built by the youngsters, and the operation of the fax machine. The children approach these objects, themes, and environments from many angles; they ponder questions and phenomena that arise in the course of their explorations; and they end up creating artful objects that capture their interests and their learning: drawings, paintings, cartoons, charts, photographic series, toy models, replicas—indeed, representatives of an ever-expanding, unpredictable series of genres.

Ultimately, like a story that reaches an appropriate ending, the exploration of a theme comes to a close. Thereafter, the objects that have been created are placed on display so that parents, other children, and members of the community can observe them, learn from them, and appreciate the care with which they have been executed and mounted. Many of these theme-inspired artifacts have made their way into books, traveling exhibitions, and wall displays in their own and other schools. Most observers agree that the works are not just cute throw-aways by young children; many are substantial and evocative creations.

Although the beautiful artifacts produced by the children command the initial attention of adult educators and lay visitors, they do not represent the heart of the Reggio enterprise. In my view, the central endeavor consists of the daily interaction among teachers, students, and sometimes parents and other adults from the community; the equally regular give-and-take among the classroom teachers and their specialized colleagues the *pedagogista* and *atelierista;* and, above all, the astonishing documentation of student work undertaken by the instructional staff during the course of each day.

The educators of Reggio Emilia have developed and continuously improved a set of techniques for taking the ideas and actions of young children seriously. Much thought is devoted to the opening exposure to experiences that might constitute themes to be developed in the coming weeks. But it is not possible to plan such a curriculum in advance. Rather, the particular reactions of particular children to particular experiences become the bedrock, the driving force of the "curriculum." The activities of next week (sometimes even the next day) grow out of the results, problems, and puzzles of this week; the cycle is repeated so long as it proves fruitful. Children and teachers are continually reflecting on the meaning of an activity, which issues it raises, how its depths and range can be productively probed.

Consider how this process works. Suppose that on the second day of school a rainbow appears, which can be observed through the skylight above the central piazza. Either a child or a teacher notices the rainbow and brings it to the attention of others. Youngsters begin to talk about the rainbow; and, perhaps at the suggestion of a teacher, a few children begin to sketch it. Suddenly the rainbow disappears; children begin to talk about where it came from, and whether it has traveled to another site. A child picks up a prism that happens to be nearby and looks at the light streaming through it. She calls over her classmates and they begin to experiment with other translucent vessels. The next day it rains again, but afterward the sky is cloudy and no rainbow is visible. Henceforth children set up observational posts after a storm, so that they can be sure to spy the rainbow when it appears and capture it in various media. And if no rainbow appears, or if they fail to capture its appearance, students will confer on the reasons why and consider how better to prepare for the next sighting of a rainbow.

A project on rainbows has been launched. In the following weeks, children read and write stories about rainbows, explore raindrops, consider rainbowlike phenomena that accompany lawn hoses and mist, record a sensational double rainbow, and play with flashlights and candles, noting what happens to the light as it passes through various liquids and vessels. No one knows at the start just where the project will eventually land; and while earlier projects clearly influence the "moves" made by teachers (and, eventually, by students), this open-ended quality is crucial to the educational milieu that has been created over the decades at Reggio.

Documenting the discussions, as well as the particular actions, reactions, drafts, and works of the children is the job of the staff. It is steady, challenging, and rewarding work. Teachers develop elaborate systems for recording just what has happened, with sufficient clarity so that anyone interested in the children's individual and collective progress can interpret the record later. The documenters frequently use audiotapes, videotapes, and still photographs in addition to paper and pen. It sometimes appears that there is too much documentation going on, and that no one will ever be able to review it all. But the documentation must be exhaustive because it is never clear *which* word, or drawing, or moment will prove crucial for the understanding of the children, the enlightenment of the teachers, and the elucidation of a puzzling phenomenon. Just as the visiting photographer must keep shooting, lest she miss the crucial moment, the teacher-as-documentarian must attempt to be all-inclusive, so that no telltale word or work will be missed.

(An amusing observation. Adults in the Reggio Emilia preschools spend so much time taking notes that sometimes children ape this activity. More than once, I have seen a child pick up a clipboard and begin to make squiggles and check marks, as if to record what other children are doing. What better demonstration of the potency of the apprenticeship! And, of course, ever alert, the teachers try to make constructive use of the child's fledgling efforts at documentation—for example, to comment when that child has noticed something special.)

Not surprisingly, most projects center on aspects of the natural world—plants, animals, and objects (like stones) and events (like rainstorms) that easily arouse children's perceptions and their feelings. But projects arise as well with reference to human artifacts, and sometimes ones of quite recent origin.

Consider the children's efforts to explain the operation of a fax machine. This project was remarkable in two senses. First, the children in Italy faxed pages back and forth with a sister preschool in Washington, D.C., and both sets of young scholars scrutinized this mysterious machine. The children's initial explanations were magical and fantastic; but the electronic, digitalized explanations they ultimately proposed were quite accurate, at least as accurate as the one I would have offered! Working together, children occasionally reach ("co-construct," to use the jargon) a level of understanding that is notable, even by adult standards.

Why this creation and recording of projects? The temptation is to look for utilitarian reasons: to instruct others (including representatives from *Newsweek*); to show parents what children are learning; to hone the skills of the observers; to encourage rich discussions among teachers; to inculcate lessons about rainbows or other group themes. Each of these factors probably contributes to the recording. But as a visitor, longtime friend, and occasional collaborator of the Reggio team, I tender a different answer.

In Reggio, as in other remarkable institutions, the medium is the message. That is, the team at Reggio has worked over decades to fashion the kind of school that best suits the entire community: teachers, parents, the physical setting, the region, and above all, the growing children. The first lessons come from the environment, one that is savored for its beauty. Subsequent lessons come from human stakeholders: children are part of a supportive extended family that is in constant communication and that seamlessly combines pleasure, responsibility, and learning.

Within this inviting milieu, rich experiences are savored and preserved, not primarily for practical reasons but rather because there is inherent value in probing everyday experiences, making them your own, and learning from them. As the Reggio documentarians might put it, their goal is to capture and make public the hundreds of languages—some oral, some bodily, some artistic—that children naturally use, produce, and share with one another.

In my own argot, Reggio encourages the cultivation and elaboration of multiple representations, multiple intelligences—and, in so doing, it furnishes a powerful set of entry points to the community's cherished truths, sense of beauty, and ethical standards. The Reggio approach invites children to explore, in multiple, comfortable ways, the physical world, the biological world, and the social world; it furnishes evocative materials with which to capture one's impressions; it shares the insights with the rest of the community; and it models a set of respectful human relations that should extend throughout the life cycle.

The Reggio team is secure in its modes of operation; its methods provide their own reward. Accordingly, the team does not necessarily engage the questions that are posed by visitors, and particularly, I suppose, by research-oriented Americans. Reggionistas (if I may coin a word) have shown little interest in documenting what children are learning in a more formal or standardized manner; in issuing a permanent curriculum; or in creating modes of assessment that will travel. They have been ambivalent about "scaling up" the Reggio message for the rest of Italy or the rest of the world. It is nice to be noticed and honored, of course, but it is not clear which educational practices travel well, nor that proselytizing represents the optimal use of the energies of the hardworking and sometimes beleaguered Reggio team. Nor has there been much effort to push Reggio education upward, toward primary and secondary school. (However, in the last few years, the left-leaning Italian central government, presided over until late 1998 by a native of Reggio, has shown unprecedented interest in the Reggio schools; it is too early to tell whether this interest will prove enduring.)

Perhaps most surprising to policy-oriented educators, the Reggio team has shown little inclination to follow up the graduating six-year-olds and learn what has happened to them in later life. If pushed, a Reggio teacher or administrator is likely to respond, "Look at how our community works. It illustrates with eloquence what happens when children have an education like this."

Of course, friends and curiosity seekers from elsewhere do want answers to these questions. Particularly, they would like to transport the key ideas and practices of Reggio to their home soil. Efforts are under way to re-create Reggio in several locales in the United States, Scandinavia, and other parts of the world; as can be imagined, a steady stream of visitors (loaded down with recording equipment) comes to Reggio. And thanks to the establishment of a parent organization, Reggio Children, there are many workshops and summer institutes, both at Reggio and in places around the world, where the Reggio approach is on display.

Transplantation will not be easy, however. Reggio is situated in an unusual corner of the world, with rich material and human resources and almost a millennium of public-spiritedness. The schools have their own decades-long history, inspired by a charismatic genius (Malaguzzi died in 1994), and a dedicated staff, many of whom have lived through (indeed, made) the history. What is perhaps most difficult to imitate, Reggio staff members live their work, spending many extra hours in the schools, and enthusiastically putting in many weekends and summers as well. Perhaps not all are married to their work, but the considerable personal sacrifices made by such educators never cease.

While some aspects of the Reggio approach can travel, the education I've described is closely tied to the specifics of the part of the world where it initially developed, and to the particular people who have been involved for decades. It is not possible to factor out just how much, or what specifically, is due to the democratic practices of the region; its civic-mindedness; its socialist government; its rich resources; its religious (yet anticlerical) background; the ideas and practices of Malaguzzi (and those of others admired by the Reggio educators, such as Piaget, Montessori, Vygotsky, Dewey, and Bruner); the chemistry of the vital team that Malaguzzi assembled; and the specific experiences of team members in Reggio, observations by longtime visitors, and formal residencies in other parts of the world. No doubt, the broad answer is that Reggio today is an amalgam of these and many other factors, which could not be replicated exactly. American notions that one can visit Reggio for a week, then replicate its key features in a year or two of experimentation back home, strike Reggio staff members as illusory; I believe that they are right in this skepticism.

Still, I do not want to suggest that Reggio cannot be re-created elsewhere, at least in part. Serious efforts have been undertaken in a number of American communities, including St. Louis, Missouri; Columbus, Ohio; Amherst, Massachusetts; Los Angeles; and the District of Columbia, under a full range of economic and social conditions. At an independent school that serves some of the wealthiest families in the country, children come to school in limousines, and parents squeeze in their voluntary "school hours" between jet-setting and charity balls. At a municipally supported school in one of the poorest urban areas of the country, children are often brought to school by distant relatives or neighbors, who sacrifice their own pleasures so that they can afford to dress the children for school. Needless to say, each "American Reggio" takes on the coloration of its setting and clientele.

Let me call attention to what has *not* been included in my description of the Reggio and Reggio-inspired schools. I have made no reference to the genes or the brains, and scarcely any reference to the minds of the children and the teachers. I did not even have to strain to effect these omissions. It is quite natural and appropriate to speak of educational institutions in terms of the culture that gave rise to them and the norms and values expressed in their everyday practices.

To focus on culture is not to deny psychology or biology; each of these vantage points is necessary. Schools in general—and equally, schools worthy of emulation—are the product of their society and culture: its goals, its values, its ways of making and interpreting meanings. Perhaps less dramatically, but equally decisively, these milieus, with their unique histories and values, determine what is likely, what is possible, and what is not going to happen in the education of their children.

The Cultural Turn

Recently, when visiting Singapore, I posed for a picture with an eight-month-old boy whom I had just met. Hoping to avoid the tears that often accompany an infant's encounter with a strange adult, I employed two established techniques. First, I did not peer into the boy's eyes, but instead allowed him to inspect me at his own pace. Second, I gave him my glasses to play with.

While nearly always effective with infants in the United States, my approach did not work with this young fellow. Try as I might, I could not get him to play with, or even to touch, my glasses. When I questioned his parents, I learned that he had been taught never to touch anyone's glasses. And when I spoke to other Singaporean parents, I was told that young children at home are not allowed to play with the objects within their grasp, except for designated toys. Two reasons were offered: the objects are too expensive; the child might get hurt. (I thought of a third: children should learn to restrain their impulses.)

This prohibition jarred my American consciousness. In my own experience, youngsters of one or two are allowed to play with the objects around the house, and adults simply remove those that might be damaging to handle. In general, Americans see exploration as a virtue; they perk up when children try to emulate acts carried out by adults in the vicinity. With certain reservations, I would say the same thing about the educators in Reggio. Certainly, they are touched when a four-year-old grabs a clipboard and pretends to make notes about the contraption that a peer has built; and they may try to convert this innocent mimicry into a "teachable moment."

My Singapore experience reminded me of an incident that occurred in China a decade earlier. My wife and I were visiting Nanjing with our eighteen-month-old son, whom we had adopted from Taiwan when he was an infant. Each day we allowed Benjamin to insert the key into the key slot at the registration desk of the Jinling Hotel. He had fun trying, whether or not he succeeded. But I began to notice that older Chinese people who happened to pass by would help my son place the key in the slot and would look at us disapprovingly, as if to chide us: "Don't you uncultivated parents know how to raise your child? Instead of allowing him to flail about and perhaps become frustrated, you should show him the proper way to do things."

I have reflected a good deal on these incidents in Singapore and China because they seem to illustrate fundamentally different assumptions about child-rearing. In the United States and elsewhere in the West, we generally encourage children to try to solve problems and to contrive objects on their own. We see it as a positive development when a child sports a pair of adult glasses or monkeys around with a key that is destined for a specific slot. Westerners have gained a certain hegemony in the contemporary world by exploring, trying out new approaches, experimenting and revising—whether in pursuing science and technology, or in exploring the ocean and outer space. We see the world as filled with challenges that youngsters will one day have to respond to; we believe in giving them a head start in facing the unknown.

Beyond doubt, those influenced by the Confucian tradition also want to prepare children for the world. Traditionally, this world has featured the mastery of long-entrenched practices and the fulfillment of long-standing adult roles, so the precise models exhibited by adults are more likely to be relevant. Moreover, because there is so much to master from the past (and, perhaps, so much to fear from an uncertain future), there seems little point in taking one's time or in leaving discoveries of essential practices to chance. If there is a reliable model around, why not transmit it to the child, so that he or she can advance smartly to the next step . . . and then to the next? For if the child is left to his own devices, he may either be retarded in his mastery of the valued practices, or, worse, head off in his own unproductive direction.

Parents and teachers will differ in their reactions to these vignettes. Some wholly endorse the Western "try it yourself" tack; others are partial to "learning from skilled models"; still others, like me, see value in both approaches, particularly when each is carried out within a like-minded community. We have ample evidence that the Confucian model produces students of high quality; in the West, the results are more variable, but the best progressive schools end up with students who are both skilled and innovative.

Indeed, in my studies of creativity in the East and West, I concluded that education could well begin with either the "mimetic" or the "constructive" approach. What is crucial is that each youngster also have ample opportunity to adopt the *contrasting* stance. Otherwise there are patent risks. The "Confucian"-trained student may be highly skilled but uncomfortable about marshaling those skills in new situations. The Western progressive student may see himself or herself as quite creative, but will all too often lack the skills to do a competent job, whether the assignment is familiar or novel.

Other blends are possible. In the West we have understood creativity largely as a result of individual initiative and solo problem-solving; the individual-centered Nobel Prize epitomizes this "Lone Ranger" stance. Confucian societies have taken a collaborative approach to the creation of new technologies, and, using this tack, have been remarkably successful in economic terms. Recently, the West has also been influenced by effective models from East Asian society. Many workplaces now delegate production to small, largely autonomous teams; increasingly, scientific work also entails collaboration among dozens or even hundreds of workers.

Informally for centuries, and more formally in recent times, the West has extended its exploratory penchant in a new direction: toward the systematic examination of other cultures. People the world over have always had some curiosity about groups that are different; and they have striven to distinguish themselves from neighbors and rivals, even as they have sometimes looked to these groups as allies or as sources for marriage partners. Yet only in the West have we developed a whole branch of knowledge that entails the documentation of beliefs, practices, and attitudes of individuals who initially appear alien from ourselves.

Traditionally, anthropologists were a breed apart. Often estranged from their own culture for one reason or another, they would spend years living in a strange culture, mastering the language and mores, developing affinities and antipathies, and then returning to lecture and write about "their" people. This practice continues but is being refashioned because of a number of factors, including doubts about the propriety of what some deem exploitation; the refinement of technical research methods (focused studies of linguistic or kinship structures); the emergence of reliable modes of documentation (filming and videotaping); and the gradual disappearance of cultures that seem as exotic to Westerners as those first encountered in the nineteenth century.

Much of anthropology is now practiced closer to home, in societies that are less alien, and in regions of our own society that prove intellectually provocative. (One can study witches or transsexuals in the next village—or in one's own.) And rather than remaining disinterested, the anthropologist frequently seeks to become involved personally with, and to come to the aid of, the population being studied.

As anthropology has become a less "exotic" practice, its methods and assumptions have been absorbed into the mainstream of social science. In the field of psychology, for example, investigators have become increasingly preoccupied with cultural questions and methods.

During its period of "physics envy," psychology attempted as much as possible to ape the methods of physical science, setting up pure laboratory conditions and removing from the experiment any vestiges of familiarity or context. This approach, dating back to behaviorist days, is still practiced in certain sectors of psychology and cognitive science. But many investigators—and particularly those focused on human development—have concluded that such decontextualized research can only get one so far. In truth, from the moment of conception, people are enveloped in the assumptions, biases, and visions of particular cultures; these predispositions necessarily color thinking, emotions, and patterns of development. It goes without saying that educational institutions are also affected significantly by the goals and assumptions of the cultures in which they are situated. Indeed, schools have no choice but to embody—or to struggle against—the values of their culture.

Influenced by the anthropologists' tools of the trade, many psychologists now leave the laboratory and study features of daily living that they had previously ignored. To cite just a few examples: Investigators watch carefully the way in which parents communicate with youngsters (and vice versa), considering both what is said (and not said) and the linguistic and nonverbal ways in which messages are conveyed. They also observe how children play with, conflict with, or motivate and instruct one another. Turning their gazes toward schools, psychologists view the classroom as a community, in which specific values are transmitted and various interactions are sanctioned or prohibited. They pay special attention to mentoring relations, within the family or beyond; they probe the role of the media in the socialization of youngsters of different ages; they examine certain classroom practices, like cooperative learning or team projects or communication via the Internet, to find out how children construct and share knowledge. All these areas of investigation throw specific cultural practices and assumptions into sharper relief.

Drawing on the Reggio Emilia schools, let me introduce some of the ways in which psychologists frame their work.

Learning is now seen as *situated*—as occurring in specific contexts, with particular identifying features and purposes, and as extending only slowly and uncertainly into new and unfamiliar environments. Youngsters at the Diana School in Reggio are predisposed to pay attention to natural events, to record them in words or works, to discuss them with others. However, it is possible that the youngsters associate these practices with their teachers and classmates: the so-called project environment is "situated" within the four walls of one school. It remains to be seen whether Diana students also raise such concerns at home, on family expeditions, or when playing with youngsters who attend another school.

Knowledge is also now seen as *distributed*. That is, it does not reside exclusively within the head of an individual; rather, it emerges jointly from one's own perspective, the perspectives of other individuals, and the information derived from available human and technical resources. This assertion proves particularly relevant to the Reggio experience. Many of the achievements of Reggio preschoolers are remarkable; they reflect understanding and artistry of a high level. Yet it is risky to assume that such understanding and skill exist within the mind-brain of specific youngsters; indeed, my guess is that by and large the knowledge is not so localized. The creations of Reggio are group productions, involving not only collaboration with peers but steady probing and support (often termed "scaffolding") by knowledgeable adults; they are dependent, as well, on the limits and capabilities of whatever medium has been employed. It is an open question how much of the understanding remains within the consciousness of a single, randomly chosen child, apart from his or her peers, adults, tangible creations, and supporting conversation.

Not averse to jargon, culturally oriented social scientists have identified processes of *legitimate peripheral participation*: the ways in which youngsters at first observe skilled adults at work and then are gradually, inconspicuously, and comfortably drawn into that labor. Learning begins with observation, evolves to guided peripheral participation, and culminates in full-fledged apprenticeship, often with explicit verbal instruction. Culturally oriented psychologists emphasize the importance of the *milieu,* the *environment,* the *habitus*—the rich, person- and prop-filled context in which occasions for learning most naturally arise. Such scholars speak about the importance of "personal knowledge," acquired by spending time in an environment of mastery. Such knowledge is difficult to capture in verbal propositions; yet it is essential to productive work in any domain, whether it be butterfly collection, tennis, mathematics, or music.

These conceptions are central to claims about the Reggio experience. The most important aspects of Reggio are "in the air." They are embodied in the attractive and comfortable physical attributes of the school, the rich displays of student work and commentary throughout, the gentle way in which adults speak to one another and to the children, the rhythm of the morning, the individually prepared and lovingly served lunches and snacks, the quiet but flexible afternoon rest periods, the energetic but not wild playground activities, the passing of the weeks and the months on a single project, even the shape of the seasons and the years. Adults set the tone; children are drawn into its spirit, and they in turn pass on their knowledge and practices to those who are even younger, whose participation is as peripheral as theirs once was.

None of these culturally tinted lenses has in itself totally transformed our understanding of children's cognitive, social, and emotional development. Much of development still occurs in the head; and in the end, students cannot use situated or distributed or peripheral or personal knowledge unless they somehow make it their own. But we psychologists have become much more aware of the social, contextual, and distributed aspects of knowledge both abroad and at home. Knowledge arises in relations among human beings; much of what we internalize comes from the models and the motifs of others; and we ourselves elaborate upon knowledge in social settings: home, school, the wider community.

Insights from Studies of Culture

Taken together, hundreds of studies of child-rearing and education in diverse cultures undermine two extreme positions. The "universalist position"—to which psychologists and biologists are partial—holds that, deep down, people are all alike in the important aspects; apparent differences are superficial and trivial. Linguists at universalistically oriented MIT used to distribute pencils bearing the legend "Context Sucks." The message: don't be tripped up by superficial cultural or contextual differences.

This position holds up well with respect to capacities that are hard-wired—for example, how we perceive objects in three dimensions; or with respect to behaviors that are necessary for survival, like sexual reproduction or securing enough food. But the position proves inadequate when focus shifts to how people use language to accomplish specific goals in a community—do they ask directly, speak enigmatically, or "listen charismatically"? Or to how they introduce children to a toy—do they simply hand over the toy, model it once, show a videotape, play together for many sessions, or teasingly withhold it from the avid youngster? In the latter cases, the assumptions of the culture lead to quite different practices, sometimes even in groups that might seem superficially akin.

The "uniqueness" point of view—favored by anthropologists and by certain multiculturalists—is also suspect. This perspective argues that each culture is sui generis and can only be examined in its own terms. Cultures develop worldviews that are so idiosyncratic that, like Thomas Kuhn's competing scientific paradigms, they cannot be translated into or compared with one another. The most to which one can aspire is to understand such cultures partially and try to convey them, typically through an artistic work or a provocative anecdote, to others even less steeped in the alien milieu. There may well be certain concepts, like Japanese *amae* or German *Gemütlichkeit* or Chinese *hao-xue-xin* that prove difficult to capture in other symbolic codes. (If I provided glosses here, I would be accused of undermining the "uniqueness" position.) And any attempt to evaluate different cultures in terms of uniform criteria is strictly taboo.

In its extreme form, the uniqueness position is equally untenable. Since human beings the world over must deal with many of the same pressures and needs, it is unproductive to assume that they cannot relate to, or appreciate, one another's stances. And partial translation is better than a refusal to translate. Moreover, many people do succeed in being bicultural, or tricultural, and in moving with increasing facility among a number of cultures; such flexible navigation would not be possible if the alternative traditions were truly impenetrable. In his comments on schooling among the Pacific islanders of Pohnpei, Oliver Sacks captures the way in which a single educational regimen can draw comfortably on contrasting cultural traditions:

> But admixed with the latest astronomy and geology, the secular history of the world, a mythical or sacred history was given equal force. If the students were taught about shuttle lights, plate tectonics, and submarine volcanoes, they were also immersed in the traditional myths of their culture—the ancient story, for example, of how the island of Pohnpei had been built under the direction of a mystical octopus, Lidakika.

There is a more productive way to approach cultural differences than the uniqueness or universalist perspective. Every culture must address certain universal needs. It has available certain resources and can secure others; it embodies a history and a set of established and proscribed practices; it is situated in a particular ecology; and out of these and other factors, it must somehow cobble together a viable way of being. For a complex of reasons, cultures arrive at different ways of living. In parts of the world that have been relatively stable for lengthy periods of time, cultural solutions are quite entrenched; elsewhere, norms and practices prove to be far more flexible or chaotic.

Some schemes and solutions will prove easy for another culture to understand; others will prove more mysterious. But with effort, goodwill, and some telling illustrations, it is possible to make progress in appreciating another culture's perspective and, perhaps, in making one's own perspective clearer to others. Such efforts are essential, particularly if one wants to develop a sense of truth, beauty, and goodness that is not hopelessly parochial.

The Cultural Perspective Applied to Education

Let me be schematic—and shamelessly anthropomorphic. Every culture must make sure that its younger individuals master certain areas of knowledge, acquire certain values, rtant that youths develop intellectually, and civically. Certain educating bodies ents, peers, teachers, masters, relatives, rious forms of technology. Certain reward s can be evoked as models, motivators, or

Given this problem space, culture y, of course, but inevitably. These choices are molded, often invisibly, by changing factors within and outside the culture, and they combine to yield its special flavor, character, or "configuration."

Take, for example, the "educating body." In most traditional cultures, parents, older peers, and religious institutions act as educational agents. In secular societies, schools take over many pedagogical functions; in a highly secular society like the United States, both peers and the media assume much of the educating role that had been handled in earlier times by the church and rudimentary schools. In the future, materials and models delivered by powerful technologies are likely to be among the chief educating agents.

Take, next, the issue of different dimensions of development. In societies that are religiously oriented and relatively homogeneous, it was assumed that moral and emotional development would be the responsibility of the schools. Secular societies have largely removed this responsibility from the school, and expect instead that it will be handled at home and in the church. This is fine, as long as there is a home with parents, and/or a church that is valued by the community. When these are absent, however, a more troubling scenario comes into play. Either no agents whatsoever are charged with moral and emotional development, or moral education occurs in a rough-and-ready way on the streets, or in gangs, or courtesy of the most compelling role models that happen to be featured that year in the media.

Consider, finally, the actual content of schooling. In many societies, decisions about curriculum are made by central authorities, and there is little public debate about the body of knowledge to be mastered. Often parents, and, when necessary, individual tutors help students master this core curriculum. Less-centralized societies will offer disparate curricula; and the manner of presentation is often left to the teachers. One often ends up with a much wider distribution of performance, some schools insisting on very high standards, others having low standards or none at all. Even within the same school, one may also encounter a wider variety of performances, since the level of attainment is a joint and still poorly understood function of student efforts, familial standards, teaching styles, teacher competencies, and societal demands.

Beyond Reggio: Other Effective Schools

As historian David Tyack has wryly noted, there is no such thing as "the one best system." At every educational level, good teaching can be practiced in various ways. Even those who attempt to re-create the Reggio model must realize that it inevitably takes on the coloration of its new surrounding, with its idiosyncratic mosaic of parents, faculty, and community.

Through my travels and reading, I have been struck by the variety of educational visions that work for different age groups, in different parts of the world. There is a joke in my trade that one should go to infant school in France, preschool in Italy, primary school in Japan, secondary school in Germany, and college or university in the United States. Without attempting to test this proposition, I want to mention a few of the compelling approaches and promising practices that one can observe in schools and other educational settings today. This brief survey calls attention to the many ways in which one can educate effectively, as well as to how different cultures place their distinctive accents on schools.

Preschools

In Japan, and in other societies influenced by the Suzuki method of talent education, children of four or five are able to play the violin in solo performances and in string ensembles. They achieve this proficiency thanks to a brilliant method of pedagogy devised by the Japanese pedagogue Shinichi Suzuki. In the years directly after birth, young children listen to recorded violin music. They also observe their mother playing a violin every day, and they themselves are allowed to handle a child-sized violin for short spells.* They are then bathed in music, as they learn to play a carefully ordered program of pieces which they presumably enjoy; this sequence has been designed to take advantage of the arrangement of strings on the violin, of finger movements that youngsters can readily perform, and of melodies that young children enjoy. They also participate frequently in performances with peers, including some a bit more advanced than they are, or a bit behind. Through this carefully controlled and loving regimen, the students become competent performers by the time they have reached school age. But little attention is paid to the inventive potentials of music making.

The Suzuki approach embodies a number of features of Japanese culture: There is the deep respect for art, and an appreciation of the practice and craft that are necessary if someone expects to enter into and ultimately master a tradition. (That the Suzuki repertoire features Western music is not of the essence; Suzuki always maintained that he could as well be teaching flower arrangement or performance on a traditional Asian instrument.) Equally important is the role of other indi-

---

*In Japan, the parent involved is almost always the mother. If she does not play the violin, she is encouraged to learn it, and to remain at least one lesson ahead of her child!

viduals in one's training. The mother is the initial educator; indeed, one of the reasons why Japanese mothers have traditionally not held jobs is so that they can concentrate their efforts on the formation of their young child. But other youngsters also play a crucial role. Children are expected to inspire and support one another, and much of early education is devoted to creating a harmonious group of peers, like the one expected at the workplace some years hence.

In the United States, some youngsters are enrolled in Spectrum classrooms, where the approach is influenced by my theory of multiple intelligences. Spectrum classes are richly stocked with materials designed to stimulate the several intelligences, as if a children's museum—with its scientific displays, live animals, artistic and musical materials, games and puzzles—had been transported into a nursery or kindergarten class. Over the course of a year children are encouraged to interact with all the materials, and thus to exercise their range of intelligences. Should they appear reluctant to work with certain materials, teachers try to "bridge": that is, they emphasize materials that the child has previously enjoyed in order to ease the transition to objects that are forbidding. At the end of the year, families receive a Spectrum profile. This document describes a child's strengths and weaknesses and suggests activities that could be undertaken at home or in the wider community to encourage the child's personal development along various pathways.

Though this state of affairs may be less transparent to Americans, Spectrum is as revealing of its cultural heritage as is the Suzuki method or the Reggio approach. To begin with, the program is based on a belief in the importance of materials and technology: children should be given lots of objects to play with, and the greater the variety, the better. Second, there is a commitment to the significance of individual differences. Every child matters, and one should try as much as possible to develop the idiosyncratic strengths of each. Value is placed on assuming new challenges; thus, special efforts are devoted to helping children move from areas where they are comfortable to ones that are initially threatening, but that should eventually be confronted and conquered. Finally, while Spectrum encourages group work, the notion of the child as an individual learner—an individual mind working with specific materials—prevails.

Certainly it would be possible to have an education that honored both the Suzuki and the Spectrum milieus—but only if one recognized the quite different pulls of the cultural traditions from which they initially arise. The respect for art and craft is greater in the East Asian milieu, while the appeal of a variety of initially engaging materials reflects a contemporary Western perspective. The intensive supporting role played by mothers in East Asia would have to be assumed by some adult(s) in the West, if the Suzuki method were to be effective. By the same token, adult Japanese would have to become far more oriented toward individual goals and needs—toward the ways in which each child differs from his peers and requires her own bridging—if the spirit of Spectrum were to be imported to a culture that has been predominantly oriented toward harmonious relations within the group.

Primary Schools

In Japanese primary schools, the first priority is to ensure that children are comfortable at school and that they can interact civilly and productively with others. Much effort is dedicated to encouraging the proper interpersonal behaviors and practices. Counter to the stereotype of rote learning in a militaristic classroom, children are posed challenging questions and encouraged to work together in teams over a considerable period of time in order to come up with solutions—including original ones. In such groups, the children not only receive ideas from each other but also learn that the group is often more effective than the lone individual. The teacher sees herself primarily as a nurturer. There is no tracking. It is assumed that children will progress so long as they work hard and receive adequate parental support at home. (If youngsters are not thriving, parents are likely to turn to private extrascholastic help, rather than attempting to affect the operations of the regular school.)

Though learning is important, the principal goal at this stage of education is to produce children who are good, responsible, and disciplined. And so the children spend much time creating a clean and attractive environment, serving as dutiful leaders or keen followers, taking responsibility for their mistakes, and helping others who have encountered difficulties. At the proper time, boisterous play is allowed, even encouraged. Again, the school is seen as a (perhaps idealized) microcosm of the society that the children will one day join.

In Chinese primary schools, children produce ink-and-brush paintings of striking beauty and delicacy. These works appear as mysterious as the performances of the Suzuki violinists, until one observes the teaching methods. As is the case with the learning of Chinese characters, the teacher demonstrates each brush stroke repeatedly, in the precise fashion in which it is to be articulated. At home as well, the children have books that illustrate the prescribed brush strokes in the prescribed order. After being exposed to "live" and "text" models, the child practices each stroke over and over again. Teachers observe these practice sessions and often aid their charges by "holding the hand." By the end of such a carefully orchestrated session, just about every one of the forty or fifty students in a class can skillfully draw a goldfish, bamboo shoot, or panda bear.

It might seem that this slavish method produces only copies. However, many students are also able to produce reasonable renditions of objects that they haven't been trained to paint and that they could not have painted before. Clearly, this careful attention to models and practicing of brush strokes develop some skills that transfer surprisingly well.

These two examples reveal sharply different accents within the Confucian tradition. Both variants respect craft, the importance of practice, the execution of beautiful objects, and flawless performance. In Japan, however, far more of the educational process is entrusted to youngsters, who learn to work together and, in fact, depend upon one another. In the Chinese instance, the teacher remains the indispensable central figure, and that figure is usually male. Given these practices, creativity is more likely to emerge from group work in a Japanese school. To the extent that creative work arises under the Chinese model, it is more likely to be individual. It may be worth observing that Japanese genius in this century has inhered in teams of technologists, while Chinese genius has more often emerged in science and in individually oriented art forms.

At the Key School (now the Key Learning Center) in Indianapolis, Indiana, and at other schools that have been influenced by the Key School model, children have regular experiences that are designed around the multiple intelligences. Each day they participate in classes (including music, foreign language, and bodily-kinesthetic sessions) that stimulate a particular intelligence. In addition, each day they participate in elective courses called pods and visit a "flow room," where they can focus on activities that highlight intelligences and combinations of intelligences that they favor. The school curriculum features periodic themes (such as Mexico, the "rebirth" of Indianapolis, patterns, birds); working alone or in small groups, students create their own projects, inspired by the theme. The completed projects are presented to classmates, described and critiqued, and the whole activity is videotaped. Projects serve as an excellent showcase for a child's interests, themes, and configuration of intelligences.

Again, the Key School reveals its American roots. There is a decided emphasis on electives and choice, with students engaging in those "flow" activities and selecting those pods for which they show an affinity. Such trust in individual knowledge and initiative might prove jarring in a Confucian milieu. Much of the education centers on projects; as in Reggio, the projects reflect students' interests. However, projects in America are more rarely undertaken by the group; they are essentially the statements of an individual child, or, less frequently, a pair of youngsters, and the projects thrive or falter as a consequence of the child's motivation. Teachers remain in the background, for the most part. And, in keeping with the pressures for accountability in American society, there is much concern with what students have learned from the projects and how this learning can be documented persuasively to the authorized (and often skeptical) educational authorities who control the purse strings.

Yet differences within America prove as vast as those between the Chinese and Japanese examples. At other schools, often in the same neighborhood as efforts like the Key School, students work on a core curriculum, perhaps one inspired by E. D. Hirsch or the privately funded Edison Project. At each age and grade level, there are prescribed lists of concepts, words, and spheres of knowledge that children should know or acquire. Youngsters are regularly tested on this information, rewarded when it has been acquired, and encouraged to study harder when their familiarity with it proves spotty. The curriculum for each age proceeds from that for earlier grades, thus avoiding unnecessary repetition or gaping holes. Especially for those disadvantaged children who do not acquire literacy in the dominant culture at home, such a prescribed curriculum helps to provide a level playing field and to ensure that future citizens enjoy a common knowledge base.

Indeed, in its own way, the core curriculum reflects enduring American values as much as does the Key School. Particularly in a diverse society, the aim of producing a single polity—"E pluribus unum"—constitutes a deep and enduring value, dating back to Horace Mann's common school of the 1840s. Moreover, a core curriculum reflects American values in another way. American educational institutions often judge their efficacy by the number of facts mastered, concepts introduced, specific behavioral objectives achieved. Americans love to count and to keep track of how many things have been learned; newspapers as well as school boards focus on behaviors that are deemed desirable and can be measured. And, less happily in my admittedly prejudiced view, these institutions often accept superficial evidence as proof of learning. Our intoxication with television quiz and game shows has affinities with one salient view of what public education ought to be like.

Secondary Schools

In Germany, a great many students prepare at the secondary level for a specific vocation. Several days each week are spent working in, for example, medicine, banking, or mechanics, learning about its content, acquiring some of the skills students need to work in it, and also learning about the world of work more generally. Much of this education follows an apprentice model: students work "on site," under the guidance of masters and journeymen who can pose problems and guide the students toward a solution, or model skills and foster the development of those skills. Students who perform well on the vocational track are assured a position after graduation in the company for which they have been working; those who pursue university education have had a useful exposure to the world of work.

The German schools, whose practices also pervade much of northern Europe and Scandinavia, embody two long-standing values of the region: First, there is the belief in the importance of the world of work and in the symbiotic relationship between the practices of study and the norms of the workplace. Second, there is a faith that good workmanship is most likely to develop if young people enter into sustained relationships with adult mentors. Indeed, in some German schools, youngsters remain with the same teachers throughout their education; this ensures that they are known intimately and supported in ways that usually come only from members of one's family.

Forty years ago, Singaporeans were so poor that many children went to bed hungry each night. Singapore has virtually no natural resources, just the minds and energy of its three million citizens. Today, Singapore ranks among the top nations in the world in productivity and income, and students regularly occupy the number one slot in international comparisons.

Singaporean students follow a carefully prescribed curriculum in mathematics, science, and technology. Teaching occurs in English, which reflects not only the colonial history of the region but also the fact that English has become the lingua franca of commerce worldwide. As in Germany, education is tracked, with those in the academic tracks having to master more challenging curricula and also more languages. Students work assiduously, on the average doing four to five hours of homework each evening. Parents study with their children, as do tutors and special teachers, and there is little tolerance for sloth in this authoritarian society. It is assumed that graduates will work for the success of the society, in general subordinating individual goals to the wider good.

At least as successfully as the Japanese, the Singaporeans have succeeded in wedding Confucian practices and values to knowledge of how to succeed in a competitive international environment. Other "little tigers" (Hong Kong, Taiwan, South Korea) have also forged an effective blend of once rival traditions—though the recent economic downturn may reveal limitations in the system. There is a strong belief in the efficacy of study, and high value is placed on devotion to learning, and on showing improvement each day; rather than being directed toward individual success (as in the case of the Protestant culture described so memorably by the German sociologist Max Weber), these virtues are yoked to the success of the society as a whole.

At Central Park East Secondary School in the New York City neighborhood of East Harlem, and at other high schools that belong to the Coalition of Essential Schools, the chief emphasis is placed not on a fixed curriculum but on getting students to think deeply and to use their minds well. Schools pledge adherence to nine essential points—for example, student as worker, teacher as coach, no teacher having responsibility for more than eighty students in all, in-depth treatment of carefully selected materials trumps coverage of many topics. As the slogan has it, "Less is more." School administrators commit themselves to developing institutional and pedagogical structures that will allow the realization of these lofty principles.

In general, at schools like CPESS, class periods are long and class size relatively small; subject matter boundaries and choices are minimized, with history-literature-art and science-mathematics often taught by interdisciplinary teams. Students are encouraged to ask bottom-line questions: Why is this important? What's the evidence? What difference does it make? Students graduate not when they have taken a certain number of courses or received certain grades but rather when they have mounted a stated number of performances and exhibitions of their work. The work is judged not only by teachers but also by citizens from the community, who bring their own expertise to bear.

Built from scratch, "alternative schools" like Central Park East Secondary School have worked out their own procedures locally over a period of decades. While cognizant of other models, their founders and administrators insist on developing their own structures and practices; and they never stop reflecting on where they have succeeded and where they have fallen short. They place a particular value on the working out of conflicts among students and, for that matter, on regularly confronting and civilly resolving faculty disputes as well. In these respects, we see distinctly American democratic values at work: a suspicion of top-down modeling; a predilection for beginning new institutions, rather than trying to reform ones that are already established; a focus on developing minds that can succeed in novel surroundings; the involvement of persons and institutions from the wider community; and the notion that the school should be an idealized microcosm of the larger society, complete with its conflicts and means of resolution.

Of course, at some American schools no need is felt for constant reinvention. In New England, elite independent schools like Phillips Andover, Phillips Exeter, and Roxbury Latin School have long favored traditional curricula and rigorous standards, as well as a rich regimen of extracurricular sports, arts activities, and quasi-scholarly enterprises like the school newspaper. Teachers are highly educated and put in long hours; the students are seen (and see themselves) as future leaders of the society. These schools can be seen as a blend of Singaporean rigor, on the one hand, and Central Park East's emphasis on analytic work and democratic practices, on the other. Many Americans aspire to education at these and similar institutions; unfortunately, because such schools are expensive and highly selective, only a very small portion of the population can attend.

A program along similar lines, the International Baccalaureate (IB), was begun in England and is now featured in hundreds of public and independent secondary schools throughout the world. The IB program also features a prescribed curriculum, along with tests that are graded by external examiners. Included are not only the predictable "core subjects" but also a range of art forms and a culminating interdisciplinary course on the theory of knowledge. The IB has particular appeal for families who move from one region of the world to another and yet look for continuity in curriculum and standards. In an increasingly globalized economy, this appeal is likely to grow. Not surprisingly, the IB is now being extended to primary and middle schools; intriguingly, the Reggio model is influencing the design of the program for the earliest years.

At the highly selective Israeli Academy of Arts and Sciences in Jerusalem, gifted students take a rigorous curriculum that spans the arts as well as the sciences. All students are required to engage in community service. Ethical issues are constantly addressed; students discuss with practitioners the moral dilemmas that arise in scientific and other professional work.

While most students enter at the secondary level, promising students from the Israeli Arab community are identified at an earlier age; these aspiring scholars receive special supplementary education (called the Discovery Program), so that they can compete successfully with the more privileged majority population. (A few years ago, an Arab girl received the highest mathematics score in the entire country.) Graduates, often successful at a young age, are encouraged to return to the school and to aid in the instruction of the next generation of talented students.

Of the schools I have discussed, none is more ambitious than the Academy, with its challenging multidisciplinary curriculum and its assumption of ethical as well as scholastic concerns. Moreover, rather than serving as a sanctuary from the conflicts of the larger society, the school is founded on a mixing of Jewish and Arab populations and on collaborative confrontation of the most vexing issues faced by the society. In the legendary Room 36, Arab, liberal Jewish, and Orthodox students argue till one A.M. and arise as friends several hours later. Clearly, the Academy embraces one set of Israeli values, those embraced by the Academy's visionary founder Raphi Amram. The Academy has already spawned cognate institutions in other nations (including Jordan) and has

forged links with high-performing academies in the United States and
other nations. In Israel, as the adage reminds us, the possible is done
today, the impossible tomorrow. The Academy provides one model—
elitist *and* engaged—of how positive energies might be mobilized in the
always embattled Middle East.

A School Vision

Beginning with the example of Reggio Emilia, I have sought to show
how good schools—in different parts of the world and in neighboring
regions of the same community—can arise from the crucible of their
cultures. Visions of school will differ enormously, depending on history,
locale, curricular needs and desires, available resources, and cultural
and individual goals. And the beliefs and attitudes embodied each day by
parents and teachers will have at least as strong an influence on the texture of the school and the kinds of youngsters that emerge.

Effective education can take many different forms, but certain features must be present. Those who run the school—or network of
schools—must have a clear vision of what they want to achieve. Mission
statements may be helpful, but they are essentially signs of the current
thinking, not agents of change. The school's stakeholders must have a
clear idea of how its classes should operate, what its graduates should be
like, how to determine whether the classes and graduates are up to par,
and what correction in course is to be recommended should these goals
not be realized.

Stated so nakedly, these features may seem self-evident to the point of
tedium. Why would one want *not* to have such agreement and consensus? Indeed, in more authoritarian contexts, or in very homogeneous
places, it may not be all that difficult to secure consensus on how schools
should operate.

However, three factors greatly complicate the task of developing a
coherent vision of schools. First of all, communities often comprise
groups that admire profoundly different kinds of schools, and kinds of
persons. It is often easier to paper over these differences, or to find a
solution that superficially pleases everyone, than to bite the bullet and
forge out a genuinely consensual vision.

Second, even when the vision itself is clear enough, how to achieve it may not be so evident; what to do when the vision seems elusive or recedes into the background is even more difficult to determine. Educators are not experimental scientists; they cannot conduct the crucial experiments with controls, and even if they could, they most probably wouldn't want to.

Third, conditions—and cultures—change. A vision that worked well a hundred or even twenty years ago may not make sense today. This is especially true of what is learned in the years directly before entry into the professional world. It might have been true that the mastery of Latin and Greek a hundred years ago, or of calculus twenty years ago, was the mark of the individual ready to step out into the world; but today problem-solving, or metacognition, or familiarity with the changing workplace, or mastery of specific intelligences might be a much more valuable attribute.

It would be congenial to the theme of this book if the missions of schools could be stated clearly in terms of roles, values, notational skills, disciplinary knowledge, and an understanding of the true, the beautiful, and the good. However, we often fail to state what is intuitive or self-evident to us. Moreover, much of the most important curriculum is hidden—rarely spoken about, conveyed instead by the behaviors and attitudes of the older individuals in the environment. It is, so to speak, in the culture, and cannot be magically transformed or transported elsewhere. The school is most likely to continue to thrive if all participants are aware of the extent to which its success depends upon the durability of a cultural support system.

•　　•　　•

As we seek to create an image of effective schools, we can be inspired by an ecumenical view of social science. To put it succinctly, we should not seek to determine whether what is within the skin (the mind-brain) or what is outside the skin (the culture with its values) is more important; we should not see neuroscience or cognitive science as at cross-purposes with, or involved in a zero-sum struggle against, cultural anthropology. *Rather, both perspectives are equally important, indispensable, and cumulative.* What is achieved (or not achieved) at Reggio, Singapore, or Germany stems partly from the exquisite particulars of each region, partly from a judicious exploitation of the mental representations, proclivities, and intelligences of young human beings. If we want to think strategically about the best education for all human beings, we must ground our thinking in the latest insights about psychology, neurology, biology, *and* anthropology; and we must seek to synthesize these findings from science with time-honored lore in ways that serve the individuals with whose education we are charged.

CHAPTER 6
Designing Education for Understanding

A Classroom Perspective

Over the last twenty years, a new kind of educational institution has arisen in the United States. It is aimed primarily at young adults who wish to secure particular skills that will help them to advance in the world. While it calls itself a university, in many ways it runs completely counter to the traditional vision of what a university is—or should be—like.

The prototypical example is the University of Phoenix. In the late 1990s, this franchised profit-making operation has spread to forty-seven sites in a dozen states, and with over 40,000 students, it has become the largest private university in the United States. Students can earn degrees in a variety of fields, including nursing, education, information technology, and business. Unlike most American universities, the University of Phoenix features neither a campus, nor a library, nor a permanent faculty. Rather than consisting of academics, the faculty is composed of individuals who are practiced in the fields being taught.

It is fair to say that there is no intellectual life at the university, in any meaningful sense of that term; ideas have value only if they can be put to immediate commercial use. Rather, the university offers students an opportunity to gain desired skills as efficiently as possible. Classes take place in the late afternoon or early evening. Students (who must be twenty-three or older) can park right near the class building, take the course, and drive home again. Much of the work can be done at one's home computer. Convenience of delivery is the hallmark. William Gibbs, the president of the company, declares: "The people who are our students don't really want the education. They want what the education provides for them—better jobs, moving up in their career, the ability to speak up in meetings, that kind of stuff. They want it to *do* something for them." And, like the customers of the most successful fast-food chains, students seem satisfied with what the university delivers.

In the preceding chapter, I described a number of precollegiate educational models and indicated how each emerged from its cultural environment. It would be easy to do the same things with the University of Phoenix—to show how institutions like this meet the needs of busy young working American adults who want to gain new skills and expertise. And I could even indicate how the university prizes the capacity to make use of what one has learned—in my terms, the capacity to demonstrate one's understanding.

My goal, however, is neither to bury nor praise the experiment occurring in Phoenix and all over the United States, in large corporations and in for-profit educational institutions. Rather, I want simply to stipulate in the clearest possible way a set of educational goals that are the *opposite* of those I cherish. The Phoenix mission is completely utilitarian; at least until this point, there is not the slightest intellectual interest in truth, beauty, or goodness—or, for that matter, in falsity, ugliness, or immorality. Nor is there interest in how these virtues might relate to one another or how they might be drawn on to help create a better community. As if to confirm this characterization, the firm recently dropped its requirement that students have some background in the liberal arts.

So much for a contrast case. Let me now shift attention to the kind of education that I personally favor.

False Starts

A sensible way to think about education is to "plan backward": to determine the kind of a person one would like to see emerge at the end of an educational regime—for example, at graduation from secondary school. The challenge then becomes to sculpt an educational approach that is most likely to achieve that vision.

It is easy to see why so many educational systems have foundered. Designers survey knowledge and skills that seem important and decide to cover them all. But time is short and there is far too much material.

Thus, the fatal weakness of an approach that strives to cover the ever-expanding knowledge waterfront.

Another flawed approach is to paper over the differences within a community and try to please all interest groups: a little bit of this, a little bit of that. This solution is particularly appealing in cases when various cultures, or warring camps, all clamor for recognition. Since no one wants to come down too hard on anyone else, the evident solution—though it ends up being patchwork at best—is to make sure that every interest group is represented, either equally or proportionally.

This studied ecumenicism proves devastating in the curricular area. We must teach science, and there are so many sciences (biology, physics, chemistry, astronomy, geology, not to mention the social sciences and information sciences) that we must make sure to touch on. We must teach the arts, and since there are so many artistic interest groups, we must be sure to include the visual arts, the dramatic arts, instrumental music, vocal music, classical ballet, and modern dance—and of course, we must be sensitive to different cultural embodiments of these several art forms.

Another solution, one all too often followed in America, is to pay lip service to the formal curriculum and bow to the standardized tests, but thereafter to shut the classroom door and to do one's own thing. Sometimes, teachers' "own things" are meritorious—after all, there are many great teachers—but the lack of coordination among classes and the absence of accountability to those "outside the door" is lamentable. It is for this reason that American students study the Pilgrims at Thanksgiving almost every year, with unjustifiable redundancy; or that, in a case I recently observed, the same information about the Wampanoag Indians is taught over and over in a Massachusetts elementary curriculum, while large parts of world and American history receive no mention at all. The lack of coordination and accountability regularly results in cases where students who move from one school to another discover almost no overlap between the two institutions' offerings.

Teaching for Understanding:
A Formal Introduction

I call for an education that inculcates in students an understanding of major disciplinary ways of thinking. The disciplines that I have singled

out are science, mathematics, the arts, and history.* Within those disciplinary families, it is important that students study substantial topics in
depth. However, it is not important *which* disciplines or topics are featured. I do not consider it essential that students survey the entire range
of sciences listed above; in mathematics, it is not essential that they master all of Euclid's proofs or every algebraic or trigonometric formula;
they need not study every art form nor every historical event.

Instead, students should probe with sufficient depth *a manageable set of
examples* so that they come to see how one thinks and acts in the manner
of a scientist, a geometer, an artist, an historian. This goal can be
achieved even if each student investigates only one art, science, or historical era. The purpose of such immersion is *not*—I must stress—to
make students miniature experts in a given discipline, but to enable
them to draw on these modes of thinking in coming to understand their
world. Later, if they want to range more widely in these disciplines or
pursue a career in one of them, they will find the time and the tools to
do so.

It is not easy to bite the bullet and to cast aside many disciplines, not
to mention the numerous aspects of a given discipline that also clamor
for attention. And that is why so few educators the world over do so.
Cultural literacy—with its promise of five minutes on every topic—
seems more inviting than in-depth knowledge of a necessarily idiosyncratic set of topics. However, in the absence of disciplinary ways of
thinking, cultural literacy lacks an epistemological home; it amounts to
a hodgepodge of concepts and facts ("Well, students, that's enough on
the Holocaust. Let's move on to holograms") waiting to be used somehow, somewhere, sometime. Moreover, absent such disciplinary texture and glue, the facts are likely to be soon forgotten. Anyone who
doubts this state of affairs is welcome to test students a few years later
on the factual material of any subject they may once have studied and
see how well they do; or, being especially diabolical, to test those policymakers who insist on stuffing the curriculum with vast numbers of
isolated facts and concepts . . . and then publish the scores attained by
these officials!

Let me introduce my alternative educational vision—one firmly cen-

---

*Mathematics should be part of every precollegiate curriculum. I mention it here as part of
my generic discussion of curriculum, but touch on it only tangentially in my treatment of
evolution, the music of Mozart, and the Holocaust.

tered on understanding. An individual understands a concept, skill, theory, or domain of knowledge to the extent that he or she can apply it appropriately in a new situation. An individual with a keen memory might well understand a topic; however, it is also plausible that he or she merely remembers the information and has not a clue about how to use it appropriately in an unfamiliar circumstance.

This formulation entails an acid test for understanding: posing to students a topic or theme or demonstration that they have never before encountered, and determining what sense they can make of those phenomena. An individual who possesses relevant understanding will be able to draw on appropriate concepts, while not activating ones irrelevant to the issue at hand. An individual with emerging understanding will at least be able to draw on concepts that bear some relevance to the topic at hand; or will indicate which information or resources are needed in order to elucidate the phenomenon. In contrast, an individual with little or no understanding will be stymied or will invoke information bearing only a superficial or tangential relationship to the theme under consideration.

Consider someone who understands the rationale underlying the program at Reggio Emilia. If he visits a new "Reggio-inspired" school that enrolls eight- to ten-year-olds, he will be able to assess whether the students' projects are sustained and coherent, whether they lead to enhanced understanding of the phenomena being investigated, and whether the documentation of those activities is accurate and useful. Should the school involve the students themselves in documentation, perhaps as the final phase of a project, that innovation might count as an appropriate adaptation of the Reggio approach with older children.

In contrast, an individual with partial but flawed understanding will more likely draw up a checklist of desired features and simply tally how many are present at the new site. Children's participation as full-fledged documentarians will probably be considered inappropriate and will result in a lower "grade" for the school. An individual devoid of understanding will either throw up his hands or will look to see whether the new site has implemented a rainbow project in precisely the way it was originally done at a Reggio school.

Note that the University of Phoenix may well succeed in inculcating mastery of certain practical disciplines. What is lacking is any concern with, or understanding of, the broader themes of life—indeed, with the questions of why the world is as it is and how life can and should be lived.

Difficulties of Understanding

Would that understanding were easy! In my book *The Unschooled Mind,* I survey a vast body of research documenting that, by and large, even the best students in our best schools do not understand very much of the curricular content. The "smoking gun" is found among physics students at excellent universities—for example, MIT and Johns Hopkins. These students perform credibly in classroom exercises and end-of-term tests. But consider what happens outside class, when they are asked to explain relatively simple phenomena, such as the forces operating on a tossed coin, or the trajectory of a pellet after it has been propelled through a curved tube. Not only do a significant proportion of students (often more than half) fail to give the appropriate explanation; even worse, they tend to give the same kind of answers as peers and younger children who have never studied mechanics. Despite years of schooling, the minds of these college students remain fundamentally unschooled.

One might hope that the problem occurs just in physics departments. But, alas, that is not the case. Similar difficulties appear across the sciences. Students who have studied evolution continue to think of the process as guided by an unseen hand—though in fact evolution results from random genetic mutations, a few of which manage to survive long enough to be passed on to succeeding generations. Students who have studied astronomy insist that the earth is warmer in the summer than it is in the winter because it is closer to the sun in the summer. If that were true, of course, Southern Hemisphere lands like Australia and Argentina would also be warmer in July.

When one examines other parts of the curriculum, similar limitations arise. In mathematics, the problem encountered by students can be described as "rigidly applied algorithms." Students memorize formulas and can then plug numbers appropriately into those formulas. But in the absence of some trigger that a particular formula is wanted, they prove unable to marshal it. And if they forget the formula, there is little chance that they will be able to derive it from scratch, because they never actually understood it. The formula was just a syntactic string that had been committed to memory.

Finally, in the traditional humanistic parts of the curriculum—history, literature, and the arts—students are sustained by scripts or stereotypes. All human beings distill experience in order to arrive at typical regularities; nearly every youngster in our society has constructed scripts about birthday parties, trips to a fast-food restaurant, a visit to a shopping mall. Having constructed such scripts, we—of any age—then interpret and remember new events, with reference to those already familiar patterns. This tack proves adequate when the new event follows the internalized scripts in important particulars. However, one cannot always count on that familiar state of affairs.

Let me give an example. Most five-year-olds have developed a *Star Wars* script. Life consists of a struggle between Good and Bad forces, with the Good generally triumphant. Many movies and television programs, and a few events in real life, can adequately be described in terms of such a script. Most historical events or works of literature, however, prove far more complex; to understand the causes of World War I or the U.S. Civil War, or to grasp the thrust of a novel by Hawthorne or Austen, one must weigh and integrate multiple factors and nuances. Students learn in class to give more complex explanations for such historical or literary events. Yet, when they are confronted with new and unfamiliar materials—say, a story from another culture, or a war in an unfamiliar part of the world—even capable students lapse to an elemental way of thinking. The *Star Wars* "good guy–bad guy" script is often invoked in such situations, even when it is manifestly inappropriate.

Obstacles to Understanding

A chief obstacle to understanding stems from the theories children develop in early life. Children do not require formal tutelage in order to develop representations or theories about inanimate objects, animate objects, their own minds, or the minds of others. Usually, these theories develop quite naturally, seemingly automatically, from the flow of experiences.

As I mentioned earlier, there is a serious problem. Some of these theories feature misconceptions that prove very robust. The misconceived theories can be thought of as powerful engravings that have been incised upon the mind-brain of the child during the opening years of life. The facts learned in school may seem to obscure this engraving; indeed, an observer may be impressed by how much information the child seems to be learning, if one weighs only the mastery of individual numbers, facts, definitions. However, all along, the initial erroneous engraving remains largely unaffected. And then a lamentable event happens. Formal schooling ends, the facts gradually fade away, and the same misconceptions—the same flawed engraving—remains unaltered.

In the case of biology, for example, the mistaken belief that evolution is a teleological process, leading inevitably to the crowning achievement of *Homo sapiens sapiens,* survives despite years of tutelage, as does the Lamarckian belief that important adaptations in one generation will be passed on to the succeeding ones. In history, despite numerous counterexamples, many students continue to believe that the world is divided into good guys and bad guys, with the struggle between these Manichaean forces constituting a staple of life. And they suffer as well from the opposed fallacies of presentism—the notion that all times are just like our own—and atemporality—the inability to differentiate events of a generation ago from those of an earlier century or millennium. For such reasons students have difficulties appreciating important aspects of the Holocaust: that it actually occurred within the lifetimes of their parents or grandparents; that it involved human beings like themselves, most partially flawed, some unexpectedly compassionate; and that attempts at genocide continue to this day, for example in Bosnia and Rwanda.

Unwittingly, teachers are complicit in the survival of early, inadequate representations and misconceptions. The villains include a text-test context, in which students are simply examined on the content of texts or lectures, without being challenged to use the information in new ways; short-answer tests, which offer a set of choices, rather than requiring students to create the choices and select among them; and the uneasy but prevalent compromise by which teachers tacitly agree not to push students too hard, as long as students return the favor. And, above all, there is that old devil "coverage." So long as one is determined to get through the book no matter what, it is virtually guaranteed that most students will not advance toward genuine understanding of the subject at hand.

This state of affairs constitutes the strongest set of arguments in favor of a curriculum that examines a limited number of topics in depth. For only rich, probing, and multifaceted investigation of significant topics is likely to make clear the inadequacy of early misconceptions, and only further exploration of those topics, under the guidance of individuals capable of disciplinary thinking, makes it reasonably likely that more sophisticated understandings will emerge. To revisit our analogy, first one must smooth out the initial misleading engraving; and then, preferably with judicious instruction, one must fashion a new and more adequate engraving.

Consideration of the obstacles to understanding provides an excellent illustration of why—as I earlier argued—education must take into account both cognitive and cultural factors. To understand the power of early misconceptions, one must adopt the lens of the psychologist and the biologist. That is, one must appreciate how such misconceptions arise early in life and why, absent aggressive interventions, they prove so resistant to change. At the same time, one must see how certain cultural inventions—the test, the textbook, the conventional superficial interactions between teacher and student—all serve to reinforce misunderstandings.

To move toward enhanced understanding, one must again adopt both cognitive and cultural perspectives. One must identify those internal representations in need of alteration; construct cultural practices that confront, rather than overlook, the obstacles to deeper understanding; and devise measures to determine whether the "corrective cognitive surgery" has been effective.

Disciplinary Expertise

In contrast to the naive student or the information-crammed but still ignorant adult, an expert is a person who really does think differently about his or her specialty. The expert has successfully achieved the desired set of engravings. Expertise generally arises as a result of several years of sustained work within a domain, discipline, or craft, often courtesy of a traditional apprenticeship. Part of that training involves the elimination of habits and concepts that, however attractive to the naive person, are actually inimical to the skilled practice of a discipline or craft. And the remaining part of that training involves the construction of habits and concepts that reflect the best contemporary thinking and practices of the domain.

For example, a crucial scientific understanding is that correlation does not mean causation. The fact that two events co-occur does not mean that one causes another, even though it may appear so to common sense. We discover, for example, that individuals who smoke over a number of years are more likely to get lung cancer, and we are tempted (perhaps correctly!) to assume that smoking causes cancer.

However, it may also turn out that poorly nourished people are more likely to get lung cancer; so perhaps malnutrition causes cancer. But because this link seems intuitively less plausible, one is inclined to consider possible intervening variables. Perhaps people who smoke are less well educated than people who don't; undereducated people are more likely to be poor; indigent people are less likely to be able to afford a balanced diet and good medical treatment. Hence, it makes more sense to see malnutrition as a correlate of poverty than as a primary cause of cancer.

Another chain of possibilities arises. Perhaps the underlying cause of both smoking and cancer is stress. People who are under stress are more likely to smoke; and people who are under stress are more likely to develop cancer. Perhaps, indeed, stress increases the likelihood that one will smoke and decreases the likelihood that one will be able to stop smoking; taken together, these two factors increase the likelihood that one will contract cancer. Now one has identified a primary variable that may be the underlying trigger of cancer—at least in the sense that its elimination might significantly reduce the incidence of the disease.

Finally, it might turn out that people whose names begin with letters in the first half of the alphabet are more likely to suffer from cancer than those whose names begin with letters in the last half of the alphabet. Perhaps there is a causal link here, but it seems probable that this is mere coincidence.

My point, here, is not to unravel the causes of lung cancer or other cancers but rather to demonstrate a certain kind of systematic and skeptical thinking that lies at the heart of the scientific enterprise. Superficially, of course, the logic of "Smoking causes cancer" and "The spelling of one's last name causes cancer" is identical. Only our common sense leads us to favor the first hypothesis over the second. But someone who has learned to think like a scientist will realize that neither statement, on its own, can be substantiated. One needs to initiate a research program, with proper control groups, to discover whether both of these hypothetical causal chains, one of them, or neither of them stands up in the face of scientific investigation.

I propose that individuals are more likely to learn to think like scientists if they probe deeply into an area (such as the causes of cancer or poverty or stress) than if they jet by a hundred different examples drawn from a dozen sciences.

Let us consider, as a contrast, the pitfalls that may undermine historical thinking. For instance, suppose that a document is discovered that purports to provide new information about the biblical King Solomon. One person unschooled in historical thinking is likely to assume that the document is authentic, and that it describes a person who is much like ourselves. Another unschooled person might conclude the opposite: that the document must be a fake, since so little writing from the time has survived; and that Solomon, being world-famous and from a remote historical era, represents an entirely different species of human being.

Neither set of assumptions is justified, of course; and the historically informed individual would think about the issues in a quite different way. She would first of all attempt to discover the conditions under which the document was found, and she might use carbon dating (or, if more humanistically inclined, linguistic analysis) to test its age. If she found evidence to suggest that the document was authentic, she would then turn to the issue of whether the picture of Solomon it presented was consistent with historical and contemporary notions of the Hebrew leader, or whether it contradicted them. This investigation might include revisiting other texts of the era, as well as commentaries from succeeding centuries. Finally, knowing that Solomon once lived, but that he represented a civilization in many ways quite unlike our own, she would try to characterize the new Solomon in a way that suffered neither from presentism ("All people are just like us") nor from exoticism ("Anyone who lived before my grandparents is as remote as an alien from another planet").

Again, such habits of mind are not arrived at easily, nor are they likely to result from a course of study that blitzes, in thirty-five breathless weeks, from Plato to NATO or from Cleopatra to Clinton. But it is the ways of thinking that are crucial here: only if armed with some notion of how historians work will a student be able to make sense of the various claims made about, say, the causes of the Vietnam War or the character of Martin Luther King, Jr. Only if equipped with some understanding of how scientists proceed will a student be able to evaluate claims about the causes of AIDS or the advisability of taking a certain hormone to increase fertility or prevent baldness or osteoporosis.

It should now be clear why a "fact-based" approach will make even less sense in the future. One can never attain a disciplined mind simply by mastering facts—one must immerse onself deeply in the specifics of cases and develop one's disciplinary muscles from such immersion. Moreover, in the future, desired facts, definitions, lists, and details will literally be at one's fingertips: Either one will be able to type out a brief command on a handheld computer or one may even be able simply to blurt aloud, "What is the capital of Estonia?" or, "Just where is Ecuador situated?" Sheer memorization will be anachronistic; it will be necessary only to show students their way around the current version of Encarta. Increasingly, the art of teaching will inhere in aiding students to acquire the moves and the insights of major disciplinary fields.

Four Approaches to Understanding

There is, alas, no royal road to understanding; or, to put it positively, many clues suggest how best to enhance understanding. I'll mention four that have seemed particularly promising to me and my colleagues at Harvard Project Zero.

1. Learning from Suggestive Institutions. Some ancient institutions, such as the apprenticeship, harbor instructive clues. In an apprenticeship, a novice spends a great deal of time in the company of a master. The master tackles new problems as they arise, drawing the novice into problem-solving (and troubleshooting) at a level appropriate to his current skills and understandings. The rising journeyman thus receives much healthy exposure to examples of understanding, as well as many opportunities to exhibit incipient understanding and receive apt feedback.

Clues may emerge from new institutions as well. My favorite examples here are science museums, as well as other hands-on museums, in which children are encouraged to explore exhibits at a comfortable pace. Of course, such an opportunity does not in itself compel understanding. Effective museum exhibitions encourage youngsters to try out their own theories and to see for themselves what works and what does not. For example, students can shoot balls through various kinds of tubes and predict how the balls will fall and where they will land. The balls can be dotted with lights to make their trajectories easier to follow. The exhibit can also include simulations or virtual realities, by means of which, again, the course of the ball can be observed, predictions checked, theories (and their underlying "engravings") revised in the light of often surprising new data.

Such hands-on experiences often reveal ways in which the children's current thinking is inadequate. And given spirited conversation, proper guidance and scaffolding, or an ingenious and reflective child, a more appropriate theory can arise. That freshly minted engraving can in turn be checked and revised in the light of new observations.

2. Direct Confrontations of Erroneous Conceptions. Going one step further, one can actually confront students with ways in which their current conceptions are inadequate. Consider a child who believes that one feels warm when wearing a sweater because the sweater itself generates warmth. Once this explanation has been offered, a parent or teacher can suggest that the sweater be left outside each evening. If the sweater itself is a heat generator, then it ought to be warm on the following morning (or at least warmer than neighboring rocks or other items of clothing). If, however, the temperature of the sweater (as measured by a thermometer) proves identical to that of surrounding entities, one has challenged the child's theory that the sweater itself generates heat.

When it comes to the rigid algorithms activated by many students of mathematics, it makes sense to create a situation in which students must think like the mathematician who developed the formula, and see whether they can themselves progress toward an appropriate formula. Consider, for example, how long it takes a vehicle to traverse a certain distance. Students can be equipped with a whole range of vehicles, a stopwatch, and a room with various racecourses and barriers. They can then be asked to predict how quickly various vehicles will cover specific distances, and what might be done to change the speed of a particular vehicle or make it more competitive.

Engaged in such an activity, many students will discover the irrelevant variables—for example, the size, shape, and color of the vehicle, the barriers, the room's dimensions—as well as the relevant one—the average speed (rate) of the vehicle. Some will move toward a formulation that approximates the classroom staple: distance covered = rate × time. And even those who do not arrive at that formula on their own will at least be more likely to understand it once it has been introduced. They have now had considerable experience in manipulating variables that are (or are not) relevant to the problem at hand.

Finally, in the case of scripts and stereotypes, the proper antidote is regular assumption of multiple perspectives. Scripts and stereotypes reflect a certain perspective at a certain moment in time. If, however, students accumulate considerable experience in thinking about a situation or event from a number of points of view, they are less likely to embrace a simplistic, one-dimensional explanation. And so, for example, students come to possess a much richer view of the American Revolutionary War if they learn about the struggle from diverse angles: the point of view of the British, who were dealing with rebellious colonies; from the perspective of the French, who had little interest in the colonies per se, but much interest in thwarting their British rivals; and from the vantage point of colonial Tories, who sought to remain loyal to their motherland.

As the educational psychologist Lauren Resnick has pointed out, disconfirming experiences do not always suffice to dissolve faulty conceptions and enhance understanding. Misconceptions can be quite robust, and they sometimes prove as insensitive to disproof as the belief system of a religious fundamentalist is to incontrovertible scientific evidence or disconfirmed predictions. Yet, for most individuals, a challenge to a deeply held belief at least compels attention; and efforts to defend that belief, or to discover a better belief, line the most promising routes toward enhanced understanding.

3. A Framework That Facilitates Understanding. With my Harvard colleagues David Perkins, Vito Perrone, Rebecca Simmons, and Stone Wiske, I have developed an approach that places understanding front and center. The key idea is that understanding should be construed as a performance, a public exhibition of what one knows and is able to do. Students ought to be exposed from the start to examples of understanding, and should be given ample opportunities to practice and perform their own understandings. Indeed, only if they have multiple opportunities to apply their knowledge in new ways are they likely to advance toward enhanced understandings in their schoolwork and in their lives beyond the schoolhouse walls.

Talk of a "performance of understanding" may seem a bit oxymoronic, since we usually think of understanding as an internal event, one that occurs in mental representations, between the ears. And we have no reason to doubt that much *is* occurring between the ears, as inadequate representations are being challenged and—should teaching and learning prove successful—more adequate ones are being constructed. Still, the focus on understanding as a performance proves salutary.

A helpful analogy can be drawn from the arts and athletics. People would smirk, rightly, if the mastery of a young art student, musician, or athlete were assessed in an examination hall on a Saturday morning, with a standardized paper-and-pencil or computerized test. Rather, what typically happens in these realms is illuminating. From the start of their training, youngsters observe more proficient (usually older) individuals performing the required actions and understandings: playing new pieces of music, practicing dance steps, engaged in scrimmages or in games against tough and wily opponents. The youngsters can see the moves that must be mastered; they can try them out; they can monitor their improvement and compare it with that of peers; and they can benefit from timely coaching.

In an "understanding" class or school, a similar ambience is created. Novices see older students and teachers engaged in the performances which they ultimately must carry out—writing essays, mounting oral arguments, debating with one another, explaining scientific phenomena, carrying out experiments, creating and critiquing works of art. They see which kinds of performances are valued and why; which criteria are imposed and why; how performances improve and how they do not; the intellectual and social consequences of enhanced understandings. Some of the mandated performances will be enactments of models already observed; but a healthy proportion will require students to stretch. "Milieu is all" in education; these students are reared in surroundings where performances of understanding have become the coin of the realm.

Our work on understanding does not simply present a vision. It also features a particular pedagogical approach, which can be applied throughout the curriculum and can be used with students of different ages and approaches to learning. This approach to understanding was not merely worked out by a group of ivy-covered professors seated in their offices. On the contrary, it emerged from a several-year-long collaborative project involving dozens of teachers in New England. In the intervening years, it has been tried out in many schools all over the United States and in Latin America.

First comes a delineation of "understanding goals." These are simple statements about the understandings that one wishes to achieve over the course of a unit. There should not be too many understanding goals; a few suffice. Let me draw on the examples elaborated on in this book:

- An understanding goal for a biology unit might read: "A student will understand the way that evolutionary forces affect individuals, groups, and entire species."
- An understanding goal for a music course might read: "Students will understand how Mozart and his librettist Da Ponte worked together to create a powerful and lovely score that captured the social conflicts of the era."
- An understanding goal for a modern-history course might read: "Students will understand the ways in which the Holocaust resembled and differed from other attempted genocides of this century."

Other examples from a range of disciplines might include what it means to be alive, the role of the Civil War in American history, how to discover the philosophical themes in the poetry of Keats, why we have negative numbers and how they differ from positive ones.

Second, one identifies "generative topics" or "essential questions." These are initial lessons or provocations that satisfy two main criteria. First of all, they must be central to the topic, with its stated understanding goals. School life is short and there is scant time for lessons or examples that are peripheral. Second of all, the generative topics must engage students. If it proves too difficult to convey a topic's interest and relevance, then one should probably seek another entry point. Of course, the better the teacher and the more trusting the students, the more likely that almost any topic or question can arouse and sustain the curiosity of the bulk of a class.

For our three chosen areas of investigation—there is no paucity of generative topics. Students in a biology class might be asked to explain why there are so many different species in the rain forest; students in an arts class might be challenged to figure out what is happening in a scene during which each of three people is singing a different phrase to himself or herself in a foreign language; students in a history class might ponder why the leaders of what many regarded as the most civilized country in the world would decide to eradicate an entire population.

Third, and most fundamental, is the identification and promulgation of "performances of understanding." To put it crisply, students must know what they have to do: they must be familiarized with the ways in which they will be asked to perform their understandings; and they must appreciate the criteria by which their performances will be judged. Far from being subjected to mysterious exams (no tests under lock and key), students should be exposed from the beginning to performances reflecting various degrees of competence; they should be assured that they will have plenty of opportunities to practice the required performances and to secure helpful feedback; and they should be confident that the culminating performances will typically be occasions for pride, rather than for apprehension or shame.

With respect to the above examples, "performances of understanding" might include a prediction of what will happen to a species given a radical shift in the local ecology; the creation of a song with lyrics that captures the generation gap in contemporary American society; and an analysis of a current virulent struggle between two ethnic groups, in terms of its similarities to, and differences from, the Holocaust.

The fourth and final component of our "understanding approach" is ongoing assessment. Most assessment in most schools comes down to a single test given at the end of a unit and kept secret until then. Students often do not know or care about the particulars of their performance; they just want to know their final grade. In contrast, in a milieu that stresses understanding, students receive continual feedback from teachers and others about the quality of their performances, along with concrete suggestions about how these performances might be improved. The criteria for evaluation are public, and students are welcome to discuss or to contest them. They have time to reflect on their performances, to practice, to receive help.

Optimally, over time, assessment no longer lies primarily with others. Rather, like seasoned professionals or experts, students gradually internalize the criteria by which they are assessed, becoming able to judge how well their performances stack up against an ideal and in comparison with performances by more and less skilled peers. That is why, incidentally, the culminating performances should be occasions of pleasure. If (like practiced artists or athletes) the students have come to understand well, then these public exhibitions should produce a state of "flow."

At first blush, our approach may seem behavioristic. Our focus is primarily on the quality of student behaviors. And, in keeping with classical behaviorist terminology, our provision of unfamiliar materials as a test of understanding may seem like a measure of the degree to which a skill has been "transferred."

But the "understanding approach" is behavioristic only in the sense that all assessments must ultimately examine behaviors; one cannot directly examine mental representations. Viewed up close, this approach reveals its cognitivist assumptions and affinities through and through. To begin with, my colleagues and I were stimulated to tackle understanding precisely because of the discovery that early mental representations are both robust and misleading; only a full court press is likely to undo them and to construct better ones.

Next, the coaching techniques that we favor are ones that point up inadequate conceptions and that encourage students to confront and revise conceptions that stand in the way of adequate understandings. Talk about assumptions is quite explicit; how students think about their own learning is a topic that fits comfortably into our understanding framework.

Finally, students are unlikely to be able to succeed regularly in responding to new and unfamiliar challenges unless they have actually altered their initial, flawed representations of the key notions in a domain. The acid test of a performance view of understanding is the development of more adequate and more flexible representations; such a test could not be conceived of in behaviorist terms.

Like any new approach, "teaching for understanding" cannot immediately be implemented perfectly; indeed, this view of understanding is itself deceptively simple and requires time to be mastered. At first, the elements are dealt with quite separately; neither students nor teachers are sure precisely why they are doing what they are doing when they attempt to put the framework into place. In contrast, expert implementation features a smooth meshing of the four component parts, so that a unit encompasses the goals, performances, and assessments as part of a seamless whole. Best of all, teachers at various levels find the framework useful and are motivated to keep using it. And so do its creators, including me.

4. *Multiple Entry Points to Understanding.* My fourth and final approach to understanding takes advantage of the fact that individuals possess different kinds of minds, featuring different blends of mental representations. People will, consequently, approach and master curricular materials in quite idiosyncratic ways. To put it formulaically, the fourth approach weds the theory of multiple intelligences to the goal of enhanced performances of understanding. Here, I believe, lies the best way for us to enable all students to achieve enhanced understanding. And, accordingly, the multiple approaches to understanding are the primary focus of the next several chapters.

Other Players

Goals must come first; and they must be kept in mind. But there are also important "other players." Let me now introduce the other members of the ideal cast.

Well-trained, Enthusiastic Teachers. To teach for understanding, the teachers themselves must be comfortable with and understand the material. Teachers need to feel expert, and they need to embody expertise in the eyes of their students. They must also believe that understanding is important and be prepared to embody that understanding in their own lives. Nothing more impresses students than the opportunity to see informed adults make apt use of the material being introduced. That is why young musicians love to watch their teachers perform, and tennis students want to play with their instructors. And that is why students soon become disenchanted with teachers who fail to "walk the talk."

As the educator Lee Shulman has insisted, knowledge of one's subject is necessary, but it does not suffice. Of two individuals who know their subject equally well, only one may know how to present it to naive students in ways that engage them, dissolve prominent misconceptions, and build up firmer and more flexible understandings.

Teachers of teachers must help their students to gain such pedagogical knowledge and to draw on it regularly in their future classroom preparations. Teachers must be ever on the lookout for the most appropriate projects, lessons, questions, and forms of assessment, ones that dovetail with a curriculum of understanding and that help monitor students' evolving understandings.

Moreover, it is not sufficient for teachers to rest on the laurels of their own training. All disciplines evolve—some, like the natural sciences, with daunting speed. The boundaries of disciplines change, and opportunities for interdisciplinary work arise both predictably and unpredictably. Teachers need to keep up; optimally, they should desire ardently to keep up. Again, students take note when teachers are themselves continuing to learn, and when they appear to be excited by new discoveries.

Of course, many teachers lack deep understanding of their topic, and some are not motivated to enhance their understandings. Education for understanding is difficult to pursue without a cohort of teachers who are committed to understanding for themselves, as well as for their charges. The good news is that there are many ways for motivated teachers to delve more deeply into their discipline and to practice their own understandings. But the motivation to do so can only come from the teacher.

Students Prepared and Motivated to Learn. A teacher's work is half done when students arrive at school healthy, secure, and eager to learn. It hardly needs to be said that many students around the world, and many in the affluent United States, do not come so equipped. It is harder to admit that even students who are healthy and secure often display little interest in what school has to offer.

Faced with students who are not excited by school, it is easy and tempting to blame parents, the students themselves, or last year's teachers. And, indeed, sometimes the job of keeping students healthy, safe, and motivated proves too difficult for any one teacher or team of teachers to accomplish. But this is a conclusion that can only be reached after the fact. From day one, teachers must seek to motivate their students, even against the odds. And their own belief in the importance and the rightness of what they are doing can be a pivotal motivator.

Master principal Deborah Meier recalls how she and her brother used to go to Yankee Stadium in the 1940s to watch the great outfielder Joe

DiMaggio. Meier admired his beauty and grace, while her brother wanted to play ball like Joltin' Joe. Meier looks back nostalgically to the way so many of her generation were enchanted by DiMaggio and eager to follow his lead. She then pointedly adds, with reference to our students today, "We've got to be their Joe DiMaggios."

With knowledge changing so rapidly, students must become able—eager—to assume responsibility for their learning. To the extent that students can craft their own goals, keep track of their own accomplishments, reflect on their own thinking and learning—where it has improved, where it continues to fall short—they become partners in their own education. Even more crucially, once formal schooling has concluded, it should have become second nature for adults to keep on learning—sometimes alone, sometimes in groups—for as long as they choose; indeed, one hopes, for the rest of their lives.

Technology as Helper. In itself, technology is neither helpful nor harmful; it is simply a tool. The most advanced and speediest computers in the world will be of little help in our mission if the software is mindless and fails to engage understanding. Conversely, armed only with their minds, a few books, chalk, and a pencil, well-informed and motivated teachers can lead their students triumphantly down the road to understanding. Indeed, Socrates had not so much as a blackboard; he stimulated understanding simply by the shrewd questions that he asked, the order in which he posed them, and his often pointed reactions to the responses of those for whom he served as gadfly.

Still, we would be ill-advised to ignore the opportunities afforded us by the sophisticated technologies of today. Videodiscs can draw students vividly into mathematical problem-solving or the art treasures of the past. Databases allow them to collect and manipulate all kinds of information about their world, their community, and their own lives. Electronic linkages allow them to share their interests with others from around the world. Networked personal computers and scanners enable them to write, make diagrams, draw, and compose music, revise their works as much as they wish, share them with peers, and make them available to experts anywhere—or indeed, to the students' own subsequent review and critique.

Note that technology does not dictate these beneficent uses. Rather, skilled educators must examine goals and determine, on a case-by-case basis, which technologies, and which uses thereof, can help them meet those goals. The search must proceed in an empirical way. Perhaps, before too long, intelligent systems will themselves be able to judge how they have been successful with students, where they have failed, and how they might be reconfigured.

A Supportive Community. Even when all the necessary components are present at school, effective education is not guaranteed. Other stakeholders have a powerful voice in what happens, what is supported, what is thwarted.

The identities of stakeholders differ widely across educational contexts. Parents, school board members, key citizens of the community, the local, state/provincial, and national ministries of education, and the general public are all factors in the equation that yields a curriculum, a means of assessment, and a cohort of graduates who do or don't possess significant understandings.

Needless to say, education cannot proceed successfully if these stakeholders are ignorant of what is going on in the classroom, if they disagree vociferously with one another, or if they collectively find themselves at odds with a goal, be it the acquisition of core knowledge or the achievement of deep understanding. Moreover, even well-intentioned policies can wreck an educational program. What is the likely fate of a program that educates for understanding, if the graduating or college admissions examinations sample coverage of routine factual material rather than probing the intellectual power of the curriculum and the students' depth of understanding?

Learning need not occur only within the four walls of the classroom. Technology can take us all over the world, and back again. Support at home is crucial. A community's citizens and institutions can make significant contributions to the education of its children. These contributions may start with field trips, but they need not and should not end there. Students ought to have available mentors, apprenticeships, work-study positions in community institutions; and experts from these institutions ought to visit schools, in reality or virtually. Workplaces are changing rapidly; many people now work from home, often by participating in electronic networks and virtual offices. Precollegiate education needs to assume the multifaceted cast and contours of the emerging new world.

•   •   •

In effect, I have presented a design for education: a central goal or mission—in this case, education for disciplinary understanding; four major ways in which to proceed toward that mission and to adjust course, when necessary; and a complex of supporting factors that can smooth the way toward the achievement of this ambitious goal.

There are, of course, many reasonable missions and goals: recall the potpourri of good schools introduced in chapter 5. One can even justify missions like that of the University of Phoenix, while recognizing that it is antithetical to one's own. Moreover, even a singular goal or mission, like the one outlined here, can (and perhaps should) be pursued in a variety of ways.

But for our study, the die has been cast. I have now described in general terms the kind of education that I want for my children, their children, and, indeed, the children of the world. It is time I specified how understanding might be achieved in three disciplinary areas: science, art, and history.

CHAPTER 7
Disciplined Approaches

Three Puzzles

During the 1830s, while Charles Darwin sailed around the world on the *Beagle,* most biologists, including Darwin himself, believed in the immutability of species. The species had been created, presumably by God, and they remained in the same pristine form forever, unless (like ancient mastodons) they perished.

Darwin began to question his convictions after he had visited the Galápagos Islands off the coast of Ecuador. He was struck by the wealth of flora and fauna that he encountered on just a few islands not distant from one another. In particular, he became intrigued by the incidence of finches; there turned out to be thirteen different varieties in close proximity. Darwin pondered the reasons that the finches had different colors as well as beaks of varying shapes and sizes. And he reflected on the distributions of other birds, land animals, and plants on these islands, and across the many other exotic sites that he had visited.

Darwin devoted the succeeding decades to related questions. Why are there so many species throughout the world? Why such a variety on just a few islands? Why does one rarely see the same varieties in environments that differ ecologically from one another? What causes certain species to die out and others to flourish? How do new species come to be? Why are offspring always slightly different from their parents? Do species that closely resemble one another necessarily come from the same single parental stock? What happens where there are too many organisms for a given space, and not all can survive?

In raising these questions, Darwin was touching on the hypersensitive topic of the evolution of species. This subject had engaged earlier thinkers, including his own grandfather Erasmus Darwin. But Charles Darwin came up with a set of answers that forever changed how informed individuals thought about the origins of species, and, most controversially, about the niche of human beings within the family of organisms.

•   •   •

In late 1785 and early 1786, Wolfgang Amadeus Mozart and his librettist, Lorenzo Da Ponte, composed an opera based on Pierre Beaumarchais's play *The Marriage of Figaro*. This French play about the Spanish aristocracy, a great success in the latter part of the eighteenth century, also proved controversial. Previously, most dramatists had portrayed a nobility that sat comfortably atop a social hierarchy; Beaumarchais created a more complex (and realistic) set of social relations, with a servant class that was enterprising, and an aristocracy that was not only flawed but that, eventually, could be undone by its own foibles.

The general plot of *Figaro* is a recognizable, typically convoluted member of the opera buffa genre, though the specifics were adventurous for the time. Figaro, a shrewd and upwardly mobile barber, is scheduled to marry the attractive Susanna. However, the domineering Count Almaviva, Figaro's boss, has his own designs on Susanna, who serves as the Countess's maid; and by tradition, the Count has seigneurial rights over her, at least until she marries Figaro. Almaviva woos Susanna, going so far as to place encumbrances on the young couple's marital design. To thwart the Count, Figaro concocts a scenario in which the Count will be led to believe that he will be able to meet with Susanna and that his wife, the Countess, will meet a lover. This scenario is not fully realized, because the Count interrupts while the plot is still being hatched.

Later Susanna pretends to accede to the Count's wishes for an amorous rendezvous. But then she and the Countess switch identities. With Figaro himself ignorant of the switch (and thus believing that Susanna is betraying him), the Count ends up wooing his wife and at the same time believing that his wife is being unfaithful.

At the end, all is righted in the world created in the work. Figaro and Susanna get married; Figaro's parents (of whose identity he was unaware) are happily reunited; Cherubino and Barbarina, a young couple who became ensnared in the imbroglio, are also married; and the Count and Countess accept their fates as the authorized protectors of the realm. In this story, true love is celebrated and, in a rare (if prescient) reversal of the social order, the servant class triumphs over the aristocracy.

The opera consists of four acts, arranged in twenty-seven scenes.* No single scene encapsulates the entire drama. Just as I use Darwin's finches to represent the themes of evolution, I use the seventh scene of *Figaro*'s first act to convey the atmosphere of the opera. I've dubbed that powerful scene, featuring Count Almaviva, the maiden Susanna, and the music master Basilio, the "Trio of Colliding Agendas." The three protagonists engage in exceedingly complex interaction and repartee which is not only amusing in itself but also moves the plot along briskly. The trio is described in detail in the next chapter; part of its score is reprinted as an appendix to this book.

The opera created by Mozart and Da Ponte was not well received on its original presentation in Vienna in 1786, but it soon came to be recognized as a masterpiece in many parts of the world. *The Marriage of Figaro* stands out by virtue of its beautiful score, its fast-moving dramatic action across several subplots, and its poignant combination of romance, slapstick, intrigue, and pathos.

To the naive ear, opera may sound like a bunch of people screaming at one another, sometimes alone, sometimes in ensemble. Indeed, though as a child I appreciated classical instrumental music, I remember my distinct antipathy for most of the operas broadcast on national radio on Saturday afternoons. But once one has the opportunity to see a performance, to understand an often convoluted plot, and to appreciate how the singers accomplish actions through words and melodies, opera can become fascinating. Pieces like the trio in the first act of *Figaro* convey past and anticipate future events, a wide range of feelings, a collection of personalities, people's innermost thoughts, and their subtle (and not so subtle) interactions. Moreover, in an effective performance, one also beholds supreme artists—the performers as well as the creators—using their chosen medium to express feelings and convey actions with finesse, elegance, and power. Finally, though

---

*The number of scenes differs slightly from score to score.

it is not the sort of thing that can be proved to an unhearing audience, the melodies, harmonies, and orchestration in the Mozart piece have struck millions of people as beautiful.

•   •   •

On January 20, 1942, leaders of the Nazi Third Reich gathered at a villa on the Wannsee in Berlin—number 56–58 Am Grossen Wannsee, to be precise. In the preceding years, the German military had conquered much of Western Europe and had also made inroads into the Soviet Union. Meanwhile, the German leadership had been trying out various approaches, in an effort to solve what they termed the "Jewish problem."

Ever since Nazi leader Adolf Hitler began his rise to power, in the early 1920s, he had made no secret of his antipathy to the Jewish people and his desire to be rid of them. During 1933–1939, the first years of his regime, Hitler and his disciples had pressured Jews to leave Germany and had mistreated them in countless ways. Once the Second World War began, in September 1939, more severe measures were taken against the Jews. Many were sent to concentration camps; many others were simply shot to death or left to die of starvation.

But Hitler and his colleagues continued to search for what they termed the Final Solution to the Jewish problem in Europe. A number of radical measures were considered, including the mass deportation of the Jews to the island of Madagascar, off the east coast of Africa, and the creation of giant ghettos or reservations—for example, in the southeastern Polish city of Lublin.

But with the invasion of Russia, and the capture of land that housed millions of additional Jews, none of these halfway measures seemed sufficient. By a series of steps still not fully understood by historians, the Nazi leadership arrived at the fateful solution to begin the systematic, as opposed to the haphazard, murder of all European Jews. The meeting at Wannsee was designed to share this decision with those officials whose fateful job it would be to translate into action a plan for the execution of millions of people. Yet the records of the meeting never actually mention the genocide.

Vantage Points:
From Puzzles to Concepts

Each of my opening examples can be set forth as straightforward puzzles:

Why do the finches of the Galápagos Islands look the way they do? And what does this tell us about the origins and varieties of species since the beginning of time?

How did Mozart and Da Ponte manage to convey so much about their protagonists' motivation and dramatic action in the course of a four-minute trio? What resources are available to creating and performing artists? And why is this music of two centuries ago so treasured today?

When and how did the Nazis arrive at the decision to begin the Final Solution, the elimination of European Jewry? How did they convey that sensitive information to those who would implement the policy? And why did so many German nationals participate—willingly and even enthusiastically—in mass murder?

Each of these puzzling "entry points" is designed to be intriguing in its own right—enough so that students (or readers) become curious about possible solutions. Students wonder, for example, whether the same variety of finches could be found on a single landmass that spanned the same geographical distance as the Galápagos do; whether one could appreciate the personality traits and motivations of the characters in *Figaro* if one did not understand the language being sung or were unfamiliar with Western musical scales; and how specifically Hitler and/or his closest associates were orchestrating the events at Wannsee. While the interest of students can be engaged in many ways, the presentation of dilemmas—or their cousins, essential questions and generative ideas—has proved an especially effective means of attracting attention.

I've used these lures to introduce our "triplet" of central examples. The finches of the Galápagos (now often called Darwin's finches) offer a concrete way in which to raise the question of the *evolution of species,* and, ultimately, to introduce Darwin's ideas about variation and natural selection. These ideas, inevitably modified in the 150 years since they were enunciated, represent an important set of scientific truths about the world.

The study of *The Marriage of Figaro,* featuring its "Trio of Colliding Agendas," serves to introduce the music of Mozart and the genre called opera. Most students have heard of Mozart, and many of them also have a notion—often quite negative—of classical music. Through analysis of how a single composition works, I hope to unravel some of the mysteries of classical music and to engender appreciation of a beautiful artifact in our world—a *work of Mozart.*

While organized killing has been a staple of human history, the Holocaust stands out in terms of the clarity of its aims as well as the thoroughness of its enactment. The Nazis aimed to eliminate an entire people—including women and children—and came very close to fulfilling their goal. They embarked upon genocide not because the Jews constituted any conceivable kind of military threat but rather because the Jews were seen as a "species" that was hardly human and whose continued existence posed a threat to the "pure" Aryan race.

Particularly because there are some who deny the existence of the Final Solution, and many who question its frightening dimensions, it is important for students to learn just what happened and why. This is a question of historical truth. The *decisions and events of the Holocaust* must be understood in their own right; insights drawn from the Holocaust might be useful in preventing repetition of such horrific actions committed by one group of human beings against another. More generally, the actions of the Germans, and the reactions of the rest of the world, raise the most profound moral questions.

In attempting to understand these three phenomena, one is drawn into the approaches taken by different disciplines. Let me first sketch out some general considerations and then turn to specific features of the three disciplines with which we are concerned here: science, art, and history.

The Disciplines . . . and Beyond

So far as we can determine, human beings have always been interested in questions of the true, the beautiful, and the good.* These questions are

---

*There is an awkwardness in using the term "good" in connection with the Holocaust. More precisely, one should always use the phrase "good/evil."

addressed in the myths of prehistory; they can be discerned in the ritual-
istic mourning behaviors of Neanderthals and in the early well-crafted
artifacts of *Homo sapiens;* and they are raised as well in the play and the
words of young children.

Over the years, cultures have evolved systematic ways of thinking
about these issues. Folk science and folk wisdom are attempts to capture
insights about what is true; and, of course, religions have mandated their
own conceptions of truth. Explicit codes, systematic punishments, and
implicit norms express what is morally acceptable and what is not.
Artists and craftsmen (and, for that matter, mathematicians) create tangible or symbolic objects of beauty, and other knowledgeable members
of the community bring to bear criteria of judgment on the relative aesthetic merits of particular creations.

There is no simple one-to-one mapping from questions to disciplines.
Indeed, most questions can be approached from the perspectives of a
variety of disciplines, even as a specific discipline can be brought to bear
on a variety of questions and concerns. Still, the ensemble of fundamental questions, as a whole, helps to circumscribe and give direction to the
family of disciplines.

Dating back at least to the time of the Greeks in the West, and to the
school of Confucius in the East, organized disciplines have grown up
around issues of the true, the beautiful, and the good. These disciplines
harbor assumptions and mandate certain practices. For example, in
Greece Socrates presented a model of how to practice philosophy; and
then Plato and Aristotle laid out the means whereby others could
become philosophers in quest of truth. Sophocles and Aristophanes
wrote compelling tragedies and comedies; Aristotle set forth these rules
explicitly for all future dramatists, thereby proposing a set of standards
of artistic beauty. By the same token, within Confucian societies, delib-
erate rules were set out about how to become a keen archer, a skilled
calligrapher, a performer of music, a gentleman. Taken together, these
constituted a definition of a good person and a good life.

Disciplines have endured over the ages, even as their identities and
boundaries have shifted. At any given moment, the disciplines represent
the most well-honed efforts of human beings to approach questions and
concerns of importance in a systematic and reliable way.

Nowadays, when it comes to questions of truth, most practitioners—
Eastern as well as Western—turn to the sciences. Methods dating back

to the Greeks, Romans, and Babylonians, and brought to a new level of precision in Europe in the seventeenth and eighteenth centuries, constitute our most trusted means of determining what is true about the physical world (physics and chemistry); the biological world (biology, botany, zoology); the worlds of remote space and time (astronomy, cosmology); and the world of human beings (social and behavioral sciences). Methods become refined, and specific theories and claims are often replaced by more sophisticated ones.

When it comes to issues of beauty, there is a division of labor. We look to artistic creators and performers for an evolving sense of what is beautiful and—by implication—what is not. Their works constitute replenishable wellsprings of instances of beauty; and, unlike ideas in the sciences, notions of beauty are not regularly supplanted. We think of Greek science as quaint; we continue to admire Greek vases and sculpture, even as our contemporary view of beauty extends and broadens the Greek ideal.

In addition, modes of analysis help us to understand how such objects are created and why they affect many of us in the way they do. Complementing artists, aestheticians help us to discover the common properties, as well as the differentiating features, of ancient literary and plastic arts, and those wrought in more recent times: Greek vases, Chinese scrolls, contemporary jazz and performance art. During periods like ours, when elite aesthetic standards veer away from traditional concepts of the beautiful, aestheticians help us to understand what is going on in the several arts.

The discipline of mathematics proves instructive in this context. At first blush, mathematics represents a search for truth—indeed, for the identification of the most permanent truths that human beings can know. Yet, the simplicity and the elegance of the truth, and the actual form in which the truth is presented, are of great import to mathematicians. In this sense, mathematics is akin to music, entailing its own sense of the beautiful—and averting what seems unwieldy.

Turning finally to the area of morality, each culture puts forth its own standards of behavior—some unique, some closely resembling those of other cultures. Even the Nazis had their own morality, twisted though it seems to us today. (The historian Daniel J. Goldhagen tells the incredible story of a German officer named Hoffmann, who had presided over the deportation and killing of tens of thousands of Jews. Hoffmann refused to sign an order agreeing not to steal from or plunder those Gentiles who came under his jurisdiction. He was insulted by the request: he *knew* that he and his men would never stoop to such dastardly acts.) Various disciplines, ranging from philosophy to literature, touch on issues of morality, each in characteristic ways. Historians play an important role in our understanding of morality, for they can help us to understand the sources of morality at a particular place and time, why certain choices were made, and what consequences flowed from those choices.

There has been a close association between the development of disciplines and the rise of civilizations. This link is in no way inevitable; after all, the Nazis practiced many disciplines at a high level, yet their expertise did not prevent them from ushering in a new barbarism. Still, the disciplines are civilizing in that they offer practiced methods for dealing with issues and questions. Shorn of the disciplines, one is driven back to common sense and its inevitable undersurface, common nonsense.

Nowadays, in a postmodern era, one incurs risks in praising the disciplines. Some question the validity of the disciplines altogether, while others rail against the undue power of those bastions of reaction, the academic disciplines. As I noted earlier, I do not agree with these critiques; yet I do not want to engage in a full-scale debate here about where the disciplines have fallen short, and where they still have value. Suffice it to say that, as an introduction to systematic thought about perennial human puzzles, virtues, and vices, I know of no reasonable alternative to the several disciplines.

The phrase "human puzzles" harbors a valuable pun, for the disciplines respond to human challenges in two senses. First of all, the questions they address have always been important to human beings. Second, they also focus on issues of what it means to be human. My three areas of investigation readily reveal their human dimensions: the place of *Homo sapiens* in the evolutionary galaxy, the foibles of aristocrats (and nonaristocrats), the stench of prejudice yoked to absolute power. But even those disciplines that seem less directly concerned with human experience—say, the physical sciences and mathematics—cast light on human beings. After all, we humans are also entities in the physical world; and the discovery of mathematical truths underscores the power of the human mind somehow to fathom the most profound regularities in the universe.

Whatever the power—even the necessity—of the disciplines, in the end, questions never stop at the boundary of a discipline. Efforts to develop decisive and personal ideas of the true, the beautiful, and the good necessarily take us beyond specific disciplines and invite syntheses. The scientists investigating Darwin's theory, the analysts of Mozart's music, the historians of the Holocaust are all attempting to answer questions about truths, though they are truths of different epistemological status. And without stretching a point too far, one can also see these disciplinarians engaged in efforts to touch on other fundamental concerns: Darwinians looking for the sources of beauty and morality in the principles of evolution (such as natural selection); analysts of *Figaro* (and the society portrayed therein) raising issues about standards of morality, political truth, and artistic truth; and students of the Holocaust pondering standards of truth and beauty in the Nazi regime.

The Patterns of the Scientist . . . and the Mathematician

Scientists attempt to explain the regularities of the world. In this undertaking, they are aided by their own observations, which themselves may depend upon quite complex measurement devices; and by the earlier efforts of empirically oriented thinkers to pose questions and secure systematic answers.

This dialectic between observational data and theoretical frameworks is crucial to the working scientist. If the scientist only makes observations, he or she may be a keen observer or naturalist, but will not have entered fully into scientific practice. That is because observations can focus on an infinite number of details culled for a variety of unspecified ends. Indeed, all of us make observations all of the time, and yet few of us are practicing scientists.

The other element of scientific thinking is a concern with placing observations within a systematic framework; in the most developed form, the framework is a scientific theory. Many people were as impressed with the variety of plants and animals as Darwin was, and not a few had attempted to group and regroup them. Darwin relied heavily on the observations of the finches made by other travelers; but it was he who placed these observations into an explanatory framework, thus crossing the threshold into scientific theorizing.

On the other hand, people interested only in theoretical issues are not scientists either. They may be theorists or philosophers, but their claims will lack grounding in concrete reality. Indeed, it has rightly been said that most sciences begin in philosophy—in the raising of provocative questions and in the sketching out of possible answers while sitting in one's armchair. Philosophy turns into science when relevant observations are fit into the current theoretical framework or an improved one. As we now appreciate, science places a special premium on observations that undermine a current theory. Progress is made not by establishing permanent truths but rather by calling into question a provisional truth and substituting one that is more firmly grounded in the evidence. This, in turn, may be replaced by yet another, better grounded claim.

Mathematics plays an important role in the more sophisticated sciences. Initially, science grows out of systematic observation and features theories that can be expressed in lay language. However, these approaches engender a science mired at a level of description that is approximate at best. For science to be precise, for all practitioners to agree about the facts of a matter, it is important for claims and predictions to be stated as unambiguously as possible. This is the insight expressed by Galileo Galilei when he famously declared that the book of the universe was written in mathematics and that its alphabet consisted of triangles, circles, and geometrical forms.

But mathematics is not merely an aid for the working scientist. Quite independently, it represents the efforts of human beings to discover (or, if you prefer a more active description, to make) and lay out with precision the abstract relationships among idealized quantities and forms in the world. Mathematicians crave patterns in the realms of number and form; they seek to demonstrate, preserve, and explain the reasons for these patterns to all who find them of interest. Mathematicians are as compelled by the beauty of these patterns as by their truth value.

And yet, paradoxically, while scientific truths are fated to be temporary, mathematical ones, once verified, remain true. That is why mathematician G. H. Hardy declared that the most marvelous experience a human being can have is to discover a mathematical truth, because it will remain forever. One can quibble here, because new mathematical discoveries or systems may reconfigure earlier truths: in a non-Euclidean universe, parallel lines *do* meet. But within the bounds of a given system, mathematical truths are permanent: the square of the hypotenuse of a right triangle will always equal the sum of the squares of the other two sides of that triangle.

Most students will not become scientists, and many will only need elementary arithmetic in their daily and work lives. And yet, to deprive students of scientific and mathematical ways of thinking is to consign them to ignorance about the world in which they live. Only with adequate exposure to these disciplines will students have any understanding of the forces that govern the physical and natural world (as opposed, say, to accepting astrological explanations); the kind of thinking that has led to current world pictures (as opposed, say, to accepting magical thinking) and that will lead to valid revisions thereof; and the role of mathematical language in fixing these truths so that all may confirm them for themselves (as opposed to arguments based on slippery language, ambiguous images, or mere authority).

Indeed, I might well have used a mathematical example in this book—say, the power of zero, the meaning of infinity, the quest to prove Fermat's last theorem. These are legitimate targets for understanding. From pondering rich examples I would like all students to gain a feeling for the regularities and beauties of mathematics and the fact that numbers and patterns can be exquisitely organized. Consistent with the theme of this book, students have no need to work through copious examples: At least through secondary school, a few well-understood examples should convey the power of mathematical thinking. Other curricular choices ought to be guided by the kinds of mathematical performances that are most likely to be useful for the world in which students will live. I must admit my discomfort that so much of what we learn in mathematics is drawn on only decades later, when we are helping our own children carry out the same lessons.

The Beauty of the Artist

The artist creates works in a genre. Usually the genre exists prior to the artist: like their predecessors, writers today create novels or poems, visual artists create paintings or pieces of sculpture. However, on occasion, artists will create new genres or reconfigure old ones. In the wake of Mozart's unsurpassable achievements, Beethoven changed the rules of classical music; a century later, in the aftermath of Brahms and

Wagner, Arnold Schoenberg created a new system of atonal or twelve-tone music.

Like the scientist, the artist moves between two worlds, but the realities of these worlds are quite different. On the one side, there are the artists' thoughts, feelings, beliefs, visions, imagination: the content of his or her conscious (and unconscious) experiences. On the other, there are the materials or media available to artists, the techniques with which they and others work in order to fashion a work of art.

Neither base alone suffices. If an artist is filled with ideas or inspirations, but lacks mastery of a medium, she will not be able to express herself (or her intended meanings) in an accessible way. Either she will be addressing only herself, or she will use a medium in a way that bewilders others. If, on the other hand, the artist has mastered a medium, but lacks in ideas or inspiration, then her work can at best be derivative; it will not sustain the interest of others.

Mozart illustrates well the working realms of the artist. In the collaboration on *Figaro*, Mozart's goal was to create (with Da Ponte) a musical work that captured the spirit and the meanings of Beaumarchais's play; in addition, Mozart had many ideas, feelings, and observations—some personal, some drawn from the general language of comic opera—that he hoped to capture in his own *Marriage of Figaro*.

Enter the mastery of technique. To produce a work, Mozart drew on the general principles of classical composition as they had evolved in Europe during the seventeenth and eighteenth centuries. With respect to the creation of a musical score, there were procedures for developing themes in a key, for modulating from one key to another, for using instruments alone or in combination, for altering rhythm and dynamics in order to achieve surprise, irregularity, or contrast. Individual and choral singers, the choice and arrangement of lyrics, a stage with its settings, costumes, lighting, acoustics—each introduced new elements that could be drawn upon in composition; in each case technical mastery of the relevant medium was necessary if a coherent and effective work was to result.

Mozart's technical knowledge may have been explicit, but explicitness is not of the essence. What was most important was that Mozart had the requisite skills to draw upon relevant techniques as needed. In contrast, the critic or aesthetician does need explicit knowledge of the artist's tool kit, and how the artist has drawn upon it to create certain effects. Accordingly, if we are to make sense of the impact of "The Trio of Colliding Agendas," we must draw upon the explicit language, terms, concepts, frameworks—more broadly, the "symbol systems"—that have been proposed by aestheticians of music.

While the target instance here is musical, the same line of analysis obtains for other art forms. Take, for example, the paintings of Picasso, the novels of Virginia Woolf, and the dances of Martha Graham. In each case, one beholds an artist with a distinct vision of the world; and one recognizes a set of techniques—graphic in the case of Picasso, linguistic in the case of Woolf, choreographic in the case of Graham—that allow the artist to bring this vision to reality. Moreover, each of these modern artists had a vision sufficiently original to change the practices of suc ceeding generations of artists.

Note, again, that neither the artists, nor their followers, required an explicit "language" or "metalanguage" to characterize their activities; it sufficed that they did their work well. But if *we* are to communicate about the effects these artists achieved, and the resources on which they drew, we (and that plural most definitely includes teachers) must draw on the language of the critic or philosopher of the relevant art form.

It would be wonderful if each growing individual had some opportunity to create in an art form. There is no substitute for drawing a portrait or a still life, composing a song or a sonnet, choreographing and performing a dance. Education early in life ought to provide such opportunities to think and perform in an artistic medium.

As future citizens grow, it is equally important that they gain access to the most remarkable works fashioned by artists. These masterworks convey the ideas and feelings of different times and places, express a range of emotions, and embody a sense of beauty and harmony that enriches the experiences of all who can appreciate them. Indeed, our sense of beauty and taste comes chiefly from those works of art that we (as a culture over the centuries) have made our own. And the vocabularies and concepts created by students of the arts allow students and teachers to make explicit their understandings—and their sometimes idiosyncratic preferences. In this respect, languages of art play a role roughly analogous to that of mathematics in the sciences.

I must stress that works of art are quintessentially individual—each is different from every other. One cannot hope to enter into a work, let alone understand it, unless one engages its particular materials. To be specific, we cannot begin to appreciate the Mozart trio unless we heed the particular characters, events, melodies, harmonies, and orchestration of that particular Mozart–Da Ponte invention. Concreteness is also where science begins; however, in the case of sciences, one always has one's vision primed for the general pattern, the set of rules that apply to all finches, all animals, all living matter. In this distinction between individual work and scientific principle lies the deepest gulf between science and mathematics, on the one hand, and art and the humanities, on the other.

The Accounts of the Historian

The historian begins with an event—a setting and a number of participants. In rare cases, the historian was present as an observer or recorder; sometimes the historian has access to eyewitnesses whom he or she can interrogate; but most often the historian must deal with documents—primary sources (as in the case of letters, journals, minutes of meetings) or secondary sources (other written interpretive accounts by participants, journalists, or earlier historians). Recently, the written record has been complemented—and enhanced—by film and video sources as well; no doubt it will be similarly enriched by electronic records and even by DNA fingerprinting.

Using these sources of data, the historian creates an account of what happened, in most cases venturing beyond simple narrative to offer explanations of why events happened in the ways that they did. Indeed, many would say that, like the scientist, the scholar enters into the discipline of history only when he or she goes beyond a mere recording of the data and becomes an interpreter of events.

The decisions that created the Holocaust throw these issues into sharp relief. Only naive or malevolent people who ignore the evidence question whether the Holocaust happened; the reports of those who survived the camps, the records kept by the Nazis themselves, the postwar testimony of certain Nazi leaders, the grisly photographs of the camps, with their gas chambers, and their piles of gold teeth, eyeglasses, and mud-caked shoes taken from victims, convince all rational individuals that mass extermination of millions of Jews—and members of other groups as well—took place in the death camps.

But when and how the "Final Solution" was arrived at remains a historical problem. In a way analogous to the challenge faced by other scholars, the historian must draw on two contrasting considerations. On the one hand, there is the documentary evidence: which orders were issued and by whom, what was said at Wannsee and elsewhere, and how veiled messages were apparently understood by those in attendance.

On the other hand, there are different ways to interpret human behavior. "Intentionalists" see the Holocaust as a direct consequence, dating back to promises made in *Mein Kampf* (1925–1927), of Hitler's resolution to rid Europe of the Jews. To intentionalists, the Nazis were only biding their time until an auspicious moment appeared for them to make good on their threats.

"Functionalists" see a less rational, more chaotic process at work. In the opinion of these scholars, the Nazi leadership was casting about for ways in which to remove Jews from European society. Deportation to either Madagascar or the Lublin Reservation might have worked, in which case the phrase "Final Solution" might now be applied to one of those ploys. However, neither alternative proved practical. At the same time, the Nazis saw that their command units were capable of massacring large numbers of Jews, without unwanted side effects. In casting about for ways to make the process more efficient, and to distance Germans from the need to pull the trigger and stash the corpses, the idea of death camps gradually arose. Once the idea arose, it still had to be tried out; had it proved too unwieldy, other "final solutions" might have been considered.

In some ways, the methods used by historians resemble those adopted by other social scientists—psychologists, economists, or sociologists. In each of these disciplinary endeavors, the analyst begins with an intriguing example of human behavior but then moves to a more general explanation of the phenomenon—for example, in terms of the explicit intentions of a certain class of persons or in terms of more general principles of group behavior. But historians are also humanists, and they share features with the artistic critic, as well: the historical event is unique, and so it must be explained in its own terms. Moreover, because historical events are unprecedented and nonreplicable, proposed explanations cannot be tested in the scientific laboratory. The patterns discerned by historians can be suggestive at best; historical accounts retain their singularity.

Nearly all humans are curious about their origins and their fate; and in that sense, the study of "our story" requires little justification. However, an appreciation of the discipline of history transcends personal curiosity. Only when they gain a sense of the diverse and often competing inputs to historians, and the conflicting ways of making sense of texts and other forms of evidence, do students begin to understand that history is not a given: any historical account must be constructed, and those who do the construction help us to define ourselves, our allies, our enemies, and our options (including our moral choices). The disciplined thinking of the historian is crucial if individuals are to draw their own inferences about what happened in an event, decide which historical analogies are apt and which are not, and express opinions and cast votes on issues of import in terms of reasonable criteria rather than sheer whim.

The historical enterprise sheds light on issues of both truth and goodness. To establish as accurately as possible what happened in a given place at a given time represents an effort to attain truth. Historians never tire of quoting Leopold von Ranke's dictum that the historian's burden is to describe the past "as it actually happened." At the same time, however, historical accounts offer perennial opportunities to consider moral options and to render moral judgments: Was Columbus a hero or a villain? Should the United States have bombed Hiroshima? Which side actually provoked the "guns of August" in 1914, and were its actions justifiable? Judging the Nazis' actions in World War II is not a historical act but one of moral evaluation. And yet, in the absence of sound historical data, such judgments deservedly command little attention.

In the Shopping Mall of the Disciplines

Even we who are not expert in the respective disciplines can appreciate the differing aims and perspectives of the scientist, the mathematician, the artist, and the historian. We contrast the data collected systematically by the scientist; the abstract patterns that intrigue the mathematician; the imaginative thoughts and feelings that inspire the artist; the reflective language of the critic; the historian's struggle to figure out which documents are important and how to evaluate human motives and "extrahuman" forces as they play out among a particular set of characters at a particular historical moment.

Youngsters face a formidable task. The questions that they themselves pose, or that are posed by an engaging teacher or text or video, are genuine. However, young students do not know about the disciplines, nor are they in a position to recognize their utility (though they may be intimidated by their rigors). Moreover, students lack the rough-and-ready intuitions that most adults have developed in a society that honors the scholarly and practical disciplines.

It is easy for students (and teachers and parents) to be confused about the disciplines. They are often seen simply as "subjects": courses to take, with discrete texts and teachers, in order to pass certain requirements. To the extent that disciplines are simply presented as sets of facts, concepts, or even theories to be committed to memory, students may remain innocent of their powers. After all, facts themselves are discipline-neutral: they acquire their disciplinary colors only when they have been pieced together in a certain way and placed in the service of a particular theory, framework, or sequence.

For the disciplines inhere not primarily in the specific facts and concepts that make up textbook glossaries and indexes, compendia of national standards, and, all too often, weekly tests. Rather the disciplines inhere in the ways of thinking, developed by their practitioners, that allow those practitioners to make sense of the world in quite specific and largely nonintuitive ways. Indeed, once mastered and internalized, the disciplines *become* the ways—in our earlier image, the engravings—in which experts construe the phenomena of their world.

For the sake of argument, let us consider the contrasting stances taken by three hypothetical practitioners with respect to Darwin's finches. The biologist asks why the finches on a few neighboring islands differ from one another in appearance. He may love (or loathe) finches, but his focus is really on more general questions: Why do closely related species (or, indeed, *any* species) manage to survive, and how does their survival relate to the fact that they are segregated geographically? His goal is to come up with truths: general principles that obtain with respect to the evolution of species. And while evolutionary biology is not generally considered to be a laboratory science, he could test his claims empirically. For example, following the practices of E. O. Wilson and Robert MacArthur, and their colleagues, he could actually observe what happens on a small island after it has been denuded of species—either through a natural disaster, like a hurricane, or through fumigation. It proves possible to observe the way in which such islands are repopulated, and how the new range of species survive, or fail to survive, subsequent disasters.

The artist wants to capture her own experience in the company of finches. She observes the finches as much as possible and perhaps examines other sources of data about birds, islands, evolution, Darwin's story. Her goal, however, has nothing to do with explanation or prediction. Rather, she wants to utilize a particular medium—it could be music, or dance, or drawing—to capture certain aspects of her own experiences, including her immediate and longer-term reactions to the finches. Members of an audience will judge the resulting work by their own criteria, among which beauty is likely to be a significant one. Critics will indicate how the artist achieved her effect and which aspects of her rendering were most likely to have impressed (or irritated) an audience.

Finally, the historian is likely to focus on what actually happened when Darwin encountered the finches. And it turns out that there is more to this encounter than meets the eye. To begin with, Darwin did not have an "Aha!" experience when he first saw the birds. On the contrary, while struck by the plethora of species in general, he simply made some notes about the finches and moved on. Only months later did he begin to think about the contrasting beaks on neighboring islands; and eventually, his colleague John Gould showed him that there were actually four separate species of finches among the thirteen varieties that he had gathered.

Establishing "the facts" about Darwin's finches turns out to be a non-trivial exercise for historians, particularly in the light of various legends and rival plausible accounts. However, even more difficult challenges are posed by another question: How large a role did the finches play, immediately and eventually, in Darwin's development of the theory of evolution? Indeed, were they necessary at all? This question prompts the historian of science to consider different models of creativity: inspirational, intentional, accidental, overdetermined. And then the historian must mount arguments about which model best fits what happened in the case of Darwin's finches. Whether the same explanation might apply to other cases of scientific discovery is a strictly empirical matter. In any event, a predictive model of scientific creation seems out of the purview of the historian—unless he hankers to create a new social-scientific discipline.

Darwin's finches may seem remote from issues of morality, especially in contrast with the issues that swirl about the Holocaust. Yet, Darwin would not have felt any remoteness. He hesitated to reveal his findings publicly (and he suffered privately) because they ran completely counter to the religious ethos of his society—and his family. Even today, few scientific issues cause as much moral tumult as the theory of evolution. While the historian may not possess special tools for making moral judgments, his accounts are indispensable ingredients in any evaluation by professional or amateur moralists.

In sum, disciplines all deal with impressions, observations, "facts," theories, competing explanatory models. But each discipline has its characteristic observations and inferences; moreover, each discipline has developed its own means, its own "moves," for making sense of initial data. Teachers of the disciplines have a formidable task. How, in a way that is comprehensible, can one convey to students that the world as they know it is really a collection of worlds? Just as the cobbler and the surgeon perceive the "man on the street" in quite different lights, so, too, the scientist, the artist, and the historian bring their own lenses and instrumentation to the experiences of every day, and to the phenomena that form the foundation of their work.

Education cannot fit every student with a full set of lenses; indeed, we are doomed to fail if we aim to make each youngster into a historian, a biologist, or a composer of classical music. Our goal should not be to telescope graduate training but rather to give students access to the "intellectual heart" or "experiential soul" of a discipline. Education succeeds if it furnishes students with a sense of how the world appears to individuals sporting quite different kinds of glasses.

From ideas that are formed intuitively, and that are often misconceptions, students need to move toward a more sophisticated set of concepts and theories. In place of engravings that do not make much sense to sophisticated observers, they must acquire new tools, those of the several key disciplines; and they must use these tools to make better engravings. At the end of the day, they should be able to emulate some scientific, artistic, and historical ways of thinking—not simply because these are exciting but because they constitute three of the most powerful ways human beings have devised for making sense of our world.

What is equally important, the disciplines serve as points of entry for considering the deepest questions about the world, questions about truth, beauty, and goodness. Evolution tells us where we came from and how we got to be the way we are; Mozart shows us what humans can aspire to, as creators and performers; the Holocaust reminds us of the evil that members of our species sometimes commit. There is never a one-to-one mapping between the disciplines, on the one hand, and issues of truth-beauty-goodness, on the other. Neither the life of the mind, nor the cartography of experience is that clear-cut. But the disciplines serve as our best, our indispensable handmaidens, as we seek to negotiate this trio of precious virtues.

In mounting this argument, I am running risks. I have presented the disciplines as more consolidated and more schematic than they really are. Historians and scientists do not agree about the best way to describe what they are doing; there are historians of science as well as scientists (like geologists) who think of their work as historical; and artists and aestheticians live in uneasy proximity to one another, at best. Each of these disciplines is itself evolving, and the descriptions I give today differ from those that would have been offered fifty years ago or will be offered fifty years from now. Still, unless we are to cordon off students from the disciplines—a terrible prospect, in my view—we must begin with a picture of each, and that is what I have sought to do in these pages.

I have been selective—highly so. Indeed, I have come dangerously near to suggesting a curriculum so focused that it perseverates on a set of finches, a trio of singers, and one fateful meeting several decades ago. Even as I move to more general concepts—evolution or the Holocaust—and to overarching disciplines—history or science—I have maintained this focus. The reader might well ask, "Why not geology or astronomy rather than evolutionary biology? Why not dance or popular music rather than the archaic form of opera, and a work over two hundred years old? Why not another social science or humanistic discipline? And why focus on one especially horrific event that affected the group to which you—the author—happen to belong?"

Indeed. There are so many topics, concepts, and disciplines that one can fill a book of this length by just mentioning them all. (When I read Hirsch-like books on cultural literacy, or the lists of learning standards developed by certain political or academic bodies, that is just what I muse.) Would that we all lived to the age of Methuselah and that we all had copious memories and keen understandings of all topics!

However, we won't and we don't; and I have elected to make tough choices. While I do not insist that my three selections are the only correct ones, I submit that they are serious contenders. And I go on to submit that any education geared toward understanding must eventually make similar difficult choices. At any event, with the die cast, I move on to a more focused discussion of how the tremendous differences among individuals can actually serve as an ally in the conveying of gritty intellectual content.

CHAPTER 8
Close Looks

Exploring Three Icebergs

In exploring rich phenomena, one must confront two realities. The first—a fortunate one, in my view—is that these phenomena are inexhaustible. One could spend a lifetime studying evolution, the music of Mozart, or the Holocaust, and still leave innumerable facets unexamined. The second reality: There is no privileged way to enter these concepts. I selected a particular triplet—a clutch of finches, an operatic trio, and the Wannsee Conference—but I could have chosen any number of alternative routes.

Borrowing a familiar figure of speech, we might think of the triplet as the tips of three gargantuan icebergs. Each offers one promising way of entering a broad, deep topic. The icebergs as a whole comprise disparate facets: an entry point (like finches or a trio); a disciplinary topic (like the theory of evolution or the historical events called the Holocaust); a fundamental question (Where do species come from? How do you convey pathos in music?); fundaments of truth, beauty, morality. Again, one could devote a lifetime to topics like these.

My project is more modest. I revisit each of the three topics in some depth, placing it in an appropriate context; remark on the issues that it raises; suggest some understandings that students might achieve as their intuitive misconceptions are dissolved. I do this as I might work with a motivated but uninformed young adolescent—and I am mindful that *all* of us remain uninformed adolescents in many respects. Later on, I show how one might be able to educate the broad range of students about these topics, exploiting their multiple intelligences, their multiple ways of representing the world.

Evolution

Ever since individuals began to think about the natural world, they have been struck by the great variety of plants, animals, and, indeed, human beings (including people of other races). How did all these different groups exist and proliferate? Can they interbreed? Why are pets different from animals in the wild? Do old species disappear and new ones come along? And if so, how?

The most famous answer—the biblical answer that there was a Creation and it took place in six days—is still subscribed to by religious fundamentalists. But among individuals of a scientific cast of mind, various theories of evolution gained popularity during the last few centuries. A strong contender was the Lamarckian view that traits acquired in one generation, as a result of an organism's experience in the world, would be inherited and passed on to succeeding generations. For example, if a parent swam a great deal and developed powerful back, arm, and leg muscles, it was more likely that his or her offspring (and *their* offspring, in turn) would be muscular, than if the parent had lived a sedentary life.

A scion of an influential family long interested in evolution, Charles Darwin cast doubt on both the biblical and the Lamarckian views. Darwin grew up a child of privilege, but not without significant personal challenges. His mother died when he was young; he was an indifferent student; not eager to enter the conventional professions (medicine, the clergy) for a man of his station, he did not know what he would do with his life.

A born naturalist, young Darwin had always been interested in living beings and had developed extensive knowledge of plants and animals. He loved the out-of-doors—riding, hunting, collecting insects. When, at age twenty-two, he was given the opportunity to serve as a naturalist on a ship that was sailing around the world, he overcame his father's resistance and jumped at the chance.

A planned two-year trip turned into a five-year voyage, during which Darwin visited South America twice. He was preoccupied throughout the journey with the need to collect living specimens, fossils of long-extinct creatures, and information about geology and ecology of the terrains he visited. Darwin was particularly struck by his experiences on the Galápagos Islands, six hundred miles off the northwest coast of South America. He noted the varied life on this small tropical archipelago, formed by volcanoes in the not too distant past, and was fascinated by the large lizards (iguanas), turtles, huge tortoises, and sea lions.

While traveling in the Galápagos, Darwin took note of a wide range of birds, including web-footed boobies, doves, and finches. The birds were so tame that one could virtually pick them up. He collected twenty-six kinds of land birds, all seemingly peculiar to the islands. The variety of finches seemed noteworthy, and so he collected numerous specimens. Some lived just on plant seeds and stayed on the ground; others, living in trees, ate either insects or leaves. The finches had beaks peculiar to their diets, either long and pointed or compact and heavy; these distinctions suggested a convenient initial sorting. (Darwin collected some birds that he did not realize were finches.) Darwin also noted the differences among mockingbirds on different islands—"each variety is constant in its own Island—This is a parallel fact to the one mentioned about the Tortoises." At the end of his stay, he began to reflect on the fact that some species present on one island were not found on others. Then, months later, on his trip back to England, he thought more systematically about the diverse fauna that he had discerned on islands so close to one another. In his ornithological notes he raised the first tentative questions about evolution: "When I see these islands in sight of each other, & possessed of but a scanty stock of animals, tenanted by these birds, but slightly differing in structure & filling the same place in Nature, I must suspect they are only varieties. . . . If there is the slightest foundation for these remarks, the zoology of Archipelagoes—will be worth examining; for such facts would undermine the stability of Species."

Back home in England, Darwin had already achieved a measure of fame. Many people knew of his voyage and were fascinated by his observations, as circulated informally and as eventually published as *Journal of Researches* and *The Zoology of the Voyage of H.M.S. Beagle*. The ornithologist John Gould pointed out that Darwin (and his associates on the *Beagle*) had actually observed a whole collection of finches that had never been seen before. Moreover, each of thirteen types represented a different species (see Figure 1). Gould divided the birds into four subgroups on the basis of their tail structure, the form of their body, and their

Figure 1. Artist's rendering of several varieties of finches.
(Reprinted by permission of Cambridge University Press.)

plumage; as Darwin put it, "the most curious fact is the perfect grada-tion in the size of the beak in the different species of geospiza, from one as large as that of a haw-finch to that of a chaffinch."

How did this come to be? Darwin had begun to question the dogma of his time: that species were immutable, created at one fell swoop and essentially unchanging thereafter. Evidence pointed precisely in the opposite direction. Rather than being fixed, there were endless vari-eties, each seemingly attuned to the niche in which it found itself. Perhaps all had had a common ancestor, which had diversified into dif-ferent species, each suited to the ecology of a particular island.

The islands served as a kind of laboratory. Each was sufficiently iso-lated that the species—and particularly land birds—could remain com-fortably on it and couldn't easily leave. One could examine the incidence of each species on an island and its resemblance to varieties (or closely related species) on neighboring islands, as well as to related species in distant regions of the world.

As a biological thinker Darwin wrestled with these clues and threads, conducting various experiments in his mind. He was strongly influenced by the work of his mentor Charles Lyell, who had pondered similar ques-tions with reference to geological shifts over the millennia. Darwin began to keep a new set of notebooks, designated by letters, in which he tried to place his observations in a broader theoretical framework. The most important one for his project was the "B notebook," in which he recorded his changing ideas on the evolution or "transmutation" of species.

As is well known, Darwin's mind was concentrated by his rereading of Thomas Malthus's classic of economic analysis *Essay on the Principle of Population.* Malthus pointed out that whenever there were too many human beings for a given quantity of land, food, or other resources to support, a struggle arose for survival—with victory going to the fittest. Darwin analogized this situation to variations within and across species. Those that were strongest—best fitted to the environment in which they found themselves—would survive, flourish, reproduce abundantly. Those that could manage less well in their surroundings could either find a new home that offered less competition or a better fit, or lose the inexorable struggle for survival to varieties that were more fit. Darwin wrote in his notebook:

> One may say there is a force like a hundred thousand wedges trying [to] force every kind of adapted structure into the gaps in the

[o]economy of nature, or rather forming gaps by thrusting out
weaker ones. The final course of all this wedgings (*sic*) must be to
sort out proper structure & adapt it to change.

By the late 1830s, Darwin had assembled the major components of
his theory of evolution in his notebooks and had tried them out tenta-
tively on a few close friends. But he hesitated to go public. His theory
challenged the orthodoxies of the time, his own former creationist
beliefs, and the still strong religious faith of his wife, Emma. And so,
rather than going public, Darwin threw out a few hints about his current
thinking. In the 1845 edition of his *Journal,* he wrote:

> Considering the small size of the islands, we feel the more aston-
> ished at the number of their aboriginal beings and at their confined
> range. . . . seeing this gradation and diversity of structure in one
> small, intimately related group of birds, one might really fancy that
> from an original paucity of birds in this archipelago, one species
> had been taken and modified for different ends. . . . both in space
> and time, we seem to be brought somewhat near to that great
> fact—that mystery of mysteries—the first appearance of new
> beings on this earth.

For nearly two decades, in conversation and correspondence with
intimates, Darwin alluded to the major project in which he was
involved, while never fully resolving how he would bring its conclusions
to the attention of the scientific and lay publics. During this period, he
dealt with every possible objection in his own mind, by rigorous argument and by collecting new data with the cooperation of colleagues in
many lands. His obsessiveness and procrastination were halted abruptly
by the news that a fellow naturalist, Alfred Russel Wallace, had arrived at
similar conclusions about natural selection. If he was to retain any scientific paternity, Darwin had little choice but to go public at once with his
controversial theory. He did so, first in a joint presentation with Wallace
to the Linnaean Society in 1858, and, soon thereafter, in his now classic
book *On the Origin of Species,* published the following year.

The bare bones of the theory can be stated readily. Individual organisms have an overriding (though unconscious) goal: to survive until they
can reproduce. If they do not do so, then they will have no successors

and their line will die out. Because resources and space are limited, not all organisms will survive; there is, in fact, a perennial, unguided struggle for existence that will identify the "fittest."

Not all members of a species or group are identical. For reasons that Darwin did not understand—because he lacked a theory of genetic inheritance—the members of a species vary in slight and unpredictable ways. Certain of those variations prove to be better adapted to their milieu, with its particular predators and its protective features, such as shelter. Given limited space and resources, these fortunate organisms are more likely to survive until reproduction, and their offspring (on the average sharing more of their attractive properties than do the offspring of other members of the species) are also more likely to survive.

As these processes repeat themselves over many generations, the configuration of individuals and species in a particular region tends to change. Certain groups flourish, while others fall on hard times. When the characteristics of two groups diverge sufficiently that they no longer reproduce sexually (or can no longer produce fertile offspring), they are no longer the same species. And when a species is no longer suited to its environment, it must either migrate or risk extinction.

This skeletal sketch itself represents only the tip of the iceberg of Darwin's theory, which itself has undergone modifications in the succeeding century and a half. We now know, for example, the means by which traits are inherited; the theory of genetic inheritance first propounded by Gregor Mendel gives us the broad framework, and the structure and replication of DNA provide the mechanism. Many now speak of a struggle among genes rather than among the organisms that house the genes. We benefit from the "neo-Darwinian synthesis" of evolutionary biology and genetic studies of inheritance.

We also know many more details about the various themes and motifs in Darwin's work. For example, earlier in this century, David Lack visited the Galápagos Islands and secured more precise information about Darwin's celebrated finches. It is now known that all the finches evolved from a common ancestor; that they were distributed across the islands in a specific pattern because of certain geological forces and geographical factors; that differences in bill size relate to species-specific food niches (for eating insects or extracting prey from crevices or eating cactus); that bill size within a species is more uniform where there are many kinds of finches living together, more variable where there are fewer species on the same island; that frequent droughts can stimulate the emergence of new species. Work on evolution, begun in the modern era by Darwin, proceeds apace. Thanks to recent studies by Peter and Rosemary Grant and their students, we have quantitative information about the exact size of beaks needed to enable birds to eat different kinds of seeds, the role of singing and physical appearance (including beak size) in the mating patterns of finches, the ways in which the variety of finches fare under changing weather conditions, and the circumstances under which a new variety of finch is most likely to emerge—sometimes with great rapidity—or to become extinct.

Darwin's is a revolutionary theory, one difficult for many people to accept because it indicates that human beings have evolved from "lower" animal forms, most recently from earlier primates; difficult, as well, because it asserts that no higher authority presides over evolution. There simply are random changes, some of which prove more adaptive than others.

It is also an inspiring theory. Darwin concluded his treatise with these words:

> It is interesting to contemplate a tangled bank, clothed with many plants of many kinds, with birds singing on the bushes, with various insects flitting about, and with worms crawling through the damp earth, and to reflect that these elaborately constructed forms, so different from each other, and dependent upon each other in so complex a manner, have all been produced by laws acting around us. . . . Thus, from the war of nature, from famine and death, the most exalted object which we are capable of conceiving, namely, the production of the higher animals, directly follows. There is grandeur in this view of life . . . from so simple a beginning endless forms most beautiful and most wonderful have been, and are being evolved.

By and large, Darwin's major assertions have survived amazingly well. There are active debates nowadays about the pace and timing of evolutionary changes; there may be periods of relative stability interspersed with eras of far more rapid evolution ("punctuated equilibrium"). Findings appear regularly that nuance our understanding of the actual course of evolution: why dinosaurs suddenly disappeared; the relationship between birds and dinosaurs; the amazing survival of a few species from ancient geological eras; the actual origins of life, several billion years ago. Just as Darwin never quite decided where a variety ends and a species begins, population biologists still wrestle about the definition of species, and the relative importance of the genes, the individual organism, and the species population as a whole.

Not every one of these discoveries relates directly to Darwinian evolution, and not every one of them requires detailed knowledge of evolutionary theory in order to be investigated. However, the line of thinking first fashioned by Darwin constitutes a necessary tool if one is to think systematically and relevantly about plant and animal life as well as the possibility of new forms of artificial life. It is for this reason that I believe a curriculum could well be constructed around Darwinian evolution. The topic opens the doors to the panoply of biological issues, and, if it is not understood, the chances are great that many issues will be totally misconstrued.

To deepen their understanding of evolution, people must take into account their own prior conceptions about the existence and proliferation of species. In our times, these conceptions are likely to amalgamate early intuitions, religious explanations, and partial knowledge of various scientific claims (particularly the notion of human beings as upright apes with little hair). Without coming to a better understanding of evolutionary processes, individuals are likely to harbor unfounded views about the natural world. Once the fundamentals of evolution (and an evolutionary mode of thinking) have been mastered, individuals have access to a set of truths about the natural world.

The Music of Mozart

Mozart was one of the most gifted artists of all time. As a youthful prodigy in the middle of the eighteenth century, he toured Europe, performing astounding feats on the piano and other instruments. He began to compose when but four or five years old; mature works date from his adolescence; by the time of his early death at the age of thirty-five, he had become one of the most prolific composers of all time. The famous Köchel listing chronicles 626 works, including several dozen operas, oratorios, symphonies, and concerti.

Mozart was not bent on becoming a musical or political revolutionary; he simply lived to make music. None of his works is better loved than *The Marriage of Figaro,* which satirizes amorous relationships among the nobility and its servant class. Although a comedy, the Beaumarchais play on which the opera was based touches on fundamental questions about social class delineations and prerogatives, and the rights of human beings—even ordinary ones—to pursue their own destinies. While the play was very popular with the public, it had been banned in many places because of the subversiveness of its political and social themes. Napoleon is said to have remarked that the French Revolution began in the pages of *Figaro.*

Attracted to this text, Mozart worked with Lorenzo Da Ponte to create a four-act opera of the same name. Not wanting to risk censorship, the artists removed most of the politically sensitive lines and portraits. After opening in Vienna in 1786 to mixed reviews, the operatic *Figaro* had a surprisingly brief run. But this work had become a staple of the repertory within a generation and in the last two centuries has been performed countless times all over the world.

Works of art call for many forms of understanding, at different levels of sophistication. There is understanding of the plot, including the choice of words, the narrative sequence, and the particular characters with their respective actions and motivations. (This understanding resembles that needed to master any text.) There is understanding of the work as a political and social creation, which engendered reactions when it was first made public and later on. (This understanding resembles that called for by any work of art that features controversial themes.) And there is the understanding that is unique to the genre: understanding of the music—how it has been constructed, which effects it achieves, how and why particular effects are wrought. In what follows, most of my examples of understanding will refer to listeners' (and viewers') appreciation of the score and performance of *The Marriage of Figaro.* And, as my particular "text," I have chosen a four-minute trio that occurs toward the end of the first act.

As I've noted earlier, the trio features Count Almaviva (baritone), a powerful noble, who wants to seduce his wife's pretty young maid; the maid, Susanna (soprano), who has no interest in an entanglement with Almaviva and is looking forward eagerly to her imminent marriage to Figaro; and Basilio (tenor), music teacher to both Susanna and the

Countess. Perhaps the least attractive character in the opera, Basilio would like to procure Susanna for the Count and be accordingly rewarded. But he is above all an unctuous double-dealer who delights in the plights of others.

Present on stage but not singing in the trio is Cherubino (soprano). As his name intimates, Cherubino is an adorable thirteen-year-old, a page boy; he is in love with all women, including the Countess and Susanna. Cherubino has been visiting Susanna when the Count approaches; Susanna beckons him to hide in a chair and covers him with a dress (or, in some versions, a blanket).

In the ensuing piece, which I've dubbed "The Trio of Colliding Agendas," each character seeks to maintain a proper relationship with the other two persons, while advancing his or her particular goals. Thus Almaviva expresses anger at the lecherous page Cherubino, but is actually wooing Susanna and attempting to forestall her marriage; Susanna pretends to faint but is actually trying to hide Cherubino and to drive Almaviva and Basilio from her chambers so that she can marry Figaro and proceed with her life; and Basilio apologizes for impinging upon their rendezvous while actually delighting in the trouble that he is observing and fomenting. It is the triumph of this trio to communicate such conflicting agendas in a powerful and witty way, while advancing the action of the opera.

For the sake of convenience I have divided the trio into nine separate sections, each with a descriptive name. In the appendix, I have reproduced the portion of the score that is discussed in the text; I have included both the original Italian lyrics and my own translation. Even readers unfamiliar with musical scores may find it useful to consult the score. You can see when the singers come in (singly or in duet or trio) and which instruments accompany the various passages. It's also easy to trace various aspects of the musical line (for example, Does it move toward the higher or the lower registers? Are note patterns repeated? and the like). Of course, it is even better if you can use the score in conjunction with a recording.

I. AGENDA SETTING (MEASURES 1–34).

Each protagonist reveals goals (to himself or herself and to the audience).

Clearly angry and as imperious as ever, the Count wants to banish Cherubino from the land. He does not realize that Cherubino is hiding in the room and therefore hears every word. He is also implicitly continuing his attempt to seduce Susanna.

Basilio enters and apologizes for interrupting Susanna and the Count. Actually, he is delighted to have barged in on them, because he loves intrigue.

Susanna wants to get rid of these intruding men, to prepare for her wedding, and to hide Cherubino. She hits upon a technique: she will express fear and feign fainting.

The men are preoccupied (the Count with banishing Cherubino, Basilio with apologizing for his intrusion); to little avail, Susanna protests several times in a quivering chromatic figure that she is feeling faint.

II. SUSANNA'S ALARM (MEASURES 35–63).

Finally, hitting a high A flat, Susanna captures the attention of the men, who then try to revive her, the poor girl (*"poverina"*), perhaps in too intimate a manner. They note that her heart is pounding (*"le batte il cor"*). The rhythmic orchestral background of constant eighth notes mimics regular heartbeats.

III. RECOVERY (MEASURES 64–69).

Susanna now feigns a sudden recovery from her fainting spell, as the score shifts abruptly to the sunnier key of D major. (Her recovery coincides with her alarm at the possibility that she may be placed in the chair on which Cherubino remains hidden.) Conveying annoyance at the men's physical intimacy with her, she raises her voice (and her musical line) and implores them to leave her alone.

IV. CALMING SUSANNA (MEASURES 70–84).

Another key change, this time back to a stable "home base" of E flat. Basilio and the Count insist that they were only trying to help, to calm Susanna down; the voices and the accompaniment deliver a brief reassuring song, spanning a comfortable interval, with a soothing, steady quality.

V. BACK TO THE PAGE (MEASURES 85–100).

Seizing the opportunity to change the subject, singing in an apologetic tone, with oboe accompaniment, Basilio backpedals on the gossip that he has been spreading about Cherubino's involvement with the Countess. In a high, preachy tone, Susanna admonishes him not to be a rumormonger.

VI. BANISH THE PAGE (MEASURES 101–115).

With quick flicks of his wrist, the Count insists that the page should be banished. All three protagonists refer to the page as *"poverino"*—poor lad—in brief duets as well as in antiphonal passages. But they repeat this diminutive with decidedly different connotations: Susanna with genuine regret, the Count ironically, Basilio (characteristically) out of both sides of his mouth.

VII. WHAT DID CHERUBINO DO? (MEASURES 116–136).

In a set of rising scalar tones, Susanna and Basilio ask for details about Cherubino: "What did he do?" and "How so?" The Count then presents a recitative of some duration, in which he relates how he discovered Cherubino in the company of the young maiden Barbarina. The self-confident Almaviva recounts how he removed a cloth from a table, thus revealing Cherubino in his hiding place.

In what is probably, in a visual sense, the most memorable scene of the entire opera, the Count reaches lower and lower, as his voice also lowers step by step for a full octave, until . . .

VIII. REVELATION (MEASURES 137–139).

Amid mounting tension in the strings and the winds, the Count discovers Cherubino, hiding in the chair in Susanna's room. The orchestra joins in a lengthy A, one long enough to allow the audience to appreciate the shocking discovery and to laugh heartily.

IX. THREE TABLES TURNED (MEASURES 140–161).

In this minute-long conclusion to the trio (the first measures of which are reproduced in the Appendix), Susanna, the Count, and Basilio sing simultaneously, revealing their innermost thoughts to themselves and the audience but not, presumably, to one another. The themes of the opening section of the trio return, both in direct quotation and in inverted form, thus bringing this piece to a sonatalike close.

The Count: Susanna is not so innocent as she appears (*"Or capisco"*— Now I get it). Ironically, he dubs her the "most innocent" young woman.

Susanna: "It can't get worse than this; woe is me" ("*Che mai sarà?*"—What's going to happen?).

Basilio: "This is getting better all the time" ("*Così fan tutte*"—That's what all the beauties [women] do).

At a first hearing, this trio can be confusing, even to a seasoned listener to classical music; and it will clearly bewilder a youngster (or oldster) who has no familiarity with (and perhaps some antipathy toward) opera. (Recall Darwin's initial confusion when faced with the profusion of birds on the Galápagos Islands.) However, because the plot itself is understandable, if convoluted, one can convey the main action of the trio readily, as I have sought to do. In times past, it would have been difficult to watch this scene numerous times, because there was no way of recording it. (Only those who could pore over the score and hear or play it could master it.) Now, of course, one can secure a videotape of a performance, and listen to the trio and watch the scene as much as one likes.

A promising way to proceed toward understanding the trio is to listen to it several times. Sometimes, one should just listen to the music. If it is not being sung in a language that one understands, reading the libretto in translation is also helpful. This immersion allows one to become familiar with the major melodies, the orchestration, the changes in key and in rhythm, what the singers are saying, the times when they are addressing one another and the times when they are soliloquizing, and the points of climax and repose. If one has a videotape player or CD-ROM, one can observe the action as well.

At other times, one should listen with more focus: while reading a score, if one can, or in the company of someone who can point out the major sections, as I have done. After a while, one should be familiar enough with the trio to know, approximately, what is being sung, by whom, and to what effect. Employing our cognitive vocabulary, one should develop a reasonably comprehensive "mental representation" of the principal linguistic, musical, and action events in this four-minute piece.

At this point, one is ready to confront a new challenge: the alignment of one's phenomenal experience of the piece with the actual tools and techniques used by the creators. (This is the listener's complement to the artist's task of using the medium to create a rich experience for the audience.) Simply in terms of the score, Mozart (and Da Ponte) have available many different components: melodies and harmonies; different keys; regular or changing meters; phrasing; various instruments and groupings of instruments; the three voices with their range, modulation, and capacity to sing together or separately. Then one adds the components of a theatrical performance: the protagonists, dressed in costume, with their actions and gestures directed toward one another and toward the audience; the sets; the lighting; the performances of the orchestra players. Evidently, one has at one's disposal a remarkable array of elements that figure in the creation and performance of an operatic work or, indeed, of any multimedia artistic presentation.

One could devote many hours to an analysis of this trio, to say nothing of the rest of the opera, which takes at least three hours to perform. In keeping with my belief that a depth analysis is more revealing than a breadth survey, I favor examination of a particular piece, like the trio, and of particular passages within the piece. For example, one might focus on the musical "moves" around Susanna's decision to feign fainting, her initial difficulty in gaining the attention of the Count and Basilio, and the verbal, musical, and gestural techniques by which she achieves this goal. A second focus might fall on the contrasting ways (notes, timing, and intonation) in which the characters sing about the "poor lad." The musical and theatrical moves when the Count uncovers Cherubino hidden in Susanna's chair constitute a particularly amusing and revealing third focus. In each case, the artists can convey mood, action, reaction, and interaction, with swiftness and acuteness, thanks to their ability to use musical and dramatic means appropriately.

There are also the amazingly rapid (and highly amusing) changes in the relative leverage of the protagonists. Susanna begins in embarrassment, gains the upper hand after she has apparently fainted and recovered, and then finds herself without weapons after Cherubino has been discovered hidden in her chambers. Basilio enters with an apology, shifts to curiosity about Cherubino's fate, and then delights in the confusion that has been wrought around him. And the Count's initial anger at Basilio's gossip about the promiscuous Cherubino gives way to a touch of humanity when Susanna faints, a reawakening of his pique as he recalls Cherubino's misconduct with Barbarina, and then a smug feeling of superiority when Susanna's apparent lover has been unmasked. Note how each of the characters is portrayed as a human being rather than as simply an index of social status; this democratic treatment is the revolutionary aspect of *Figaro*.

Much of artistic accomplishment can be conveyed without technical jargon. That is as it should be; artists do not expect their audiences to be composed of aestheticians. Yet, for teaching purposes, it is valuable if students know or can learn something about musical techniques and their names. Even if a student cannot read a score, being able to detect a key change or a change in orchestration or an alteration in rhythm or meter is crucial if he or she is to appreciate the sequence of events in their aesthetic as well as their chronological dimensions. Indeed, the more he or she knows about how music and drama work, the more value an audience member is likely to glean from a performance.

The trio is the tip of the iceberg that is *The Marriage of Figaro;* it occupies but a few minutes in a lengthy and complex work. It is heard in isolation only as part of an artificial exercise like this one. Its effects take on an entirely different coloration when they are apprehended in the course of a complete performance of the work. The genius of Mozart and Da Ponte may be thought of as holographic in nature. The trio is in no way a substitute for the work; and yet, if the trio is apprehended as part of the entire work, one can move back and forth between part and whole. One can "listen backward"—knowing that Susanna is innocent in the matter of Cherubino—and "listen forward"—anticipating that Almaviva will eventually be undone by his lecherous designs. As one oscillates between the trio and the rest of the work, one can appreciate numerous resonances of character, gesture, melodic motifs, and orchestration. In this sense, the trio does constitute a "hologram" of the larger work.

The musical and dramatic relationships between the trio and other solo and ensemble set pieces in *Figaro* are well worth exploring. (How tiny a slice I've presented is conveyed by the fact that the hero, Figaro, is not even mentioned in the trio—although, just as clearly, he remains on everyone's mind throughout the opera.) The work offers at least two dozen other set pieces of comparable length on which I could have focused. And each of these both epitomizes and adds to the ensemble of resources used in the work.

Alongside *Figaro* there are other icebergs of comparable size: *Don Giovanni* and *Così Fan Tutte,* both full-scale collaborations between Mozart and Da Ponte, the latter work exploring the very misogynistic sentiments voiced by Basilio at the end of the trio. Add to these the works of other composers—or creators in other art forms—and one begins to gain some sense of the panorama that awaits the student who seeks to understand the realm of the arts.

Though awe at this impressive panorama is appropriate, it is important not to lose sight of manageable issues. The task of Mozart and Da Ponte was to take Beaumarchais's play, execute some shortening and some censoring, and figure out a manageable number of players and scenes. Having decided to feature this interaction among three players (plus a fourth who does not speak and an unseen fifth who is a prime agent of the action), they then chose to create a musical trio. The resulting piece reflects thousands of (conscious and unconscious) decisions that they made, both before composing and, presumably, after they had an initial score and had seen early rehearsals of the work. We have the unique privilege of enjoying the work and then, donning the cap of the student, seeking insight into its effects. And once we have worked through this exercise, we can apply the techniques to other works of music, by Mozart and others; and perhaps transfer some of our acquired aesthetic sensitivity to other art forms as well.

The theory of evolution captures a momentous truth; Mozart's music is an example of beauty. It is not always possible to convince someone of a truth, and it is probably inappropriate to try to convince someone that a work is beautiful (though many students appropriately take note of works that are loved by their teachers and other respected adults). "About taste," as the Romans said, "there is no disputing." One might add that one can never fully explain why something is perceived as being beautiful. The task of the educator is to call attention to works that are worthy of study and to show, in as much detail as practical, how important effects have been achieved. Sometimes a sense of beauty comes before understanding; sometimes, a sense of beauty follows detailed study; and at times, individuals may properly conclude that they simply cannot appreciate what others consider to be lovely.

I accept that some persons cannot perceive the beauty of a work of classical music, a Chinese scroll of the Sung dynasty, or a performance of the Japanese dramatic form Kabuki. But, to put it bluntly, lack of appreciation has no meaning if no effort has been made to understand. What one must do in the arts is to attempt to enter into the world of the work, and of the artist, to grasp what is being attempted, to familiarize oneself with the tools, and to try to "perform" one's own understandings—for example, in the present case, explaining why the orchestration differs in the various sections of the trio, or tracing the relationship between the melodies at the beginning and the end of the trio and those encountered elsewhere in the opera.

Having made a good-faith effort to understand, one may then justifiably return to one's intuitive judgments of delight, indifference, or even repulsion. Certainly, we all have preferences. In my own case, there are many artists whose work I simply do not cherish, even though I've made the effort to enter into their worlds; equally, there are artists whom I have grown to love, and others from whom I have become alienated over the years. As a general rule, however, time spent entering deeply into the works of esteemed artists repays itself. Even if, in the end, one does not fall in love with the work, one can admire its craft and one can appreciate why others do find the work to be intriguing, powerful, beautiful.

The Holocaust

The Holocaust is the name conferred upon a series of horrible events that occurred in Germany and other countries, chiefly those to the east of Germany, as part of World War II. Adolf Hitler, a self-educated rabble-rouser with keen political instincts, joined and soon became the leader of the National Socialist (Nazi) party; he and his Nazi circle came to power, legally, in Germany in early 1933. Anti-Semitism, a key tenet in Nazi ideology, had deep roots in German (and central European) culture. It was also fanned by Germany's military defeat in World War I and the reparations imposed on the nation thereafter, a state of affairs often blamed upon internationalists, Communists, and the Jewish people—three groups often conflated in the Nazi psyche and in Nazi propaganda.

When Hitler came to power, it was still unclear (perhaps even to him and his henchmen) to what extent he intended to act upon his anti-Semitism. Hitler moved cautiously at first, in part because he did not want to engender unnecessary opposition to his regime, in Germany and abroad. For example, since Hitler wanted to host a triumphant Olympic Games in Berlin in the summer of 1936, he concealed his racist views and programs in the preceding months.

Still, the Nazis' intention of disenfranchising the Jews became unmistakable during the middle and later 1930s. A series of ever harsher laws drove German Jews out of the mainstream of their society. Many left Germany, and many more tried unsuccessfully to escape or buy their way out. The Nazis set up concentration camps, in which various political dissidents, those deviant in other ways (sexual, physical, psychic), and people whose crime consisted in their Judaism were first detained, then tortured, and eventually murdered. In November 1938, following the murder of a German diplomat by a distraught young Jew whose parents had recently been deported, the Nazi party was authorized to undertake a plundering expedition throughout German cities. On the so-called Kristallnacht (Night of Broken Glass), Jewish stores and synagogues were destroyed, and many individuals (including relatives of mine) were trampled to death before the horrified eyes of their families.

Finally, following the outbreak of World War II in September 1939, plans gradually fell into place for a "final solution" to the Jewish problem.* Within nine months, the Third Reich had sufficient power on continental Europe so that it could do pretty much anything it wanted to. The first step was to rid Germany totally of its remaining Jews, one way or another; a second goal would be to rid all Europe of its Jews as rapidly as possible.

In retrospect, it is tempting to conclude that the Nazi party always favored extermination of the Jews. Leaders (and many members) were simply waiting for the total power (so that public opinion no longer mattered) and the method (lethal killing by gas) that would enable them to accomplish their goal. Indeed, as early as his book *Mein Kampf*, Hitler spoke of the need to get rid of the Jewish scourge—the primary threat to "Aryan purity." Antipathy toward the Jews was a staple of Nazi rhetoric throughout the 1930s; and when World War II broke out, Hitler explicitly said that now he would be able to make good on the promise that he had already made, "the annihilation of the Jewish race in Europe." In 1940 and 1941, officials often referred to the "doubtless imminent final solution of the Jewish question."

Yet this conclusion that the Holocaust was premeditated does not withstand scrutiny. As mentioned in the last chapter, Nazi officials seriously considered a number of other measures for "solving" the Jewish

*In using the expression "fell into place," I do not intend to minimize the active agency involved in these decisions. Historians still differ on who made these decisions and how they were transmitted to others who would implement them.

problem. One measure, which seems ludicrous today (though less unthinkable than what actually happened), was a plan to move all Jews to the island of Madagascar, off the east coast of Africa. This plan foundered because of Germany's inability to defeat Great Britain and thereby dominate the seas. Another measure, which the Nazis actually began to put into practice, was to move Jews to large reservations or ghettos in Eastern Europe, such as the city of Lublin in Poland.

These and other contingencies were under active consideration during the summer of 1941, a time when Germany was excited by the initial success of the campaign to conquer the Soviet Union. However, a number of factors seem to have dampened the enthusiasm for what can now be considered halfway measures, and to have raised the possibility of a solution that was truly final.

Among the factors that turned the tide toward the Holocaust were, first of all, the large number of Jews now under German domination. In addition to a few million remaining in Western Europe, there were now 5 million to 6 million in Eastern Europe, far too many to "store" in a ghetto or resettle on a distant island. The difficulties of setting up a ghetto and controlling the inevitable disease and political unrest had also been underestimated. In addition, there was the fateful decision to allow Polish, Romanian, and other foreign agents to eliminate Jews, and the concomitant order for Germans to kill all the Soviet Jews that came under their domination. Nazi observers were struck by two hitherto undetermined facts: it was not that difficult to get either foreigners or Germans to murder large numbers of Jews; yet it was logistically difficult to do so through shooting or starvation. A search began for a means of killing that would be less jarring for the executioners.

Hitler had ruminated openly about the Jewish question in January 1941 and said that he was "thinking of many things in a different way, that was not exactly more friendly." He declared that he would begin to "play out his prophecy in the coming months." By the end of that month, the deputy chief of the Gestapo, Reinhard Heydrich, had submitted his proposal for the "final solution project."

At some point between the summer of 1941 and the end of 1941, a final decision was made and events fell into place. Most assume that the decision could not have been made without the explicit approval of Hitler and his henchman Heinrich Himmler, the leader of the SS (Hitler's elite protective force), and that the actual agent who articulated the solution and organized the death camps was Reinhard Heydrich. Probably Hitler gave his final approval in the summer of 1941, a time when he spoke about a "new Garden of Eden" in the Reich. An important marker was Reichsmarschall Hermann Göring's authorization to Heydrich, on July 31, 1941, to prepare a "total solution" (*Gesamtlosung*) of the Jewish question in Europe; also important was the fact that orders to eliminate large numbers of Jews were becoming commonplace, including formulas, for example, that one hundred Jews be killed for every German killed.

It is also agreed that some important "experiments" had to be pursued. In mid-October 1941, the first deportation trains left Germany; women and children were being sent to the cynically labeled work camps; in December, the first massacres of German Jews had taken place in Riga, and the first gassings using the chemical Zyklon B had been carried out in the death camps at Chelmno and Belzec, without significant repercussions.

Which leads us to the fateful Wannsee Conference. This meeting, called by Heydrich, was initially announced in November and was scheduled for December 1941, but was then postponed until January 20, 1942. In attendance were the state secretaries of the German ministries, representatives from occupied territories, and various other functionaries. According to one report, of the fourteen principal figures at the meeting, eight held doctoral degrees from major Central European universities. The official purpose of the meeting was to discuss "the Final Solution of the Jewish question." Luncheon was served.

Our knowledge of the meeting comes largely from a protocol written by Adolf Eichmann, head of the Gestapo's Section of Evacuations and Jews; he later admitted that he had used euphemisms in his account. Because of prior documents that had already been sent to those in attendance, including virtually public ones that had discussed the killing of Jews by soldiers, discussion proceeded as if attendees already knew that the decision had been made to eliminate European Jewry. Heydrich began by discussing Göring's plan for the Final Solution—how to deal with the 11 million European Jews then under Nazi domination. Evacuation of Jews to the East had now replaced emigration of Jews from Europe as the general mode of operation. The focus of the meeting then moved to logistics: what procedures should be followed; who should do what in each of the occupied territories; who should be counted as Jews, and who not.

Revealing their awareness of the unprecedented nature of the pro-
ceedings, those in attendance at the meeting studiously avoided the
words "kill" or "murder." Speakers referred instead to "solutional possibilities," but that expression, Eichmann acknowledged, meant "killing
possibilities." Heydrich also stated that, of the Jews conscripted for
labor, "a large number of them will drop out through natural wastage."
This statement also referred to death, and was meant to contrast with
what would happen to those who did not waste naturally: they would be
gassed to death.

Reports about the meeting spread to the individuals who would conduct the exterminations and to the locations where they were to take
place, and other subsidiary follow-up conferences were held. Within a
month, the death machines commenced operation.

With frightening efficiency. In mid-March 1942, most of European
Jewry was alive. Less than a year later, in mid-February 1943, at least 3
million Jews—men, women, and children—had been murdered in cold
blood—half of the ultimately 6 million Jewish victims of the Holocaust.
All this was undertaken with as much secrecy as possible; as Himmler
proudly told his lieutenants in October 1943: "in our history, this is an
unwritten and never to be written page." Following the war, the tri-
bunals set up by the victorious Allies concluded that Hitler had ordered
that no one should be informed about the death camps unless they had
to be.

Ever since the truth of the death camps became known more or less
in its entirety, humans of reason have asked how and why these events
came to pass. As noted earlier, intentionalist historians trace the genocide to explicit, long-term plans on the part of Hitler and his closest
Nazi henchmen. The functionalist historians (sometimes called the
structuralists) are less impressed by long-term consistency and the
operation of direct "top-down" chains of command. They call attention
instead to the struggle among rival camps within the Nazi hierarchy to
gain the approval of Hitler and his inner circle; to a series of ad hoc
actions that were deemed unsuccessful or insufficient; and the final des-
perate lunge toward a decision that would render all other options
unnecessary.

Whichever of these general orientations is more plausible, it is
equally important for historians to reconstruct what happened at a more
local level. Once the Final Solution had been arrived at, in effect, in the

middle of 1941, there was still the question of whether it could be made to work, and if so, how.

Here the historian must rely on his tools—his equivalent of the biologist's observations and theories, the musician's plots, performers, and scoring options, and the aesthetician's concepts. Believing that they were engaged in a decisive historical enterprise, the Nazis kept painstaking records of many matters—though, of course, most of these records were not meant for public consumption. Historians dispute which records are reliable; whose testimony is credible and whose is not; how to piece together the facts of a conference whose attendees knew at some level that they were carrying out a program of unprecedented scope and barbarism, which could never be unambiguously traced to them. And historians must wrestle as well with those events that were never literally recorded but for which there is overwhelming circumstantial evidence.

Once these elements have been selected and evaluated, historians must then piece them together into a plausible overall account. Each statement or account by a recognized scholar not only occupies a niche but also helps to redefine an issue's scope for successive scholars. Thus, Raul Hilberg was the first to write extensively about the Holocaust, and to lay out the massive and highly bureaucratic nature of the procedures devised to murder the European Jews; Tim Mason identified the rival schools of intentionalists and functionalists; Christopher Browning detailed how specific events of 1941 were decisive in launching the Holocaust; German scholars in the early 1980s struggled mightily with one another about the uniqueness of the Holocaust and whether it could be attributed specifically to German history and character; Charles Maier summarized the debates among German historians about the "unmasterable past." Recently, in a much-discussed work, Daniel Jonah Goldhagen has directed attention to the willingness of numerous ordinary Germans to join, sometimes with enthusiasm, in the murdering of the Jews. And surrounding these historical events are literary accounts by individual survivors like Elie Wiesel and Primo Levi, as well as major films such as *Sophie's Choice* (based on William Styron's novel) and *Schindler's List* (based on a book by Thomas Keneally).

Just as Darwin's views on evolution must be viewed with reference to those of other earlier and subsequent scholars, and *Figaro* has been subjected to many artistic and musical interpretations, accounts of the

Holocaust are now framed against the background of the enormous literature on the topic. For anyone who becomes engaged in the literature of one of these fields, it is not easy to keep one's attention on the "raw data"—the finches of the Galápagos, the songs of the Trio, or the protocol from Wannsee. Each has been colored by conversations among generations of scholars and interested laypersons—and, not least, by powerful artistic portrayals. However, for the purpose of education, it is important not to let the secondary literature swamp the primary phenomena.

In understanding evolution, one may begin with the variations in one or more species or subspecies, focus on some surprising patterns and exceptions, and then oscillate between observations and the overarching theoretical framework. In understanding the music of Mozart, one may begin with a particular piece, such as "The Trio of Colliding Agendas," and then explore the rest of the opera and its relation to other works in the repertory. The resonance between the particularities of a piece and the composer's overall oeuvre provides a provocative dialectic. Finally, in the case of the Holocaust, one begins with a specific event and a finite set of characters (the conference at Wannsee); and one then attempts to place this event in the context of a genocide, and, perhaps, of other crimes of comparable awfulness.

Wannsee represents a sobering introduction to history, its events and its interpretations. Once one has grasped the fundamentals of the Holocaust, other questions arise. Genocidal efforts of this and earlier centuries are often compared to the Holocaust, and debates flare up about whether the Nazi Holocaust ought to be thought of as unique or as one of a number of equally or comparably pernicious episodes in human history, including events in this century. And is it possible to "transfer" some of the tools used to study Wannsee to the description and interpretation of quite different events—those that occurred at Fort Sumter, South Carolina, in April 1861 or at the Bastille in Paris in July 1789 or in Tiananmen Square in Beijing in June 1989? Are these episodes simple markers for the convenience of historians, or does history grow out of such specific sites and actions? And how does one make sense of other ideological forces in history—other hatreds, such as those in the Middle East; other economic and social theories that took a political turn, such as those propounded by Marx and Engels; and other movements on which one may look more favorably, such as civil rights and feminism?

The Holocaust may have passed into history, but its shadow haunts us today. Memorials continue to be set up around the world, and nearly every one of them engenders controversy, particularly when explicit or latent neo-Nazis insist on being heard. The reasons why one group would decide to annihilate another elude most sane individuals—yet we must confront just this human possibility when we consider what has happened recently in Bosnia and Rwanda.

Probing more deeply, one must ask what it is about human beings that causes hatred and conflict, and what options are available to victim, victimizer, and other human beings. Questions about responsibility and guilt also linger. Recent continuing debates about the roles of other Germans, French or Austrian citizens and soldiers, and the Swiss bankers who were in charge of the Nazis' money and the art and money they held or stole reveal the complexity of this set of events. One cannot participate in such discussions in the absence of a developed understanding of the events of the Holocaust.

Finally, the Holocaust raises moral issues in most acute form. On what basis did the Nazis do what they did? What was the contribution of eugenics and other pseudoscientific rationales? Does might make right—and should it? Who could have stopped the Nazis, and why didn't they? Who has the right to punish those involved in the implementation of the Final Solution? What are the responsibilities of those—in Germany, Europe, and the United States—who stood by and did little or nothing? When, if ever, does the "statute of limitations" on responsibility run out? Of course, analogous questions can be raised with reference to other historical events, ranging from the slaughter of Chinese nationals by Japanese invaders in the 1930s to the treatment of African slaves and Native Americans by the colonizers from Europe.

Attaining historical mastery of the Holocaust is not equivalent to understanding its moral dimensions. Indeed, its moral dimensions can be discerned as effectively through an examination of artistic works or personal memoirs or monuments. Nor do historians have a privileged role in making moral judgments; all of us have the right, as well as the obligation, to do so. What is key, as I see it, is that issues of morality are best approached through concrete events involving human agents. Such events need to be understood in their particularity, and in turn we should draw on them to guide our own decisions and actions. The Holocaust does not belong to a single people, any more than does

American slavery or Christian charity; it belongs to all human beings.

One hopes that individuals today will not have to deal with events of the Holocaust's horrific nature, although if past centuries are any guide, some of us will have to do just that. No one can know for sure how he or she will behave in such extreme conditions. But I have to have faith that a deeper understanding of how humans acted—or failed to act—can have some influence on what we ourselves do.

The most important understanding about the Holocaust, in my view, is that it is what some human beings did to other human beings. Any one of us could have been victim or victimizer. Even if one does not deny the historical reality of the Holocaust, even if one takes the position that it was absolutely wrong, one still has not understood it fundamentally if one continues to believe that it involves a different species, living in a different world. Indeed, as many have noted, the Holocaust was possible in part because the Germans did see the Jews, and certain other groups, as members of a different species. In this way, they were not only cruelly bigoted; they also overlooked a basic fact of science, that all humans belong to the same species.

Aliments for Informed Citizens

To be an informed member of our world today, one needs to have background knowledge: Who was Darwin and what is evolution? Who were Mozart and Da Ponte and what is *The Marriage of Figaro?* Who was Hitler and what happened during the Holocaust? Here is the strand of merit in E. D. Hirsch's call for cultural literacy. But what one needs is of far more importance: some understanding of what is implied by these names, terms, and concepts.

Alas, there is no royal road to understanding—no mediation or medication that allows one to absorb the iceberg in a moment. At first this seems a handicap. How easy if understanding could simply be assimilated, like a good meal, and if the same diet worked for everyone. However, as I've often observed in these pages, individuals harbor many misconceptions and misunderstandings; these must be dealt with if deeper understanding is to emerge.

Nor can we ever exhaust these topics. Presumably, as long as there are reflective individuals, they will return to questions about evolution, music, and man's inhumanity to man. Indeed, the more deeply one probes these topics, the more enigmatic they become (in a sense); we can never know for sure how large a role the finches played in Darwin's epochal discoveries; or why Susanna's predicament affects us as it does; or how Hitler's dream became humanity's nightmare. But the purpose of education is not to provide ultimate answers; it is to enhance one's sense of understanding without dashing one's sense of mystery and wonder.

The very multifaceted nature of these themes and concepts presents an opportunity. There is no need to look for the single, privileged approach to important concepts, for none exists. Rather, such foundational ideas can and should be approached in a variety of ways. And here, at last, we can draw upon our knowledge of the different kinds of minds that we possess, as well as our knowledge of the differences among human beings: differences at least as great as those found among Darwin's finches, among Mozart's protagonists, among the victims and victimizers of the Holocaust.

CHAPTER 9
"Multiple Intelligences" Approaches to Understanding

Three Uses of Intelligences

By now, my educational vision should be clear. Deep understanding should be our central goal; we should strive to inculcate understanding of what, within a cultural context, is considered true or false, beautiful or unpalatable, good or evil. Stressing that these are merely examples (though considered ones), I have called for a curriculum that fosters understanding of the theory of evolution, the music of Mozart, and the recent historical event called the Holocaust.

But can we draw on our expanding knowledge of human development, individual differences, and cultural influences as we seek ways of enhancing the understandings of large numbers of students? If so, we are finally in a position to assemble the pieces of the puzzle of effective education.

To put it succinctly, such an education should be constructed on two foundations. On the one hand, educators need to recognize the difficulties students face in attaining genuine understanding of important topics and concepts. On the other hand, educators need to take into account the differences among minds and, as far as possible, fashion an education that can reach the infinite variety of students.

Here the theory of multiple intelligences can become a powerful partner in effective teaching. I contend that a "multiple intelligences perspective" can enhance understanding in at least three ways:

1.By Providing Powerful Points of Entry. The pedagogical decision about how best to introduce a topic is important. Students can be engaged or turned off in quick order. Also, because of what psychologists call the primacy effect, students are likely to remember the opening illustration or attention-grabber. The theory of multiple intelligences yields an abundance of ways in which to broach a topic.

2.By Offering Apt Analogies. Unfamiliar topics or themes are often first grasped by analogy to a topic that is better known or understood. Models drawn from familiar territory can also help students gain a first understanding of an unfamiliar terrain.

Of course, every analogy has strengths and weaknesses. Since, by definition, analogies and models are drawn from remote realms, there will be important differences, as well as telling similarities, between the unfamiliar topic and the more accessible vehicle being used to illuminate it. Instructors must convey the power of the analogy; no less, they must indicate its limitations and the ways in which it might mislead.

3.By Providing Multiple Representations of the Central or Core Ideas of the Topic. For pedagogical purposes, any topic or theme should feature a few important or central ideas. Teaching will be considered successful to the extent that these ideas have been grasped and can be drawn on appropriately in new situations.

Often instructors will think about these core ideas in a particular way. Yet, I doubt that there exists *any* seminal idea that can be thought of in only one way. Indeed, I would go further. It is a characteristic of powerful ideas that they can be represented in more than one way—that they can be embodied in a number of "model languages," a term I shall discuss later. A mark of the expert is that he or she can create a family of representations, a set of model languages, a variety of takes on the core idea—and can go on to evaluate candidate new accounts of the topic.

There are numerous ways in which one can approach and introduce directly our target triplet of evolution, Mozart, and the Holocaust. As I have already said, each of these resembles an iceberg; no single observer can do more than survey parts of it. Until now, I have deliberately focused on a generative introduction to each topic—finches; an operatic trio; the Wannsee Conference. From now on, I will deliberately draw examples from a variety of sites on each iceberg. And so, for example, in speaking about biological science, I will sometimes touch on the introductory example (finches), sometimes on the entire topic (Darwinian evolution), sometimes on more general considerations of scientific exploration and explanation. I will follow a similar sampling strategy with reference to Mozart and the Holocaust.

I adopt this ecumenical approach for two reasons. First, I want to show that a "multiple intelligences" approach is flexible; it can be employed in studying sharply focused topics as well as generic ones. Second, not every aspect of multiple intelligences can be used with equal effectiveness for every pedagogical goal. Put concretely, while there is more than one entry point, analogy, or model language for each topic, there is no reason to suppose that there will necessarily be seven or twelve or thirty-seven for each. The pedagogical challenge is to figure out *which* entry points hold promise for particular understandings; to try out a candidate entry point; to reflect upon successes and failures. The same reflective challenge obtains in the selection of apt analogies and model languages. I have sought to use examples that make sense, not merely to invent examples that, checklist-style, will occupy every space in a preset grid.

Even though I make no claim to being exhaustive, I do provide numerous examples in the pages that follow. This is for a reason. All too often, the theory of multiple intelligences has been invoked to convey trivial examples, or to present important examples in an offbeat or anecdotal way ("Let's sing our times tables, children!" says the teacher; and then an observer claims that musical intelligence has been used to teach mathematical thinking). Here I offer an existence proof: A multiple intelligences approach can be drawn upon in a thoroughgoing way to present ideas that are consequential. And while I have in mind teachers working in classes with students, I believe that this approach can be of use to *anyone* seeking to master *any* significant topic . . . including someone who has not been inside a classroom for decades.

Multiple Entry Points to Rich Topics

Taking off from the theory of multiple intelligences, in a rough-and-ready rather than a slavish way, one can find at least seven powerful entry points to diverse concepts. These opening gambits help to introduce important and challenging topics.

Narrative Entry Points. Perhaps the most effective way to involve a large number of learners is through vivid, dramatic narrative. People of all ages find stories inviting. Narratives, of course, activate the linguistic as well as the personal intelligences; and it is also possible to convey narrative in other symbolic forms, such as mime or cinema, that engage other intelligences.

Each of our three cases lends itself readily to narrative entry points. With the example of evolution, one can tell the fascinating story of Darwin, a young man with promise but also with personal weaknesses and foibles; his epochal voyage on the *Beagle;* his struggles to formulate the theory of evolution; his illnesses, which perhaps reflected those struggles; his reluctance to make his awesome conclusions public; the strange coincidence of Wallace's codiscovery of evolution and the uncharacteristically gentlemanly resolution of this struggle for priority; and the pitched battles that followed upon the public unveiling of the theory in 1859. How ironic that a shy man who shunned publicity would inspire so compelling a drama.

The narrative can extend beyond Darwin himself. There are other fascinating protagonists in the story of evolution, including his predecessor Lamarck, his contemporary Wallace, Thomas Huxley ("Darwin's bulldog"), and Darwin's own evolutionist grandfather, Erasmus. And stories can transcend individuals; it is inviting to cover the saga of a particular group of species (such as the finches across the Galápagos chain), or even the grand story of evolution itself—the story begun so vividly, if nonscientifically, in the opening verses of Genesis and in other myths of origin.

Mozart and his family (featuring an ambitious and difficult father) furnish a promising narrative, as Peter Shaffer showed in his play *Amadeus.* So do other characters in the *Figaro* story. Da Ponte, for example, ended up teaching Italian at Columbia University; Beaumarchais became a secret arms supplier during the American Revolution; and Mozart seems to have been in love with Nancy Storace, who played the role of Susanna in the original production of *Figaro.* There is also the story contained in the Beaumarchais play, and even the story of how the play was turned into the opera, with sharp condensation and the deletion of most of the "politically incorrect" material.

However, from a musical point of view, narrative takes on a different meaning. Now the reference is not to plot and character but rather to

motifs—how they are introduced, elaborated upon, revisited in different guises and for different expressive purposes. The overture, for
example, introduces a number of different themes—joyous; touched
with intrigue or tension; and plaintive—primarily in the triumphant
key of D major. These themes, moods, metric patterns, and figures are
played with throughout the opera; they capture portions of the action,
and themselves are acted upon by the composer in order to achieve contrasting effects.

We even can trace the course of a theme in the "Trio of Colliding
Agendas." Basilio commences the trio with a simple descending scalar
motif of three notes (the last one repeated), spanning a triad (F, E flat,
D, D), which competes for attention with the chromatic motif of
Susanna. The descending motif is immediately inverted, when both the
Count and Basilio seek to help the fainting maiden. Basilio picks up the
theme again, in a lower key, this time in an ascending passage, when he
insists that he is only here to help Susanna; and he returns to the original
descending figure when he explains apologetically that he was only com-
municating hearsay about Cherubino. Finally, the concluding minute of
the trio, with each of the three protagonists baring his or her soul, is
similarly based on variations of this set of three notes, sometimes sung
in ascending, sometimes in descending, order. I could go so far as to dub
this trio "The Song of Three Notes"; its story is the story of the ways in
which three successive notes in a major scale can be used to convey
diverse feelings and actions.

Like evolution and Mozart, the Holocaust proves a vast recruiting
ground for compelling narratives. Few characters from modern history are as fascinating, if in a morbid way, as Adolf Hitler. His story, that
of the Nazi party, and its more sensational leaders—Field Marshal
(later Reichsmarschall) Hermann Göring, chief propagandist Joseph
Goebbels, and Heinrich Himmler, the architect of the Holocaust—
engender enduring interest.

Narratives can also encompass a broader range. There is European
history, German history, the history of the Jewish people, the history of
anti-Semitism. At a more narrowly focused level, there are intriguing
stories about individuals, including survivors, martyrs, and those who
protected Jews and others under threat from the Nazi regime. And as we
have seen, it is possible to tell the story of a specific event, the Wannsee
Conference—in terms of what was and was not explicitly said and in

light of the horrible events that led up to and flowed from it. Indeed, a cinematic or theatrical treatment of the Conference can prove as effective as an annotated version of the protocol prepared by Adolf Eichmann. Such a film was made by Heinz Schirk in 1984.

To recapitulate: The decision about how to introduce students to a rich generative topic or a provocative question proves pivotal. Because stories hold much interest, they offer an inviting entry point. For each of the topics under consideration here, ample opportunities exist for the creation of arresting invitations, which should generate initial curiosity and help to sustain interest in the topic.

But a variety of additional promising entry points exist. More briefly, I will introduce each and suggest some ways to apply it to my triplet of topics.

Numerical Entry Points. Some students like to deal with numbers and numerical relations. In the case of the theory of evolution, they might find it provocative to trace Darwin's own thinking during and after his tour of the Galápagos Islands. Struck by the variety of finches on closely related islands, Darwin tried to figure out the nature of the distribution and the reasons for it. In subsequent conversations with John Gould and others, he revised his numerical classifications; one can read the slightly differing accounts in the manuscript of his journals, in the published version, and in *On the Origin of Species.* A century later, the evolutionary biologist David Lack revisited the islands and made a targeted analysis of the number of species on each, even as he offered his own explanation for the observed distribution.

Nowadays, like the rest of biology, the study of evolution has become highly quantitative. Mathematically oriented students find plenty to cut their teeth on: mathematical models of evolutionary processes or of shifts in population, and programs that produce artificial life. Without going into technical details, I can mention that Dolph Schluter has collected data on the range of beak sizes in all the ground finches on the Galápagos Islands and created a program that calculates how many species of finches a hypothetical island could support. The program yielded the surprising finding that there should be three species of finches, each with a beak suited to cracking one of the three kinds of seeds finches eat in the Galápagos.

Any work of music is presented in certain meters and is organized according to specific rhythmic figures. One might take a look at two arias in *Figaro,* lay out their respective meters and rhythms, and speculate about why Mozart chose these numerical patterns. Indeed, in the motif of three ascending or descending scalar notes in the "Trio of Colliding Agendas," one has available a large number of arrangements that can be experimented with in different keys, rhythms, and note lengths.

Fixed by the indelible figure of 6 million murdered Jewish men, women, and children, the story of the Holocaust is a story of numbers. One could examine the populations of various groups—Jewish, gentile, and Gypsy, say—before and after the Third Reich. In some regions and countries, nearly all the Jews were destroyed, while in others most were saved; indeed, the issue of where achievement of "the Final Solution" was likely to be most effective proved central at Wannsee and subsequent policy discussions. Even the way the figure of 6 million was arrived at, and how accurate it is, has been a subject of controversy among the historians of the Holocaust—and among those who would deny its existence or question its scope.

Logical Entry Points. Related to yet distinct from an interest in numbers is a preoccupation with logical propositions, their interrelations and their implications. Evolution can be expressed in syllogistic form:

> If there are more individuals/species in a territory than can be supported;
> and if there are variations among individuals/species;
> it follows that those variants that survive best in a particular environment will be able to reproduce and flourish.

As can the Holocaust:

> If one wants to remove all Jews from Europe;
> and if they can neither be moved elsewhere nor allowed to die natural deaths;
> it follows that one must devise a procedure for eliminating them.

Less strictly syllogistic, the logic in *Figaro* grows out of the relationships among the various plots and subplots. There are the love relationships at the start of the opera (Almaviva and the Countess; Figaro and Susanna); the desired relations (Almaviva seeks Susanna; Marcellina wants to marry Figaro; Cherubino is in love with all women); the changes of circumstance (Marcellina discovers that she is Figaro's mother and should therefore marry his father, Bartolo; and Cherubino and Barbarina are also paired). As in most comedies of the era, it is imperative that the villains get their comeuppance and that everyone ends up with the person to whom he or she rightly belongs. An initial imbalance must give way to a final balance in the crucial interpersonal ties. Those of a logical frame of mind are attracted by the challenge of delineating the limited number of ways in which the various tensions, antipathies, and passions among the characters can be resolved.

There is a logic, as well, within any musical composition. One can trace the relationships among the Count, Susanna, and Basilio over the course of the first-act trio, and see how they are altered by events—the fainting of Susanna, her sudden recovery, and then the untimely revelation that Cherubino is hidden in Susanna's chair. Indeed, dramatic moments occur precisely when the relationships of the characters are suddenly changed—as when, in this instance, the men are proved right and the woman is unmasked (though only temporarily). And there is even a logic in the musical scoring. If a piece modulates to a distant key, or the rhythm suddenly shifts, it is assumed that eventually, at an appropriate moment, key and rhythm will return to home base.

Existential/Foundational Entry Points. Of enduring interest to some individuals is the possibility of tackling deep questions about existence: the meaning of life, the necessity of death, the passions and vagaries of love and hate. The theory of evolution tells us about human beings as a species in nature; in portraying the spectrum of human emotional life, Mozart illustrates the wonderful creations of which human beings are capable; the Holocaust documents the awful potentials of humans, as well as offering some inspiring instances of kindness, courage, and heroism.

As for more specific existential questions, the theory of evolution provides the best scientific answer to the question of who we are as a species, what is our background, and what figures to be our future. Though evolutionary theory is often set in opposition to religious explanations, there is no necessary conflict between these stances. One can believe that evolution is God's plan, and that God has set in motion the elaborate calculus of mutations, struggles for survival, and the temporary ascendancy of certain species in certain niches. Indeed, the Catholic

Church has recently made its peace with the account of origins offered by evolutionary theorists and has laid out proper spheres for faith and reason.

Alfred Tennyson wrote of the "flower in the crannied wall," "*if* I could understand / What you are, root and all, and all in all, / I should know what God and man is." For those who discern significance in fine detail, the finches offer an inviting occasion to ponder questions of existence. The secrets of life and the mysteries of biological evolution can be epitomized in the varying sizes and shapes of beaks found on the variety of birds spread across the Galápagos.

Figaro traffics in such powerful themes as love, intrigue, power, and social hierarchy. Like other convincing dramatic vehicles, it explores the relationships among human beings, in all their subtlety, complexity, foolishness, and occasional nobility. Such themes are dealt with darkly in tragedy, with greater lightness or irony in comedy. In the closing measures of the trio, each of the characters confronts the puzzles of his or her current existence: Susanna is asking what will become of her; Almaviva is coming to grips with the reality of his rival Cherubino, and the injustice of his intended conquest of Susanna; and Basilio is confirming his cynical views both of women and of life in general.

The Holocaust presents the most extreme human attributes: hatred, cruelty, evil; power used maliciously; some instances of courage and decency. It compels us to consider how a nation could come to the point where genocide became state policy; and how specific individuals could, sometimes eagerly, become the vehicles of that policy. It raises equally profound questions about what civilization *is*. The idea of genocide took form in a nation that many people considered the pinnacle of civilization; the plan was vetted by individuals holding doctorates from major universities; and the murders were carried out by individuals who somehow managed at the same time to pursue interests in literature, art, music, and religion. And especially for all those who were personally involved in the events, the Holocaust raises the most fundamental questions of meaning. How can one find reasons for living in the face of such horrible human actions? Herein lies the urgency of writings by Elie Wiesel, Primo Levi, and other survivors.

Aesthetic Entry Points. Works of art are apprehended in terms of their organization, sense of balance, and appropriateness, as well as more specific features of color, shading, tone, ambiguity of meaning. Each of our three topics can be introduced through works of art: evolution, through documentaries or animated scenarios that illustrate the forces of nature at work; *Figaro* through various dramatic, operatic, and balletic interpretations; and the Holocaust through cinema, ranging from Leni Riefenstahl's propaganda movies to Steven Spielberg's recent *Schindler's List*.

Unlikely aesthetic presentations may exert powerful effects. Robin Lakes's *Dissonance* seeks to convey the experience of the concentration camps in dance. Consider this description:

> In the first section . . . we see the dancers in a series of split-second flashes of light dying horrible deaths. A man suspended on a wire is electrocuted in his desperate attempts at escape. Bodies fall from the flaming ovens into a pile. The images are powerful in their detail; we feel the man's spasms against the fence as death throes, we feel the limp bodies stiffening into the contorted shapes only corpses could retain. . . . scenes gradually lengthen into scenarios—prisoners on their way to concentration camps, couples separated against their will . . . nameless victims have become real, identifiable people before you. . . . you really feel as if you might have a number tattooed on your arm. The arms of barbed wire in front of you could as easily be enclosing you. You could as easily be dressed in the dancer's rags and bandages.

Yet to think of art simply in terms of familiar genres is too limited. Key ideas and examples also have aesthetic properties. The shapes of plants, birds, and other animals, and their change over time, invite investigation; the shifting morphologies constitute arresting displays. Many of the individual features of *Figaro*—the melodies and harmonies, the lyrics, the characterizations, the scenery, the gestures, even the revealing pauses—call for artistic appreciation and analysis.

When it comes to the relationship between the Holocaust and artistry, one must tread carefully. I suggest two points. First, the designers of the death camps saw themselves as fashioning a system with its own form. From the deceptive legend above the camp entrance ("Work makes one free") to the passage of individuals through the camp, to the way in which the gas was released, to the disposal of the charred bones and the preservation of the gold teeth, the architects sought to satisfy certain design criteria. Indeed, Heydrich and Himmler were driven to the creation of death camps precisely because the earlier forms of killing and burial were considered too hard on the murderers' sensibilities; the death camps allowed them to participate in a relatively sanitized and distanced process.

Second, the Holocaust raises in most unflinching form the question of the relationship of art to issues of life and death. As the British critic George Steiner (among others) has reminded us, we must understand how SS men could preside over the acts of the greatest brutality and then return home to their families, listen to Mozart on the gramophone, or perform at night in string quartets. One must take note not only of the many artists whose works were burned by the Nazis but also of those, like composer Richard Wagner, who were placed on a pedestal, and of those, like conductor Herbert von Karajan, singer Elisabeth Schwarzkopf, or filmmaker Leni Riefenstahl, who hitched their professional destinies to the Nazi star. And finally, one cannot forget that Hitler was once an aspiring artist, that he treated his architect, Albert Speer, like a son, and that he thought of his speeches and his architectural creations as contributions to German culture.

"Hands-on" Points of Entry. Young people, in particular, are stimulated by the opportunity to work with physical materials. Since the processes of evolution ordinarily occur much too gradually to be observed, it is necessary to take a more aggressive or imaginative approach. The opportunity to breed Drosophila (fruit flies) has long been exploited in biology classes. Precisely because the species is in many ways a simple one and its life cycle is brief, it is possible to monitor the changing of traits and the way that these changes affect the life course and morbidity of different strains. Virtual reality and other computer simulations also give students the chance, for the first time ever, to experiment in an active way with the factors that control evolution: for example, the struggle among species, or the gradual isolation of variations until separate (reproductively exclusive) species have emerged.

Those with means can explore other manifestations of evolution directly. Every year, many tourists and study groups visit the Galápagos to see for themselves the biological diversity that struck Darwin and his shipmates. And it is also possible to confront other aspects of evolution by visiting the rain forest, probing streams that have been polluted, or examining those experimentally denuded islands where attempts have been made to simulate or observe evolutionary processes.

Works of art provide the readiest forms of hands-on (or mouth-on) involvement. Anyone can listen to or sing along with parts of *Figaro*. And particularly since the advent of computer music, one can perform parts of the score using different instrumentation and also conduct experiments with contrived endings and combinations of themes. There are also numerous roles that one can assume in the production of a complex work like *Figaro*, which calls not only for singers but also for instrumentalists, conductors, dancers, a lighting crew, scene designers, program creators, a dramaturge, and a prompter.

Hands-on involvement with the Holocaust must be approached carefully, especially with children. In some Holocaust exhibits designed for young people, each visitor receives upon entry the name and photo of an actual European Jewish child. At the end of the exhibition, the visitor learns the fate of that child. Certainly this form of temporary identification constitutes a powerful, if unsettling, experience.

For older individuals, it is instructive to learn about, and perhaps participate in, a re-creation of the classic "obedience to authority" study. In this psychological manipulation, devised in the 1960s by social psychologist Stanley Milgram, an unwitting subject (A) is instructed by a white-coated experimenter to deliver a series of electric shocks to another subject (B). Unbeknownst to A, B is actually a confederate of the experimenter and is not experiencing shocks. Despite the simulated cries of the confederate, and evidence from the instrument panel that the shocks had reached the danger level, most Americans who served as subjects continued to deliver the shocks. Residents of other countries behaved similarly.

Only after the conclusion of the experiment did subjects learn that the shocks were simulated. They had actually been involved in a provocative experiment: a study designed to explain why so many Germans had followed orders that, at some level, they sensed were wrong. The Milgram studies revealed that subjects were not happy about what they were doing but that many felt they had no choice once the experiment had begun. They lacked a procedure for "opting out." Interestingly, most behavioral scientists had predicted that only psychopaths would continue to deliver shocks; this single set of experiments has revised many people's views of how (a)typical was the behavior of Germans who became "willing executioners."

Interpersonal Points of Entry. So far, the entry points reviewed have been ones that touch the individual learner. Some students, however, want to learn in the company of fellow human beings. Some like to cooperate with peers; others like to debate, argue, present conflicting agendas, occupy various roles.

Projects are excellent vehicles for such interpersonal entries. By participating in projects that are engaging and that last for days or weeks, students can interact with others, learn from one another's words and actions, capture their own reactions to a topic, make their own idiosyncratic contributions to a group effort. When projects feature drama, students can assume different roles and learn how a situation looks and feels to other participants.

Earlier illustrations can be readily reconfigured to involve groups. For example, students can collaborate on works of graphic art that treat a powerful phenomenon, create a drama that fleshes out various narrative lines, debate existential questions or logical conundrums, or carry out a biological or social-psychological experiment.

Returning to our three themes: students of evolution could re-create the debates that followed publication of Darwin's theory; fabricate a new ecology and enact the ways in which different species fare under these contrived conditions; or plan an expedition to the Galápagos, complete with a survey of the current distribution of finches, tortoises, and iguanas.

Studying Mozart, they could create an ensemble and enact a scene from *Figaro;* more ambitiously, they could compose and perform an operetta about the clash between social classes or generations. They might try to reenact the "Trio of Colliding Agendas" with different performers, varied readings of the scores, contrasting interpretations of the motivations and goals of each character, even a new three-note motif.

The Holocaust provides many opportunities for role play. Students could enact plays based on the Holocaust (such as Hochhuth's *The Deputy,* or Goodrich and Hackett's *The Diary of Anne Frank*). They could re-create dramatic scenes from the Holocaust, such as the defense of the Warsaw Ghetto, or debates within families about what to do when they were about to be separated from one another, or the reactions among members of a unit when a solitary soldier refused to join in the massacre of Jews. Returning to our central example, they could reenact the planning for Wannsee, the conference itself, or Eichmann's subsequent account of it to the Israeli court that tried him in 1961. Or they could dramatize the reactions of the Wannsee participants had one of them objected strenuously to the genocidal orders from the German command.

Once again, there is no formula for generating promising entry points; one must draw on judicious blends of analysis and imagination, followed by mindful experimentation. Nor is there any obligation to use all entry points. The advantage of multiple entry points is simply stated: what works for one student with one topic is likely to be different from what works with another student on another topic or with the same student on another day. A varied approach greatly increases the likelihood that one will engage a range of students and that they will sign on for the longer run and move toward performances of understanding.

Powerful Analogies and Metaphors

Once interest has been engaged, it is time to up the ante, to bring students into full contact with the principal content of rich topics. This deeper penetration can be effected in two ways: through powerful comparisons (described in this section) and through complementary attempts to represent the core aspects of the concept (the focus of the section that follows).

Stripped down, analogies are simply examples drawn from another realm of experience, a realm presumably more familiar to the students than the topic at hand. Metaphors (and similes) again illuminate the less familiar topic in terms of the more familiar.

Recall that Darwin himself was guided toward his discovery by his reading of the economist Malthus. Darwin came to appreciate that the historic (and prehistoric) struggle among individuals and species paralleled the situation described by Malthus: a rapidly growing human population facing limited resources. Darwin explicitly used the analogy in his writing.

It did not take many years for scholars and laypersons to discover, or think they had discovered, evolution at work in many aspects of life. Observers described the market economy as a struggle among participant individuals and corporations. This view is often called Darwinian because its proponents embraced the metaphor of "survival of the

200 Howard Gardner

fittest." However, any struggle involving conscious human beings in a historical moment also *differs* from Darwinian evolution. Biological evolution occurs as a result of the struggle among individuals (and species) with different genetic constitutions over many generations, without any conscious knowledge or choice among the participants in the struggle.

Individuals are particularly vigilant concerning changes in domains of interest to them. Youngsters, for example, observe changing fashions in dress and hairstyle. Listeners observe the way in which particular themes evolve in a piece of music, as well as the ways in which beats or vocal styles characterize one decade as compared to the next. Readers of literature notice changes in fictional genres and character types, which nowadays often reflect what is appearing on the movie or television screen. Sometimes these changes will be so gradual that they are scarcely apprehended; at other times, they will be swift, dramatic, and short-lived.

Each of these examples can be thought of in Darwinian terms. Indeed, the contrast between gradual and rapid cultural evolution is roughly analogous to the current debate between evolutionists who favor a gradualist explanation and those persuaded by the theory of punctuated equilibrium. But because any comparison will be inexact, it is equally important to call attention to its potentially misleading aspects. For instance, evolution is often seen as a ladder, an image that deceptively implies that the species at the top are the "highest" or best.

The case of Mozart suggests many interesting analogies. From his very early life, Mozart's career was like that of a meteor: a very rapid rise, followed by a disappearance into space—one that, in my view, ultimately led to heaven. His productivity, on the other hand, was very steady: like a bird carefully building each new nest or a squirrel burying each new nut, he proceeded from one composition to another in workmanlike fashion, seemingly oblivious to the turbulence in his personal life.

Mounting an operatic presentation resembles many highly complex tasks. One can compare it to the design and construction of a building, the creating of a new weapon, the launching of a business. Many discrete roles can be assumed by one or several individuals; and each artistic decision affects the whole work.

Finally, a particular work like *Figaro* also lends itself to comparisons. The imbroglios in this eighteenth-century social tableau are reminiscent of other complex plots—for example, the Los Angeles–based movie plots of *The Big Sleep* and *Chinatown*. The relation among scenes and acts resembles the courses of a long meal: major courses, interspersed with shorter palate cleansers as well as periods for conversation or dancing. And pieces like the trio recall particular events in life. There are times when rumors lack proof and yet have the aura of truth. There are times when each of several acquaintances is playing with the same basic elements (say, ideas, rather than notes) and yet none is ever cognizant of that fact.

Debate about the uniqueness of the Holocaust raises the question of the appropriateness of analogies. Since analogies always involve differences as well as similarities, I see no problem in searching for revealing comparisons.

Hitler's desire to eradicate the Jewish people resembles other efforts to annihilate all traces of an unwanted body, whether in the destruction of a work of art or science, the disposal of a corpse, the killing of all cancer cells, or even the removal of the final traces of an old civilization, as happens when ruins are razed and distributed. The actual devising of concentration camps and death camps proceeded much in the style of trial-and-error experimentation: the designers tried out various patterns until they found one that satisfied the most crucial requirements. The analogy between work and death was drawn out deliberately; the Nazis sought to apply the principles of factory production to the packaging of death. And the experiences of inmates resembled a nightmare that never ended, or one that ended not with awakening to a bright day, but only with a brutal death.

If Aristotle was correct and metaphor is a sign of genius, no wonder it is challenging to discover the most apt comparisons. Certainly, skilled teachers and researchers struggle to discover fruitful, apt analogies and metaphors. Awareness that each comparison has its limitations is important. Once students enter more deeply into a topic, they should be encouraged to come up with their own analogies and metaphors. Not only are these likely to work for the particular individual; but students' discussions of the virtues and limits of particular comparisons can prove enlightening.

Multiple Representations of the Core Ideas:
Introducing the "Model Language"

We are now at the pivotal point in instruction where interest has been gripped by compelling entry points, and where the key ideas have been broached through various comparisons, analogies, and metaphors. Yet the most demanding task remains: how best to convey the definitive features of a theme, idea, or phenomenon?

For discussion purposes, I can lay out the most important ideas connected with each of our "iceberg" topics. In the case of evolution: variation, struggle among organisms, natural selection of those that survive to reproduce, and the best long-term fit to a particular environment. In the case of Mozart's music: appreciation of the major contours of the plot; sensitivity to the motivations and goals of the characters; grasp of the principal musical means available to the composer; appreciation of, and pleasure in, the ways in which music conveys pivotal actions and feelings. In the case of the Holocaust: the anti-Semitic program of the Nazis; the weak position of the Jews, particularly once war had commenced; the failure of various provisional "solutions" to the "Jewish question"; the decision to pursue systematic genocide; the means designed to achieve that goal; the actual operation of the death camps; judgment about culpability.

Deviating from established wisdom, I do not believe that there is a single best representation for any core idea or set of ideas. The notion of such a representation is an illusion, usually derived from a particular history of contact with a concept—how the teacher has first encountered it, or how it was initially presented or written about. For example, if one has seen evolution represented as a branching tree, or a memorable performance of *Figaro* at New York City's Metropolitan Opera, or photographs of liberated inmates at Auschwitz, then one may believe that this "mental representation" offers the optimal way to convey that particular topic. In contrast, I argue that the best representations are multiple. And so our search should be for the *family of representations* that can convey the core ideas in a multiplicity of ways at once accurate and complementary.

The "multiple representations" perspective balances the "analogy and metaphor" tack. In making an analogy, one chooses a vivid element from a deliberately different or distant sphere of reference. In the case of multiple representations, one chooses elements from spheres of reference that apply readily and unproblematically to the topic at hand.

Here I introduce the idea of a *model language*. In scholarship, models are abstractions from the topic or discipline at hand; there can be models of the atom, of historical revolutions, of classical tragedies. Models may occur in ordinary language (of the sort used in books like this) or in any other symbolic form that can be readily interpreted by knowledgeable persons. In science, models are often presented in graphic or numerical or logical form; in the humanities, models are more likely to be presented in language, though other symbol systems are sometimes used; in the arts, models typically appear in the garb of the particular artistic symbol system. That is, a model of a painting, or of a school of painting, would appear in graphic form; a model of a work or genre of music would be expressed in a musical score (or, less commonly, in some sort of graphic format that—like a weather map—portrays different forces, directions, and motifs).

Let us turn, then, to model languages that can capture and convey core aspects of our three specimen cases. As an instance of scientific scholarship, evolution lends itself to expression in terms of a set of propositions. The syllogistic statements introduced earlier represent one secure way of capturing the central idea of evolution.

But key facets of evolution can also be captured in natural language, as Darwin first did, or in pictorial language. One common means is to present a branching model of evolution, with a single ur-species giving rise over time and geographical space to a number of secondary branches. Some of these branches thrive and proliferate; others remain relatively isolated and endure; a larger number do not survive in their particular niche.

Readers of Darwin tend to think of the branching tree in the static form he himself employed, the spindly drawing from his notebook (Figure 2A) or the geometrically parallel structures from his published work (Figure 2B). Film, video, and computer simulation can also indicate how species arise, evolve, and ultimately proliferate or disappear. As for other facets of the evolutionary process, ranging from the incidence of certain traits (like the beak sizes of various finches), to the laws governing transformations of shape, to the changing ratio of different species in a fixed ecology, various kinds of algebraic, geometric, and calculus languages can be employed as well.

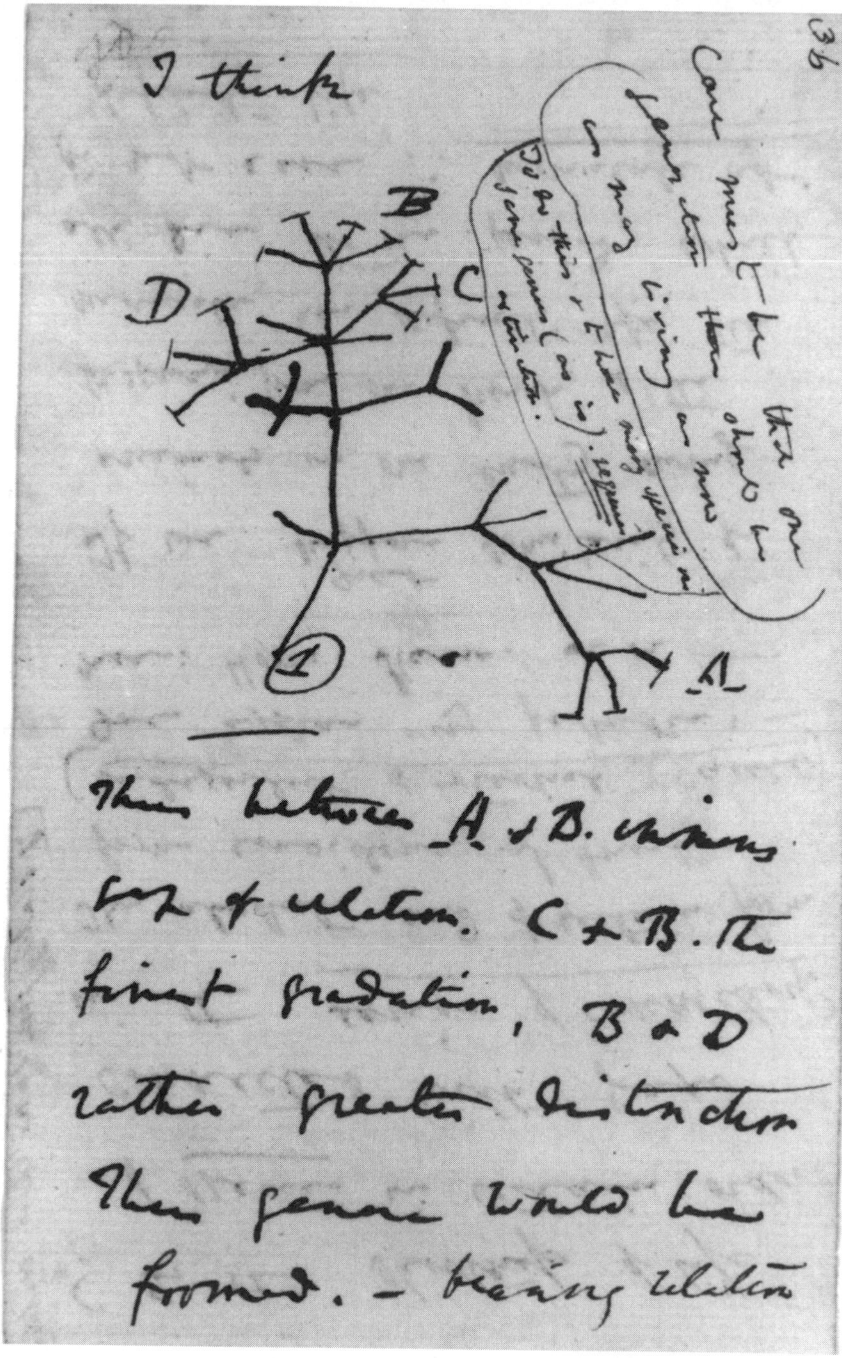

Figure 2A. An early attempt by Darwin to sketch the branching tree of nature. (By permission of the Syndics of Cambridge University Library.)

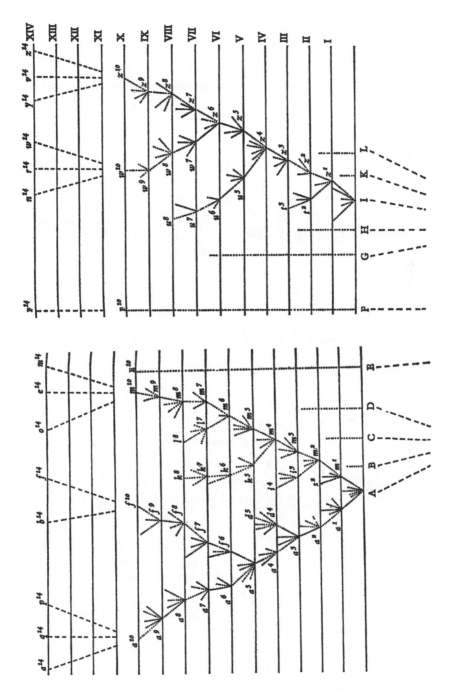

Figure 2B. Darwin's published diagram of divergence of character, principles of natural selection, and extinction. (From *On the Origin of Species*.)

To underscore the central point: None of these model languages constitutes the last word on evolution. All contribute. And so, it is that individual—initially the expert, eventually the student—able to move comfortably among the multiple representations, drawing on them when appropriate, who can be said to have a full understanding of the concept.

Different model languages will not capture identical aspects of the concept. Geometry will capture shape; film will capture motion; logic will isolate causative factors. Indeed, each of the model languages has its own genius; each is privileged for certain purposes, while less useful or relevant or exact for others. The individual who can appreciate these individuating features and piece them together ends up with the most versatile, flexible, and desirable understanding.

Just how do these models and model languages come together? This question is difficult to answer, both in terms of psychological modeling and in terms of actual pedagogy. It is certainly easier to have available an ensemble of model languages than it is to tie them together into a meaningful synthesis. My own answer—admittedly an insufficient one—is that there is no privileged approach to creating "interlingual fluency." Rather, the more time and effort one devotes to understanding each of the several model languages, the more likely it is that one will make appropriate connections (and separations and dissociations) among them. One settles into increasingly comprehensive models of the topic at hand; but promising new model languages can unsettle one's representation and ultimately hone a fresh representation that is even more powerful.

Model languages work differently with respect to different cases. The life of Mozart and the plot of *Figaro* possess features that are readily covered in natural language, in logical analysis, and in graphic form. And what of the distinctly musical features of a long and complex work like *Figaro*? To be sure, musical scoring provides a convenient way to express motifs, "responding" countermotifs, and the shifting uses of themes, keys, registers, instruments, and soloists.* However, other languages can contribute, even decisively. There are many books about music, including some that contain very few scores or score fragments. The course of motifs can be well conveyed by geometric figures or less formally sketched "field forces." These renderings resemble the "artful

---

*Note that there are now many rival musical notational systems.

scribbles" of abstract expressionists like Jackson Pollock or Franz Kline, or the more diagrammatic languages of Piet Mondrian or Sol LeWitt. And should aspects of *Figaro* be converted to movement or dance, various dance notations can bring out important features of the score.

Indeed, if one were faced with the task of conveying to a naive listener what *Figaro* (or even one trio) is like, it would make little sense simply to hand him or her a score. Much more powerful would be the devising of a simpler symbol system that denoted only the principal characters, actions, and musical motifs and forms. In only a few pages, such a representation can provide a very powerful characterization. And, not incidentally, a summary representation of this kind created by the student would serve as a pertinent performance of understanding at the conclusion of a unit—provided, of course, that it was accompanied by a good legend or key.

Since the Holocaust occurred within living memory, many kinds of representations can be readily identified. The testimony of eyewitnesses remains the most potent kind of "live" representation of this horrendous chapter in human history. Photographs and documentary as well as dramatic films provide other powerful ways of presenting and contrasting key ideas.

More abstract forms of representation can be used as well. Key factors can be analyzed in logical or numerical form, and graphic representations can be made of the identity and interactions of key players. Indeed, there are maps and diagrams of the concentration camps, their lines of supply, relation to battle routes, and the like. These, too, can be presented in static or dynamic form.

Even our target example of the Wannsee Conference allows itself to be captured in diverse model languages. One can give a straight narrative account; offer a dramatic reenactment; analyze the different logics that gave rise to decisions; examine, numerically and logistically, the steps needed to realize the Final Solution. And the attendees' immediate and later emotional reactions (or lack thereof) provide an entirely different kind of mental map of the Holocaust.

It may be feared that these various forms of representation could reduce the Holocaust to a set of formulas and thereby trivialize it. I suppose that this is a risk, and one that should be guarded against. But it is probably a greater risk for someone to have a single representation that is limited or misleading in various ways.

All three of our examples lend themselves readily to contemporary media such as CD-ROM, videodisc, hypertext, and so on. Often these appeal to the student. *But they can be too rich*—one can draw too many inferences and construct too many mental representations from such multisensory, multimedia displays. Often more useful are attenuated or uncluttered representations, which sacrifice richness, so that the learner can focus more readily on features that are truly central to the concept under investigation.

Remaining Issues

I have suggested the multifarious ways in which important topics can be approached, presented in terms of analogies, and crystallized in a series of discrete and complementary forms of representation. I believe that such an approach is most likely to result in learning that is deep, genuine, and enduring—learning that will reach a variety of students in ways that are meaningful to them and that allow them to build on their understandings, to perform them publicly, and to stretch them in new and appropriate directions. There is no need for all students to begin or end with the same representation as do others; at a premium, rather, is an increasingly rich representation that is meaningful to each student and that can be communicated to others.

It will not have escaped the reader's attention that my account has been presented in words. I am comfortable in that medium, and it is also the medium in which books are written. I hope that I have used words in a way that is sufficiently evocative to suggest the power of nonlinguistic symbolic systems as well.

We are left, however, with several outstanding issues:

1. How does one orchestrate these three approaches to important ideas?
2. How does one spread this orientation to the rest of the curriculum—and what might the limitations be?
3. How does one assess the success of such an approach?
4. How might this approach be misunderstood?
5. In the end, what is the status of the true, the beautiful, and the good, and of their possible interconnections?

Orchestrating the Three Approaches

My mode of presentation implies a distinct order: begin with entry points, then offer analogies, then converge upon multiple representations of the core idea. As a schematic, this rough itinerary has much to recommend it.

The art of teaching, however, consists precisely in resisting formulas. It is important to underscore that the three perspectives are not completely distinct: multiple representations use analogies, entry points can also convey key constructs, and so on. The teacher's job resembles that of a master orchestrator, who keeps the whole score in mind and yet can home in on particular passages and players. He or she should come up with questions, units, and performances of understanding that fit together comfortably, engage the students, and, ultimately, aid the vast majority of them to achieve deeper understandings of the topic. Within that broad prospect, the teacher can and should be encouraged to be as versatile as possible.

The Rest of the Curriculum: Possibilities and Limits

Even in a curriculum that focuses on understanding, there will continually be pressures to cover more topics, or to cover the existing topics in different ways. Compromise has to be the order of the day.

That said, I believe the general approach outlined here can be applied to a wide variety of topics in the arts, the sciences, and the humanities. Indeed, my three examples have been chosen precisely because they can stand for many others: evolution, for a range of theories and concepts in science; *Figaro,* for innumerable artists and works of art; the Holocaust, for a range of historical events and forces.

But while understanding should be a universal goal of education, it requires a stretch to apply these methods equally across the curriculum. Certain aspects of mathematics are algorithmic; certain segments of foreign language study simply require drill and memorization; much of arts education involves steady practice of component skills and gradual success in integrating them.

However, even in these apparently less flexible areas of the curriculum, the current "model," if you will, has utility. New concepts proliferate across subject matters. Whether one is studying infinity, zero, differentiation, or proof in mathematics, the "understanding approach" should prove useful. By the same token, such unfamiliar concepts in foreign languages as the imperfect past tense or the ergative case can be judiciously introduced to speakers of English by the set of perspectives sketched here.

Measures of Success. If one's goal is understanding of key concepts, then there is only a single way to gauge success: students must be given many opportunities to perform their understandings under varying conditions, and to receive regular, useful feedback as well. Initially, these performances are likely to be prescribed in terms of what students are supposed to do and the criteria by which they are to be judged. With time, several trends ought to emerge: more facets of the assessment will be undertaken by students themselves; the students will have more opportunity to join together various concepts, themes, and ideas; they will show in a greater variety of ways what they have learned; and, most important, they will find occasions to stretch their understandings, to see how they do or don't apply to new instances.

It would take many pages to indicate the ways in which one can probe understanding of each of my three icebergs—to say nothing of other icebergs, let alone the relationships among them. Still, I have made a start. Nearly every example of an entry point, analogy, or model language suggests a possible form of assessment; taken together, they provide a sizable ensemble of means for measuring students' understanding.

Let me suggest just two possible assessments of understanding for each of our topics. One could assess understanding of Darwin's finches thus: create a hypothetical chain of islands, each with its own ecology, and ask students to predict what would happen, over time, to a small set of insects transported to each of those islands. Or students could be given data from a recent visit to the Galápagos and asked how Darwin would have made sense of the current distribution of flora and fauna.

Turning to the Mozart trio, one could take a duet from a different kind of opera—say, Puccini's tragedy *Tosca*. This composition features a struggle between the passionate singer, Tosca, who is in love with the painter, Cavaradossi, and the tough and lustful chief of police, Scarpia, who desires Tosca. The student could be provided with necessary background material and asked to analyze the duet's events in terms of both plot and use of musical materials. Or students could be asked to create their own duet featuring two contrasting personages.

Finally, in the case of the Holocaust, one could describe what happened to Armenians in the early decades of this century. The Turkish government, for its own purposes, ordered the annihilation of the Armenian minority and largely succeeded in its goal, using many of the same techniques that the Nazis later "perfected." Students can debate the similarities and differences between the two attempts at genocide, or can create works of art that appropriately commemorate these events.

Possible Misunderstandings of the Approach. Inasmuch as new ideas are typically misunderstood, it is well to be on the lookout for possible misapplications of the approach I describe. It would be a complete travesty to take any topic and attempt to lay out seven (or ten) entry points, seven (or three) metaphors or analogies, seven (or twenty-two) model languages or multiple representations. Just as my three topics are meant only as illustrations, so, too, the lists developed here are only exemplary.

In each case, the ultimate selection of entry points, analogies, and model languages must proceed in an intuitive—indeed, artistic—manner. There must be a constant dialectic among the ideas to be stressed, the modes of instruction that are comfortable for the teacher, and the identified interests and needs of the students. It is perhaps understandable that teachers might begin by looking for a few entry points, analogies, and model languages, suited to the topics to be probed. However, as teachers become more expert, they are likely to arrive at personal approaches to every topic.

It would also be a misunderstanding to assume that every entry point, analogy, or model language is equally appropriate for a particular concept. Just as disciplines constitute different lenses, highlighting separate aspects of a topic, so, too, each entry point, analogy, and model language calls attention to certain features while minimizing others. Indeed, this difference in emphasis constitutes one of the most powerful arguments for taking several approaches to a topic.

Finally, it is important to say a word about the relationship between the theory of multiple intelligences and the pedagogical approach set forth here. I would like to think that the theory of multiple intelligences has created an *intellectual atmosphere* in which it is natural and productive to speak of different entry points, analogies, metaphors, multiple representations, and model languages. Variety is the message of the day. Yet it would be a distortion to relate specific entry points, analogies, or model languages directly to specific intelligences. The links are at best suggestive. For example, while narration has ties to linguistic intelligence, it has powerful links as well to logical, personal, and existential intelligences; and, by the same token, while spatial intelligence suggests visual representations, these can range from graphs to photos to films to hypermedia presentations.

No doubt, at some level, the intelligences of which we are capable determine how we make sense of the world. It would be fascinating to detail the relationships among the structures of the mind-brain, the physical properties of our world, the perspectives of different cultures, and the particular symbol systems and disciplines that have developed over time. I am quite sure that there are some relationships and that both striking similarities and revealing differences appear from person to person and across different cultures. But, alas, this book is not the place to trace these connections or differences. The most I can say here is that a plurality of minds begets a plurality of ways to make sense of various worlds.

Once More: the True, the Beautiful, and the Good. I initially introduced our three cases as prototypical examples of the classic domains of truth/falsity, beauty/ugliness, and goodness/evil. As one enters into the details of each case, it is perhaps inevitable (and not inappropriate) that these broad organizing labels will be obscured or even forgotten. But here, as my discussion of pedagogy draws to a close, it is apposite to revisit these enveloping themes.

Cultures evolve notions of what is important; they find it imperative to pass on that lore to their young. To be sure, the ways in which these topics are construed and described will change over time; in particular, concepts like truth, beauty, and goodness now harbor an old-fashioned varnished-wood air in our largely plastic culture. Nonetheless, unless we are to make them at random, our choices reflect our values; and no culture can endure unless it attains some success in passing on its chosen verities, beauties, and desired modes of behavior.

If one comes to understand evolution, one will have some purchase on an important truth about the origins and fate of our species; and one will see the weaknesses in rival Lamarckian theory and in fundamentalist religious accounts.

If one comes to understand the music of Mozart, one will have encountered an unambiguous and powerful instance of beauty in the Western canon. One will appreciate, as well, the limitations of lesser Western composers like Ditters von Dittersdorf, and of less ambitious genres and works, such as those found on the pop charts. For those who doubt my characterization, I am happy to wager on which works are likely to be listened to with pleasure and enlightenment a century from now. (Our "post-postmodern" descendants will have to cash in our respective debts or credits.)

Finally, if one comes to understand the Holocaust, one will have a better purchase on the nature and dimensions of human evil: its sources, its extent, and the measures one might take to combat these human potentials, in others and in oneself. And within this bleak picture, one will have descried rays of hope, in the exemplary behaviors of certain soldiers, civilians, and political and religious leaders.

Ultimately, society's answers to questions about truth, beauty, and goodness are important, but our personal questions and answers are more important. Connections and reverberations among the true, the beautiful, and the good are as important as their distinctive features. The issue of how one might set up programs that facilitate such understandings—cultural and personal—assumes center stage in the pages that follow.

CHAPTER 10
Getting There

A Tale of Two Scripts

Two contrasting scripts can lead to education for understanding. According to the "centralized agency" script, there should be coordinated planning throughout a student's education. Such coordination is most likely to come about at the instigation of a single overarching authority. According to the more flexible "local initiative" script, education for understanding is most likely to come about if teachers and students are engaged in exploring topics of enduring interest, and if they have the opportunity to dig as deeply as they wish, without the pressures of a mandated syllabus and a clock that is ticking loudly.

What are the less palatable consequences of each course? The costs of a centralized agency are loss of autonomy and constant pressures to "cover the prescribed material." Local initiative risks repetition from year to year, parochial and idiosyncratic preferences or omissions, and/or the absence of meaningful, consistent standards for evaluating student performance.

Most countries have followed the path of a required curriculum. In the best-case scenario, students do well on international comparisons and a sense of common culture is established. However, deep understanding of topics is typically sacrificed, even if such depth is a stated goal of the system. The United States, and a few other countries, have so far opted for locally developed curricula. Optimally, students probe deeply into topics and gain a genuine love of learning. But all too often, students acquire a hodgepodge of knowledge, or, even less happily, little reliable knowledge or understanding.

Is it possible to navigate between these polarities? Earlier, I discussed education for understanding in a particular class or school. Now I turn to how one might achieve comprehensive education for understanding on a large scale. While aspiring to make such an education widely available, I concede that this goal might not appeal to everyone. And so I also sketch a system of "multiple pathways," in which citizens of a country may choose among a number of routes to quality education. At their best, such pathways combine the strengths of centralized and localized approaches.

A K–12 Pathway to Understanding

A crucial ingredient of successful education is the "pathway." In choosing a pathway, members of a community agree about the goals of the system and the steps to be taken to achieve those goals. Such planning involves a determination of what should occur at every age and grade level, and how that set of practices fits into the broader picture. Teachers and parents of children at every age level should know what has come before, why it was done, and what is anticipated at subsequent ages/grades. Any practice that cannot be justified in these terms should be reexamined critically and probably scuttled. Neither mindless repetition nor careless omission of important material should be tolerated.

Agreed-upon standards and milestones should not be kept secret, nor restricted to those who can decode educational jargon. On the contrary, the behaviors and understandings expected should be publicly demonstrated, discussed, argued about, celebrated when successfully realized, adjusted when they prove ineffective or too difficult to achieve. If primary students are supposed to be able to determine whether an unfamiliar, unidentified entity is a plant or an animal, every family should know this goal; if graduating secondary students should be able to take either side of a contemporary dispute about artistic censorship and defend it publicly, relevant practice should begin years before. (As always, these are just examples.)

Thus stated, the idea of a pathway may seem uncontroversial. However, in truth, it has rarely been realized as fully as it could be. In jurisdictions without centralized curriculum, education is prone—often fatally—to redundancy or omissions. In jurisdictions with centralized curricula, the chances of designing and implementing a pathway are ostensibly greater. In practice, however, there is often a division of labor:

The early years are devoted to "basic skills," the later years to disciplines, without efforts to coordinate the questions, the themes, and the desired outcomes over the long haul. Also, the early years may accentuate social or emotional facets of development, while the latter years are almost exclusively focused on preparation for examinations. (Recall the teachers' quip: "In the elementary grades, we love the children; in high school, we love the disciplines; in college, we love ourselves.") The means of assessment is typically a written test, with the "items" kept a carefully guarded secret; rarely are full-scale performances carried out publicly, critiqued, and celebrated by the community. These factors render pathways less effective than they might be.

Where pathways have been considered, they have almost always been construed in geographical terms: a student goes to Madison Elementary School, to Madison Middle School, and then to Madison High. Such geographical pathways still make sense where they are possible. However, the advent of powerful technologies opens up the possibility of "virtual pathways." Not only can students now attend schools that are not physically nearby, but members of pathways may learn from and remain in contact with "partner pathways" the world over that share their philosophy and their problems. (People can now have lifelong "mouse pals.") This access is especially important when students move from place to place or when the particulars of their home pathway have been suddenly altered.

I personally favor a "pathway for understanding." Let me indicate just one of its dimensions. Education in this pathway ought to be inspired by a set of *essential questions:* Who are we? Where do we come from? What do we consider to be true or false, beautiful or ugly, good or evil? What is the fate of the earth? How do we fit in? What is the earth made of? What are we made of? Why do we live, and why do we die? Are our destinies under the control of God or some other "higher power"? What is love? What is hatred? Why do we make war? Must we? What is justice and how can we achieve it?

These questions, and others of comparable scope, are raised and pondered by human beings everywhere. The questions are natural ones for young persons to pose. However, they are rarely articulated in explicit philosophical terms. Rather, they are posed in the language of fairy tales, myths, "pretend" play, and, in a cinematic age, films and video. At later ages, people do ask these questions directly—in discussions at a bar or café, in college bull sessions, on phone-in talk radio, at times of personal or societal crisis. And they continue to pose such questions in various symbolic forms, including mythology, religion, the arts, the sciences, and philosophy.

Here we can see the potential power of a pathway. Once a set of schools in a community has decided to connect to a pathway that asks such questions, they can be posed from early on in school and then revisited regularly in ways that are appropriate for students. Students' capacities to field such questions can be monitored by parents, teachers, and the students themselves. The commitment to essential questions has the flavor of a "centralized agency" policy; but the particular ways in which such questions are posed over the years are best determined by local initiative.

The Power and the Perils of Disciplinary and Interdisciplinary Study

The scholarly disciplines represent concerted efforts by individuals (and groups) over time to address essential questions and answer them, however provisionally. Significant works of art and theories of science represent specific efforts, in disciplinary and interdisciplinary form, to embody tentative answers. Starting in the early years of school, individuals must become sufficiently literate and numerate so that they can begin to partake of the disciplines. Next, they must acquire some mastery of the disciplines so that they can participate—as observers, or, better, as active practitioners—in the most ambitious and successful human efforts to answer those essential questions, and so that, ultimately, they can arrive at more personal and more comprehensive responses.

And so, to revert to my target examples, Darwin's evolutionary theory represents a profound answer to the question of the origins of human beings. To appreciate Darwin's theory, one must acquire certain literacies as well as the capacity to think systematically about scientific questions—for example, how to isolate the variables that might over time bring about different species of finches. Mozart's works (and characters) wrestle with questions of love, fidelity, power, and people's relationships to one another. To enter Mozart's world, one must be able to integrate knowledge of the human sphere with the capacity to assimilate musical themes, harmonies, and rhythmic patterns. The Holocaust raises issues of human good and evil in their most naked form. To understand that event, one must become familiar with the circumstances of a particular historical era and then acquire the tools to evaluate rival accounts of its causes and consequences.

This way of thinking can provide a rationale for many curricula. Literacies are not mastered as ends in themselves, but rather as means of opening the disciplines up to students. Nor are disciplines themselves the goals. Rather, scientific thinking, artistic interpretation, and historical analysis constitute privileged ways into phenomena like evolution, Mozart, and the Holocaust; indeed they constitute the most sophisticated means for addressing the questions that preoccupy human beings.

All too often, means and ends become confused in this area. American presidents call for a nation where eight-year-olds can read. This is, of course, a worthwhile goal, but it does not address the major problem in the United States (and in some other countries): individuals *can* read *but they do not*. (In fact, the average American reads about a book a year. The figure for teachers is roughly the same.) Individuals should be motivated to read because they are curious about essential questions and because they are convinced that some inroads can be made through reading pertinent works of nonfiction and fiction.

Again, the pursuit of disciplines and disciplinary thinking is not controversial, except perhaps in certain postmodern educational circles. But the *purposes* of pursuing disciplines are often forgotten. One should not take chemistry in order to satisfy Andrew Carnegie's notions of how many hours of science are required in high school (the so-called Carnegie units, established by the Carnegie Foundation), or to gain admission to a certain college or professional school. Rather, the rationale and the reward for studying the disciplines should be enhanced access to, and stronger purchase on, the major questions of human life. If you want to understand what it means to be alive, study biology; if you want to understand the composition and dynamic of the physical world, study chemistry, physics, or geology; if you want to understand your own background, study national history and immigration patterns and experiences; if you want to gain intimate knowledge of the feats of which human beings are capable, study and participate in art, science, religion, athletics, and perhaps even developmental psychology.

The purpose of disciplinary study in the precollegiate years is not to develop miniature scientists, historians, or aestheticians. Rather, the goal is to make youngsters comfortable with the intellectual core, the analytic power of several ways of approaching the world. Youngsters need not know the technical details of biological processes, procedures of musical composition, or historiographic debates. They *should* understand how disciplinarians approach questions; and they should gain deep familiarity with a few evocative examples.

By and large, such generative questions do not come wrapped or marked with a specific disciplinary coding; and in most cases interdisciplinary work provides a privileged way to secure rich answers to essential questions. But one cannot plunge directly into interdisciplinary study. First one must master more than one discipline, so that one can link mastered disciplines productively.

These remarks may seem at odds with the widespread call for integrated curricula, thematic curricula, interdisciplinary curricula, to be put in place, often, as early as elementary and middle school. I have no objection per se to such curricula, which are often well prepared and inviting to students. I have strong reservations about calling them *inter*disciplinary.

Why the objection? To use the word "interdisciplinary," one must show that particular disciplines have been mastered and appropriately joined. (One would not call a person trained in only one legal system an international lawyer—and one would hardly call a person who had never studied the law an expert in international law.) Such interdisciplinary synthesis is simply not feasible for most youngsters during the middle years of childhood, or for most of their teachers. Rather, I see most so-called interdisciplinary curricula as commonsense or "proto-disciplinary" activities. Instead of drawing on or preparing disciplined thinking, these approaches tend to ignore the pre- or proto-disciplinary distinctions that young children are becoming able to master. They simply introduce an attractive topic—like the nature of silence, or the rain forest, or a Native American ritual—and allow children to read or write or draw about these topics as they wish.

Elementary school and middle school children are just beginning to get a sense of the difference between issues subject to empirical investigation (the actual incidence of specific finches on different islands) and those that are merely a matter of opinion (their own hunches about why beaks have the shapes that they do); or between events that happened (a rare case of survival at Auschwitz through collusion with the guards) and events that are fictional (a short story about a child who survived the Holocaust by living like an animal in the woods). The question to ask about these self-described interdisciplinary curricula is, Do they help students make such foundational disciplinary distinctions? And in many cases, the answer is no.

Still, there is good news on this front. It *is* possible to create thematic middle school curricula that begin to train disciplinary thinking. Ann Brown, Joseph Campione, and their colleagues have created "communities of learning" in the San Francisco area. In such communities, students divide regularly into groups and explore various aspects of a provocative question—for example, "How do different kinds of animals reproduce?" The youngsters read, write, research, and report data; they model these modes of inquiry for one another, providing critique and encouragement. They argue about data and about interpretation. They establish criteria for what counts as a good summary, a provocative question, a thoughtful answer. Through such activities, youngsters are gaining a feeling for how to think like a biologist or naturalist or journalist.

A similar effort, the CSILE project (for Computer Supported Intentional Learning Environments), has been undertaken by Marlene Scardamalia and Carl Bereiter in Toronto. In this technology-rich approach, students can research any topic of interest. They explore on their own or with classmates; they write notes to one another, communicate with peers elsewhere, and also question experts in person or on line. They create multimedia hypertext documents that record the results of their inquiries and that, Reggio-style, present the group's understanding of a topic. Through these activities, youngsters are learning about styles of research in history, science, or social studies; they are enhancing their skills as summarizers, questioners, and reporters; and they are co-creating a body of knowledge that exceeds the expertise of any single individual.

Do such youngsters learn about the parallels as well as the differences among different families of disciplines? Probably not on their own, unless they are unusually independent and innovative thinkers. However, the habits of reading, writing, collecting and reporting data, and linking these activities systematically serve them in good stead when they undertake more formal disciplinary studies in later years.

Only then can we begin to speak legitimately of "hyphenated" disciplinary curricula. By the time they enter college, having achieved some mastery in at least two disciplines, students can commence genuine *interdisciplinary* work. They can, for example, study the intoxication with eugenics in Nazi Germany, drawing on their biological as well as their political and historical understanding. An issue like the Nazi program of eugenics can be understood only if one is able to deal simultaneously with scientific (and pseudoscientific) information about genetics, the political considerations entailed in ideological struggles, and the relevant historical and scientific texts and records.

Other options are available. Students can also gain from *multidisciplinary* stances. In these cases, no explicit effort is made to synthesize two disciplines. Rather, the student simply studies a topic as it is seen by representatives of relevant disciplines: for example, the Renaissance as it is understood by a historian and a literary critic; or the meaning of life as seen by a biologist and a metaphysician. Of course, students have the privilege of creating their own interdisciplinary synthesis, but that is not the explicit purpose of the course. Finally, there is *metadisciplinary* work—actual discussion of the nature of disciplines and how they might be combined: as it happens, exactly the activity being undertaken on this page.

Without apology, I confirm that I am a defender of the disciplines. But this does not mean that I defend the way that disciplines are typically taught in secondary school or in college. In most cases, the way history or biology or geology is taught is dictated by what professional disciplinarians do. To put it metaphorically, the shadow of graduate study dominates college teaching, and the shadow of college dominates high school teaching. Regrettably, this practice means that most individuals are being trained as apprentices for careers that they will never follow.

At a premium should be disciplinary instruction that will be of value primarily to those who will go on to other careers. We need citizens who can think scientifically about new discoveries (cloning) and new personal choices (whether to undergo genetic screening); citizens who can think historically about their own society and who can draw on historical and political insights as they determine how to vote on referenda or how to choose among candidates with different philosophies and policies; citizens who recognize morality and beauty (and their absence) and who will pursue these virtues in their own lives. These goals require curricula and instruction that expose the core ideas and approaches of the major scholarly disciplines, not ones that seek to cover every topic or that prepare one for graduate study. Happily, these core aspects change less rapidly than do particular findings and perspectives; consequently, there can be some stability in how ordinary citizens come to absorb disciplined ways of thinking.

A National Standard or National Standards?

An oddity of the U.S. Constitution has made discussion of national curricula and assessments controversial in the American context. Because control of education is left to the states, and because fear of the federal government is perennial, relatively few successful federal programs in education have been mounted. The major exceptions have been protection of students' civil rights, and financial support for disadvantaged students.

But a sea change may be occurring in the United States. For the first time in our history, a majority of citizens see virtue in national tests, and perhaps even in national curricula. Still, there remains enormous opposition to such endeavors, particularly among those at the extremes of the political spectrum. Those on the left fear a curriculum that is too jingoistic or simplistic, and testing that will further stigmatize those who are already at risk. Those on the right fear a curriculum that invades personal areas (such as values), or that dictates what Washington bureaucrats and elected officials want, rather than accommodating the diverse voices and interests of "the American people."

On most days, I could live with a national curriculum. I believe that there are many things that every child should know and be able to do; I believe that the American system could benefit from the coherence and rigor of a national curriculum; and I doubt that most of America's two and a half million–plus teachers desire, or are in a position, to create curricula and assessments that make as much sense as those drafted by expert teams of scholars and master teachers.

Yet there is one hitch, and it may prove decisive. I would favor a national curriculum and national standards *only* if I—or others of like mind—could play a substantial role in their creation. When I consider how I would feel if the national curriculum or tests were placed in the hands of individuals with whom I have no ideological or educational commonality, I become an opponent of attempts to create national or federal standards. I could not subscribe to the recommendations of the "Jesse Helms" or "Louis Farrakhan" curriculum team.

Context may be helpful here. Education is politicized everywhere, but rarely as much as in the United States. In most other democratic (and even some nondemocratic) countries, a relatively nonpoliticized ministry or civil service endures despite changes in government. In the United States, however, education at every level, federal, state, and local, is suffused with political considerations. Newly appointed heads of bureaucracies—urban superintendents, chief state school officers, or secretaries of education—routinely (and often energetically) overthrow the policies of their predecessors. In fact, President Reagan appointed his first secretary of education, Terrel Bell, with the understanding that Bell was to close down the department (the boss's instructions were ignored); and other secretaries of education have called for the department's abolition—though, typically, only after the completion of their own stint in the cabinet.

The reason for this disaffection is worth noting. In the United States, secretaries of education (or heads of the National Endowment for the Arts and National Endowment for the Humanities) are usually at ease when their departments carry out their bidding. But when, either during or after their incumbency, the departments proceed in novel directions, the erstwhile heads do not hesitate to denounce them. In this way, they are no different from me. I want national standards only so long as they bear a reasonable resemblance to standards that I personally embrace.

Note that these issues are not exclusively American. Other societies are beginning to decentralize their educational systems; and many find appeal in the current American intoxication with vouchers or charter schools. The market model does not stop at national boundaries. But once the hegemony of a centralized agency has been broken, all the virtues and vices of a local initiative system must be confronted.

Multiple Pathways

Ideally—if I could be the benevolent dictator—I would like all children to receive the education that I have described in these pages. I think it is the best education, for now and for the foreseeable future, and I am working toward its realization. Indeed, recent events constitute a powerful argument for "understanding" as an education for all human beings.

Ten or fifteen years ago, it was said that America's economic woes were due to its inadequate schools, while the triumph of East Asia was due to its excellent schools. Now, at the cusp of the millennium, the United States is the nation most successful in the economic sphere, while few if any would argue that its schools have substantially improved. Indeed, recent international comparisons suggest that American schools are mired in mediocrity, if not worse. Clearly, the link between a certain kind of education and economic prosperity is tenuous at best.

Just because of America's current hegemony, however, the country finds itself in a unique position. It does not have to model its educational system on those of other, putatively more successful countries. It does not have to excel in—or even accept—other countries' tests. This country is at liberty to embrace the system it wants and devise measures it finds suitable. For the reasons stated in the earlier part of this book, an education aimed toward understanding is best suited for a world that is changing rapidly. It makes sense, for other countries as well as the United States, to establish pathways for understanding.

But I am not a dictator; in fact, I am a democrat. I still want my children to have the education of my choice, but I am realistic enough to recognize that the rest of the world will not necessarily endorse my preferences or the reasons for them.

Is there a way out of this dilemma? My solution is a surprisingly simple and straightforward one. We should move toward the creation of a manageable number of distinct pathways.

Analogies can be found in airline or long-distance telecommunications companies. There is no need for a single national airline carrier or telephone company; we know the limits of these monopolies. On the other hand, it is not necessary, or even advisable, to have dozens of airlines or carriers from which to choose.

The rational educator in me suggests that half a dozen pathways, designed according to quite specific guidelines, would be the best alternative, particularly in a heterogeneous nation like the United States. The pathways will have different textures: or, to use my implicit metaphor, they should be variously "landscaped." In the shadow of the year 2000, here is a plausible set of six pathways:

1. The Canon Pathway. Inspired by Allan Bloom, William Bennett, and Lynne Cheney. For those who desire a system that features traditional American (and Western) historical and artistic values. Students from all over the country will have read the same books and be able to discourse on American constitutional and historical issues. Citizens of France will most readily recognize and perhaps resonate to this pathway, though of course French "Canonites" will be reading Victor Hugo and Jean-Jacques Rousseau rather than James Madison and Mark Twain. Similarly, other things being equal, for Brazil, Singapore, or South Africa.

2. The Multicultural Pathway. Inspired by James Banks, Jesse Jackson, Ronald Takaki, and many recently formed university departments. For those who desire a system that features the nature and identities of America's chief racial and ethnic groups. Students will study their own cultures and compare them with other groups, particularly those that have hitherto received unfair treatment at the hands of America's majority population.

3. The Progressive Pathway. Inspired by John Dewey, Francis Parker, and Deborah Meier. For those who desire a system in which individual differences and growth patterns are respected, the curriculum grows out of community concerns, and democratic values are lived, not merely studied. Students will be genuinely involved in community activities and will seek to create and sustain a school community that embodies democratic values.

4. The Technological Pathway. Inspired by Bill Gates, Louis Gerstner, and much of the American corporate-financial world. For those who believe that America must maintain its competitive edge, and that mastery of technologies represents the best way to ensure a well-trained and flexible workforce. In these schools, the particular curricula will be less important than immersion in a full range of technologies. Students will learn to use these technologies—for example, to create and critique media products.

5. The Socially Responsible Pathway. Inspired by assorted civic organizations, including environmentally oriented groups, agencies that foster social entrepreneurship, and the Educators for Social Responsibility. For those who are conscious of the world's enormous social and economic problems and want to encourage the development of human beings who will be actively involved in improving the world. In these schools, the curricular focus falls on national and global issues that are susceptible to solution.

6. *The Understanding Pathway.* Inspired by Socrates and presented in this book. For those who believe that human beings have a desire to explore and to understand the most fundamental questions of existence, and that curricula ought to be organized around the tackling of these epistemological concerns—familiarly, the true, the beautiful, and the good. Students in this pathway visit and revisit these classical questions, armed, in succession, with literacy skills, disciplinary skills, and the possibility of multidisciplinary or interdisciplinary approaches. They exhibit their understandings publicly; they are motivated to ponder these questions, and their interconnections, well after formal schooling has ended.

Of course, my list of six pathways is illustrative only. I could as well have spoken of families of schools that are already successful: Steiner "Waldorf" schools, Montessori schools, and Comer schools; networks like the International Baccalaureate and the Coalition of Essential Schools; Catholic and other sectarian schools. I might have listed theme-based pathways, focused on the arts, or business, or health. I might instead have described "The Spiritual Pathway" or "The Citizen Pathway" or "The International Pathway."

Unum Out of Pluribus?

One argument holds that we should allow a hundred, or a thousand, pathways to bloom. Indeed, this is what has happened in American collegiate education, which—somewhat paradoxically—is considered far more successful than our primary and secondary education system.

With respect to the precollegiate level, I reject this argument for two reasons. First, I believe that a system that is basically public ought to have responsibility for inculcating the values of citizenship—of what it means to be an American (or a citizen of France or of Singapore), an inhabitant of a country that claims to embody certain norms, practices, and values. Second, I believe that a public system needs standards that are public and that can be monitored by external bodies charged with accountability.

Neither of these goals can be realistically pursued if we allow every pathway—indeed every school—to pursue its own ideals (or its own demons). (This is the risk raised by the rapid growth of charter schools.) What is feasible is to have more than one pathway within the nation. The designers of an "officially qualified" pathway should commit themselves to the transmission and inculcation of certain basic national values, in that particular pathway's dialect. And it means as well that the designers issue the standards to which students will be held; that these standards be susceptible to public critique and debate; and that students who do not meet them will not be allowed to graduate from the pathway, though they may be granted multiple opportunities to succeed.

To choose one example (not at random!), let me reflect on the obligations of an "understanding pathway." To qualify for public support in the United States, the proponents of such a pathway would have to articulate those understandings that are important in this society—for example, an understanding of principal foundational documents, our current system of government, our history of diversity, tolerance, and intolerance. Further, the brief on behalf of the pathway would have to lay out particular curricular foci for different ages and describe the performances of understanding that would demonstrate students' sufficient understanding of the Constitution, our various governmental institutions, our democratic debating and decision-making procedures, and current discussions of freedom, tolerance, and justice. Finally, the brief would have to spell out the consequences for students who did not demonstrate such understandings, and describe the steps the school would take if a significant proportion of students was not achieving success.

A focus, a pathway, a commitment to American democracy, high standards that exist in more than name—none of these is problem-free, but each seems manageable and worth pursuing. Still, even if this general scheme were accepted, many questions arise. Should one be allowed to combine pathways? Should one have the right to reject pathways, or to create one's own? And what are the consequences if a pathway (or one or more of its instantiations in particular schools) fails to measure up to its commitment?

I believe that a system of multiple pathways ought to be administered with some flexibility. Schools or pathways ought to have the option of applying for waivers, if they have good reasons for so doing, and if they can demonstrate that they are successful in terms of a reasonable set of crite-

ria. My own guess is that upwards of 90 percent of schools and districts
will be content to choose one of these half-dozen or so alternatives, and
that the remaining handful of holdouts deserve a hearing. Pathways ought
to be given a reasonable amount of time to improve and to benefit from
feedback when goals have not been met. If, however, a pathway lacks the
capacity to educate its own students, it ought to be closed down.

Above I reiterated my own preference for "education for understanding," while conceding that not all individuals will choose to march
under this banner. A compromise might nonetheless be possible. One
could commit to an education for understanding, while retaining the
right to place a certain spin on it. Thus, I can envision "understanding
pathways" that highlight the arts, or technology, or social responsibility.
More difficult to envision are pathways that strive both to cover material and to "uncover" it. Such a pathway may perennially pull in opposite directions, and end up with a student body that needs to "recover"
from the experience.

Just how flexible can we afford to be? As psychologists have had
opportunities to observe—and, occasionally, even to prove—human
beings do not necessarily work in a rational way. I must confess my
doubts that Americans could produce and adhere to six interestingly distinctive pathways. We run the risk that candidate pathways will be like
Detroit's new cars: similar enough to make the same kinds of boasts, yet
different enough to assert their own recognizable identities. Such an
outcome would represent little progress, in my view.

Leadership Challenges

Direction of any institution requires leadership; the creation and sustenance of new pathways (individual schools or entire clusters) will
require leadership of high caliber. Certain aspects of leadership are specific to situation, but others prove universal.

Effective leaders have a sense of what they want to achieve and how to
get there. This sense is often conveyed best by means of a story—a dramatic creation that outlines the goals, introduces the principal protagonists, describes the obstacles en route, and proposes how these
impediments can be circumnavigated. When one is leading an institution
that exerts major influence over human lives, one's story ought to touch

questions of existence and identity: Who are we? Where do we come from? Where do we want to go? And why?

Being a good creator, teller, and modifier of stories is a job requirement for the leader bent on bringing about change. But glibness and image are not enough. Effective leaders must "walk the talk." They must indicate, through personal actions, what they would like to achieve and how best to achieve it. They must be able to make decisions, sticking by them if possible, revising them when necessary. If leaders cannot exhibit what they mean, they are ineffectual; if their own actions contradict what they advocate, they are hypocritical; but if they can embody their stories in their own daily lives, then they will be rightly seen as authentic and as empowering others to join their quest.

Faced with the challenge of directing one or more schools devoted to understanding, the leader might begin with discussions of the goals of education in the past, which of these goals and means remain, and which need to be refashioned in light of new considerations. (I began this book with such an exercise.) Optional routes for achieving the goals ought to be the next topic on the table. I use the word "discussion" advisedly; one is far more likely to secure a staff's genuine engagement (and even enthusiasm) if its members are part and parcel of the envisioning and planning process.

An education based upon questions, understanding, in-depth probing, and mastery of disciplines is most likely to be realized if it is not simply described in the abstract. Teachers and parents need to be reminded of their own education—what worked, and why; what passed them by or was soon forgotten. They need to be familiarized with new pressures and opportunities in the world, ones that were invisible (or were less visible) during their own school years. They need to think about the kinds of contemporary issues that they understand, and the ones they wish they understood. Especially in the area of human change, an actual demonstration of what can be done in analogous surroundings is worth many words and exhortations. Thus, school personnel should visit other sites and reflect on what they've observed.

Of course, these remarks do not apply only to an understanding pathway. A leader who wants to stimulate movement along any pathway must engage in an analogous set of activities. Thus, a technologically oriented pathway should give participants many opportunities to make use of the current tools; a multicultural pathway will need to ensure that its planners and staff are diverse in background and ideas.

Throughout this process, the task of the leader is to articulate the vision, to encourage associates to express their reservations and hesitations, to show where such objections are mistaken and to take them into account when they are justified. As much as possible, the teachers themselves should participate in learning of the kind that is desired for the students. To be specific, teachers in an understanding pathway need multiple opportunities to perform and to stretch their own understandings of relevant materials and procedures. Only then will there be much chance that they can help students do the same.

In general, human beings learn best from landmarks, heroes, positive (and negative) examples of behaviors and attitudes. The leader can serve as one point of comparison for those who would bring about change; but even the leader will have limitations, blind spots, preferred lenses. It is important to show that others, at comparable schools, can also embody an education for understanding. And most important of all is the realization that individuals within the school can carry out a revolution—and survive to tell the tale.

Battle Scars and Occasional Medals

I have been deeply involved in efforts to move toward the kind of education described in these pages. Some of these efforts have been directed toward schools in which the idea of multiple intelligences is taken seriously; some have taken place in schools in which education for understanding is the goal; and some involve comprehensive, broad-based school change, as in my collaborative efforts with James Comer, Theodore Sizer, and Janet Whitla to create a K–12 pathway designed for "Authentic Teaching and Learning for All Students" (known acronymically as the ATLAS Communities Project).

Let me mention some of the principal lessons—cautionary and occasionally inspiring—that I have learned from these efforts:

The Importance of Leadership. In the absence of serious and sustained leadership, efforts to bring about change will not take hold. The leadership need not always come from the designated leader; sometimes leadership can feature a group of parents, a team of teachers, or even an outsider who regularly visits, provokes, and joins forces with the local agents of change. In these latter cases, the "authorized" leadership cannot be in active opposition; reformers can manage for a while under a policy of benign neglect. But if leadership is not present and active over the long haul, then changes are likely to be short-lived and may sometimes even leave the educational community in worse shape than before.

With respect to my own vision, I have a recurrent nightmare: One day I return to a school at which I've worked, and I overhear someone say, "Oh, 'Education for Understanding'—we used to do that!"

The Need for Long-term Perspective. It is ill-advised to institute change for change's sake, or to mix a whole set of programs. Actions should be taken with a view to the long-term goal—for example, an education that focuses on "uncovering" rather than "coverage." Frills and diversions must be avoided.

A long-term perspective requires markers that indicate whether, and to what extent, the "school's story" is being achieved. For example, if the school's vision encourages "uncovering," then there should be clear markers in student work (e.g., essays and projects) that reveal when students are able to go deeply into particular disciplines, when they are no longer restricted to the collection and spewing forth of disparate facts. Absent such specific markers, the overarching vision is likely to serve as a Rorschach blot, eliciting reactions ranging from "We could never do that" to "We're already doing that." Experienced school watchers will confirm that these apparently contradictory remarks sometimes emerge from the same set of lips within a very short interval!

The Need for Flexibility and Small Victories. If one pursues the vision with excessive rigidity, it becomes difficult to deal with inevitable shifts in personnel, pressures, and local and national signals. Sometimes, one has to temporize. And it is especially important not to attempt to achieve everything at once—doing that, one is bound to fail. The prescient leader makes sure that at least some of the initial efforts will succeed, so that students, teachers, and parents do not lose heart. Having students put on one project for the year, with plenty of help from parents and teachers and much rehearsal with feedback, is likely to lead to a feeling of accomplishment—and the willingness to tackle additional projects next year. Requiring five student projects the first year is likely to exhaust the teachers, produce many frustrated students and parents, and, perhaps, incite the feared backlash.

Anticipate Setbacks and Be Prepared to Deal with Them. One should be upbeat when possible; pessimism saps energy and undermines momentum. One should make it clear that experimentation is the order of the day; everyone will make mistakes, and the world goes on. The important point is to learn from mistakes, not repeat them, and then to move on to a more promising tack. As the cyberspace expert Esther Dyson quips, we should all "make new mistakes." And one should learn how to frame a setback as a learning opportunity rather than an occasion for despair. If, for example, test scores go down one year, study the tests, see where the problems lie, and try to adapt the curriculum so that it helps students to deal with trouble spots on the test.

Even apparent victories may be only temporary. There *will* be setbacks. The chief question is whether these are treated as opportunities to learn; as way stations en route to more reliable success with more students; or as an occasion to backbite, backslide, or give up.

Allow Time for Reflection. The push for action is sometimes powerful, particularly when it comes from impatient supervisors and parents. But unless one has the opportunity to think about what one is doing and to reflect on what went well, what went poorly, and why, the chances for a long-term improvement curve are slight. Time for individual and joint reflection must be built into the schedule; if it is not, then genuine change is most unlikely to occur.

Build on Strengths. Every community, every faculty member, every student has strengths. Identify and build on those strengths; don't fret about areas of weakness. In a community of any size, the strengths of the members will be complementary: leveraging them is better than having somehow to convert weaknesses into strengths. This search for compensatory strengths can extend beyond the building; complementary capacities can be found among parents, in other schools, in the larger community, and on the Internet. So, if your school is stronger in liberal arts than in the sciences, begin the explorations for understanding with the arts; if there is a history of high-quality student essays, begin ongoing assessments in that arena. Then find partner schools with contrasting strengths; the institutions can learn from each other.

Pay Attention to Implicit Messages in the Institutional Culture. What one says one believes is important; but what one does on a day-to-day basis really matters. I have already mentioned the implicit messages of the leader; those sent by teachers, parents, and older students are equally telling. Nothing can boost the cause of understanding more than the sight of the teachers themselves striving to understand new material. And nothing more totally undermines this process than teachers who prove unwilling to deepen their own understanding or to share their intellectual doubts (and delights) with others.

Create a Community That Cares. The most important message in a school community is that the adults in a child's life care—fully, even irrationally—about that child. Nowadays everyone mouths the clichés "Every child can learn" and "It takes a village to raise a child." But only those milieus that go beyond the catchphrases, that provide support and love for each child, unconditionally, succeed in the long run in developing youngsters who care about learning and about one another. It matters when teachers know their students well, can ask about their interests and families, comfort them in times of trouble, spur them on to greater efforts; it matters when peers work together on a school improvement project or come to the aid of a student who has suffered a personal loss; it matters when the members of a community, ranging from dining hall attendants to visiting parents, are courteous and helpful to one another.

While these sentiments invite consent, it is reassuring to have empirical evidence to support them. Thanks to the research of Eric Schaps and his colleagues, we know that the communities of caring result in positive school outcomes in the elementary years. Research by Linda Darling-Hammond and her associates confirms that small and caring communities have similar positive effects in high school.

Visit and Be Visited. When one is embarking on a journey, it is a very good idea to have an anticipatory glimpse of the destination. There now exist many schools that embody some of the practices I have described (as well as practices associated with "rival" pathways); visit those schools—in actuality or through the Internet—and learn from them. Invite veterans from those schools to visit your own campus. And, as soon as you feel comfortable doing so, invite "critical friends" to your school and take advantage of their candid feedback.

Cultivate New Energies. It is easier to launch a new school than to change an existing one. New schools can usually choose their personnel, and they benefit from the energy that comes with starting from scratch. Conversely, old institutions carry lots of baggage; it is more difficult for them to renew themselves.

Here imaginative leadership comes in. Even when the site and the players are the same, it is still possible to tap new energies. These energies can come from without (from visitors and visits, exciting books or provocative movies) or from within (a new agenda, a new spirituality, a new vision). Cultivating one's own mind and the minds of one's students is the most exciting endeavor that I can think of—so long as I do not begin to take it for granted.

Commit Yourself to the Process of Change. Build change into the institutional culture and become a learning organization. Most of us were raised on the idea that there was a certain way to do things. Mostly, that way was adequate; if not, then we learned how to do something new, and that would suffice. We might call this the "unschooled" view of change.

Alas, that view won't do anymore. Change is constant, and no solutions, however effective today, will survive unaltered in the long run. People and institutions that can learn to deal with change—indeed, to welcome it—stand the best chance of surviving and thriving.

Accordingly, though with difficulty, an institution that has learned to do things one way must learn to do new things in a new way. But this involves an appreciation that—counter to the unschooled view—*this* new way will never have an end. Rather, the *new* new way consists of a continuing process of learning, reflecting upon learning, and then learning some more. Ultimately, this new process should become reflexive—that is, educators should automatically and naturally reflect on their course. And perhaps the process will also become joyful, marked by "flow," as the fresh challenges come to mesh with the increasing skills of the individuals and the heightened awareness of the organization as a whole.

I call on educators to make a new covenant. Too often, teachers have allowed those outside the classroom to set the public agenda for education. They have gone along even though they do not agree with the standards and tests imposed by external authorities, in exchange for freedom to do pretty much what they wish inside the classroom.

In the long run, this policy is neither wise nor sustainable. It breeds hostility and hypocrisy. Educators should be prepared to state publicly what they themselves wish for their students. As their part of the "new covenant," they must be willing to state what would count as evidence of success, and what they are prepared to do if success is not immediately achieved. In taking this courageous step, in seizing responsibility, educators would begin to establish that they are professionals, capable of monitoring their own calling. And they would claim (or reclaim) authority over their work.

"Scaling Up": Three Helpful Ingredients

Nowadays, one cannot participate in conversations about schooling without encountering the phrase "scaling up." As the argument goes, we have examples of schools that work, even schools that flourish under trying conditions. The problem, especially in the United States, has been that these successes are isolated. And so the challenge for policymakers is to figure out how to achieve success on a wider scale—how to "retail" success.

In many cases it is possible to produce quick jags in school performance. Programs that increase early literacy, measures that lengthen the school day or the school year, teaching to the test, reducing class size significantly—these and other maneuvers are likely to yield indicators that a school has improved.

However, the ultimate success of a school depends upon the quality of its personnel, the thoughtfulness of its programs, the sustained involvement of parents and the larger community, and the willingness to make mistakes and to learn from them. None of these is susceptible to a quick fix. Jurisdictions that have high-quality schools and high-performing students have not achieved this status overnight. Rather, they have devoted years to articulating a program and making sure that it is carried out systematically, thoroughly, and reflectively. This approach may not appeal to those who need to win the next school board election, but it is the only viable one to follow over the long haul.

Moreover, scaling up is not a magical process, unconnected to the local scene. In the end, scaling up entails scaling *down*—to specific pathways, specific schools, specific classrooms, and specific teachers, families, and students. Ultimately, scaling up entails improvement of particular institutions, one at a time.

A hopeful note. The articulation and pursuit of a manageable number of pathways can be a productive first step toward the attainment of good schools. The schools benefit not only from a clearly stated program but

from the existence of other schools from which they can draw sustenance and with which they can exchange ideas, practices, and resources.
And pathways need not engage in endless struggles with dissatisfied parents; alternative pathways are available.

Three ingredients can be helpful:

A Clearly Articulated Program. Such a program should furnish a fairly
detailed vision of the child's experiences as he passes through the years,
as a learner in the school. This picture should be as vivid as possible, but
not so prescriptive that it saps the individual initiative of teacher or
student.

A Consistently Held Focus. A pathway's educators should agree about the
most important element on which to focus. At Project Zero, we have
found that "ample instances of student work" provide the ideal focus.
Student works are tangible; they can be critiqued and can be compared
with the works of others as well as the student's own previous work;
progress can be monitored; and such achievements can be related to
later milestones in the student's life, including his own transition to the
world of work.

Conviction That One Is Involved in a Movement. Reform can be a lonely
undertaking, and the feeling that one is engaged in a solitary uphill fight
can be discouraging, even devastating. Progress is more likely to occur
within schools, or across networks of schools, and scaling up is more
likely to become a reality, if the players feel that they belong to something important and if they secure the emotional rewards that come
from engagement with a cause. The fatal limitation of a carrot-and-stick
approach to school reform is that this behaviorist tack ignores what
motivates human behavior in the long run: a feeling that one is engaged
in something of consequence, and a belief that what one does matters—
to the community, to the students, to oneself.

The Roles of Business

In the post–Cold War era, business has become an enormously powerful force worldwide, rivaling political entities as the "locus of attention and action." In the United States, business has become extremely concerned with the quality of education; by and large, businesspeople believe that the workers of the future are not being adequately prepared. (Such an interest is not unprecedented; many of the innovations in education in Japan in the post–World War II era were provoked by the business community.) While businesses continue to want workers who will show up on time and be honest and reliable, they are also demanding higher levels of literacy. And at several echelons of employment, businesses seek individuals who will be creative, who will be able to solve and anticipate problems and work with others in a resourceful and cooperative manner. The most forward-looking companies, such as Microsoft, Merck, or Monsanto, are particularly likely to favor such "knowledge workers."

I believe it is appropriate for an educational system to address these needs, at least in a general way. (I do not believe that business should have the right to dictate what education should be like, any more than law, medicine, or journalism has that right.) Moreover, given the vast resources that businesses have at their disposal, and the meager government financial support given public education (particularly in the inner cities), it is appropriate for business to participate in the improvement of education.

But how? Many in business favor the creation of for-profit schools or school systems; others favor the awarding of vouchers so that students can attend any school, for-profit or not, independent or public.

I cannot subscribe to this way of thinking. I believe that education is inherently a public responsibility: it must be addressed by public institutions and underwritten by public funds. (This does not mean that I oppose independent schools; my children and I have attended both public and independent schools.) The need to educate for citizenship, to provide good schools for children of all backgrounds, and to expose students to their fellow citizens should not be evaded in a democracy. While some businesses might go about these tasks in a responsible way, the business of business is to make products that sell and to make profits for their owners. I am not alone in seeing these goals as interfering with important traditional aims of education—and particularly with the aims that I have set forth in this book.

To be sure, some experimental schools (including ones created by for-profit corporations) will do an excellent job, and some of them will exert a benign influence on other schools as well. However, these successes are likely to be temporary, depending upon the extra energies of founders, hand-picked teachers, and, not infrequently, large infusions of venture capital. We do not need more isolated successes; taking a leaf from Singapore or Japan, we need a public school system which in general does a better job of educating our children.

While they should not be running schools, businesses can provide important support for them, both in this country and abroad. They can contribute expertise in teaching and assessment; they can help with school-to-work transitions; they can invite students to participate in business initiatives, as apprentices or trainees. They can also help with funding, both by contributing general support to schools in their neighborhood and by underwriting specific programs. And when schools are charged with managing their own fiscal affairs (as has been happening with greater frequency), businesses can provide models, technological adjuncts, and just-in-time assistance.

To my way of thinking, business can make its biggest contribution through the creation of products—especially technologies—that help educate students effectively. Until now businesses in the United States have been involved in three visible activities: creating textbooks and curriculum packets; designing tests; and producing technologies, like television, video cameras, and personal computers. None of these devices or creations have brought about remarkable improvements, either in this country or abroad.

If they took the goals of this book seriously, however, businesses could make manifold contributions. For the first time, it is possible via technology to teach individual students in the ways that they learn best; to fashion future instruction based on the record of earlier successes and failures with those students; and to allow them to show what they have learned in ways both comfortable for them and susceptible to external evaluation. The technology to do this can be conceived but it has not, to my knowledge, been realized.

Education for understanding depends upon the creation of materials that are engaging, that allow for probing and synthesis, and that afford plenty of opportunities to perform one's emerging understandings.

Some CD-ROMs created commercially hold much promise for engaging students and for allowing productive probing. However, they may also stimulate students to go off in idiosyncratic directions and deviate from the curricular goals of the school; in other words, they often lack a "righting mechanism."

To convert these inviting entertainment (or "edutainment") materials into effective educational vehicles is a daunting assignment, which has not yet been successfully executed. To be sure, individual teachers of genius know just when to use—and when not to use—glitzy inventions. But those geniuses do not require fancy technology anyway; their "technologies" are in their heads and their hands (and, perhaps, in their hearts).

The challenge is to create pedagogical and curricular interfaces that mobilize the genius of the technology and the curiosity of children in the service of deeper understanding. Here is a perfect opportunity for business to do what it is suited to do. Such a mission also provides the right flavor of collaboration among educators, researchers, designers, and individuals in marketing and sales. Profits might not come instantly, but the first technologies that can demonstrably improve the learning of mathematics or history or genetics in a non-hothouse atmosphere will attract consumers from all over the planet.

Businesses can also aid with scaling up. Many businesses have succeeded in spreading promising practices on a wide scale. While it would be wrong to manage schools as if they were businesses, some business techniques—such as those associated with total quality management and with learning organizations—may well be transportable from corporate headquarters to PS 101. Businesses can share their own experiences in dealing with constant change and in making sure that desired changes spread effectively throughout an organization. Commercial technologies can also help schools to connect with one another and to share materials, resources, and assessments. Finally, a central focus—for example, on improving the quality of student projects—may benefit from the experiences of business in making high-quality products and offering satisfying services at the workplace.

Finding an Appropriate Niche

Taking a leaf from the study of evolution, let me recast my message here as a search for appropriate niches. All of us want good educations for our children, and many of us care about the education of other children of the world. But we do not necessarily agree on the nature of quality education. The job of educational designers is to come up with prototypes that will satisfy most customers. In a complex society like ours, there are numerous people who have strongly held and fundamentally different views of what a good education is. Rather than allowing these constituencies to haunt one another, or to compromise in nonproductive ways, it seems more sensible to create a small number of prototypes and let families (and communities and even nations) discover the niche that best suits them.

The same way of thinking must be applied at the school level. Schools cannot be all things to all persons. They are better off developing a vision and a story that make sense in their context, and inviting those who share it to join and contribute to their community of learners. The process of school change is one of constant discovery and rediscovery of who one is, and of what one can be. Effective leadership stimulates that discussion and often helps individuals to find themselves, either confirming their identity or opening up the possibility of a new one.

Finally, there is the question of the proper role for various bodies within the society. Many individuals and groups, sensing the inadequacy of schools, want to be helpful; too many also believe that they could solve educational problems in a flash. Their challenge is to figure out where they could best make a contribution to the schools, rather than to arrogate all powers to themselves or to wash their hands entirely of the problem. The challenge for schools is to accept this help graciously when it is appropriate, to reject it when it is manifestly inappropriate, and to engage in continuing dialogues that are aimed at bringing educational visions into better alignment with one another.

CHAPTER 11

In Closing

One Hundred Years of Education . . . and of World History

Let's imagine that I was living at the end of the nineteenth century and had decided to write a book about education, with an eye toward the coming century. What considerations would enter into my deliberations?

To begin with, "writing" would have quite a different physical context. In all probability, I would be seated at a writing table, using a quill or a fountain pen, or perhaps one of those new mechanical typewriters. If I mailed the manuscript to my publisher, using a few pennies' worth of stamps, it would have traveled by train, and reached its destination some days later. There was no thought of electric typewriters, let alone computers; even the most forward-looking correspondent could not have anticipated mail being carried the world over by airplane, or through instant facsimiles or electronic mail. Even today, seated at my word processor, I have difficulty thinking of written messages—let alone books!—in the absence of paper, as just a series of electronic blips.

And what about the portrait of education in such a book? Certainly there are many features which I could not have anticipated: televisions in most classrooms, computers in most schools, children coming to school in buses, teachers and administrators flying to conferences across the country and even abroad. In 1896, the U.S. Supreme Court held that public facilities could be "separate but equal"—the civil rights revolution, affirmative action, and multicultural curricula could not have been conceived.

What issues would have arisen in the classroom of 1900? The national and international political scenes were very different. The American

Civil War was still a recent memory (and the Spanish-American War had just been fought), but wider European and global wars seemed a thing of the past. (Indeed, one unwitting cause of the imminent "Great War" was incredulity that such large-scale conflict was still possible in the modern era.) Few anticipated fascism or Nazism; Communism and socialism were the pipe dreams of a smattering of odd intellectuals.

As for science and technology? Albert Einstein was just finishing his university education. No one anticipated the revolution that he—and his quantum-mechanical successors—would bring about in our conception of the physical world. Nor did anyone imagine the weapons of mass destruction that could be constructed as a result of our understanding of nuclear energy. Darwin's ideas were becoming widely accepted—though, as Frank Sulloway has shown, far more readily by laterborns than firstborns!—yet the work of Gregor Mendel on genetics and heredity was still not known. As for the role of DNA, the molecular revolution, antibiotics, genetic engineering, and cloning, manuscripts on these topics would have been rejected by a journal editor as subjects for science fiction.

Yet, during the same century that has seen such epochal events and scientific advances, the texture of daily schooling has changed relatively little, particularly at the precollegiate level. The opening grades still stress the literacies; as for secondary school (which only a small percentage of Americans attended in 1900), the prestigious Committee of Ten (which included five college presidents) had just enunciated a curriculum of core disciplines that remains substantially with us today. Current teaching involves lecturing, workbooks, tests, and a few laboratory experiments that would have been old hat to many educators a century ago.

And what about human beings' conceptions of themselves, of ourselves? During the past century, we have accumulated fresh examples of the marvelous performances of which humans are capable: in the arts (the music of Stravinsky and the Beatles, the writings of Joyce, Proust, Woolf, the films of Ingmar Bergman and Charlie Chaplin); in the sciences (the insights of Einstein, the discoveries of DNA and molecular biology, the theory of plate tectonics); in technology (antibiotic medicines, antipsychotic drugs, computers, airplanes, and television). And we have had ample confirmation of the evil of which individuals are capable—individually and en masse (the Germans under Hitler; the Russians under Stalin; the Chinese under Mao Zedong; the Cambodians under Pol Pot—alas, an unanticipated long-term consequence of bipartisan U.S. foreign policy in Southeast Asia under Presidents Kennedy, Johnson, and Nixon). So many discoveries can be used for good or for ill—nuclear energy, genetic engineering, the mobilizing of public opinion, the mass testing of students.

Life a century ago, to say nothing of life two millennia ago, was very different. And growing up in East Asia or sub-Saharan Africa is a very different experience from growing up in Western Europe or the United States. Yet, the human brain and the human mind have not changed during these periods—scarcely blips in the history of our species, let alone in the history of life. As human beings, we do not differ fundamentally from the humans portrayed in the Bible or in Greek drama. The most remarkable achievements of the past—the philosophy of Socrates, Plato, and Aristotle; the literary achievements of Sophocles, Aeschylus, and Euripides—reflect minds of the highest order; and note that I refer only to representatives of a tiny spot in the world: Athens, a few centuries before the birth of Christ.

As human beings, despite the remarkable changes of recent times, we remain cognitive and emotional siblings of those who lived in Stone Age caves, those who settled the Fertile Crescent, and those who built the first cities in the Middle East, on the Indian subcontinent, and along the rivers and coasts of South America. We can understand many of their pains, disappointments, fears, aspirations, desires, and dreams. It would perhaps be more difficult for them to empathize with us, because the superficial appearance of our world is so alien from anything that they could have imagined.

Yet so-called Stone Age persons are able to make the transition. This is one of the remarkable findings of Carleton Gajdusek, a Nobel Prize–winning virologist who brought almost sixty boys and girls from Micronesian and Melanesian tribes to the United States and raised them in a family setting in suburban Washington. Not all the transplanted youngsters thrived, but many of them have gone on to productive careers in the West or back in their homelands. Thanks to this informal experiment, we receive fresh confirmation of the remarkable flexibility of *Homo sapiens*. Many, perhaps most, can catapult from a culture that lacks all but the simplest technology to one dominated by machines that can radically alter our "common sense" of time, space, and human capacities. Whatever their constraints, our brains and minds can adapt to a dizzying variety of ecologies and cultural norms.

Here, then, in a nutshell is the situation faced everywhere by educa-tors. All human beings inhabit the same brain, mind, and body, roughly speaking. Certain timetables and capacities—and incapacities—are built into our species. At the same time, as a consequence of the vagaries of history and geography, we are born under conditions that vary enor-mously, subject to the influence of equally varied norms and values. Educators must honor universal constraints. At the same time, they must raise youths who can cope with their particular society in a partic-ular historical moment, and, indeed, pass on its chief precepts and prac-tices to succeeding generations. This, in fact, is what I (now an elder) have tried to do in this book.

The enormous changes taking place in the world magnify this task. We must prepare to live in a world whose contours we cannot antici-pate. The best preparation, in my view, is to understand deeply the insights about the world and about experiences that have accumulated over the millennia. I am reminded of an exchange between T. S. Eliot and a younger colleague. The colleague suggested to Eliot that modern people know much more than did the ancients. Eliot agreed, but then added with characteristic asperity: "And they are what we know."

Once More, My Vision

As "dry land" for this endeavor through turbulent waters, I have turned to a trio of ancient touchstones: what is true (and what is false), what is beautiful (and what is not), what is good (and what is reprehensible). With suitable qualifications, I have nominated topics that qualify for spe-cial consideration within our Western culture: the theory of evolution, the music of Mozart, and the events of the Holocaust. I have argued that people in our society ought to attain a masterful understanding of topics like these; and that such mastery can only be achieved if one is willing to devote time and energy to their exploration. At the same time, I have stressed that these choices are illustrative only. (Alas, this will not keep some people from misrepresenting my work; those who scan critical reviews and other secondhand accounts will no doubt read somewhere that the Europhile Howard Gardner has mandated a curriculum based on three of his personal obsessions.)

So let me say, one more time: It is important that a culture identify the truths, beauties, and virtues that it values, and that it then dedicate resources to inculcating their understanding in young learners. A culture must acknowledge that these virtues are always being redefined, but that such definition and refinement are a worthwhile pursuit. In the end, individuals must arrive at their own syntheses of these virtues—and, I would hope, commit themselves to making virtuous additions to their world.

Two towering facts complicate this task. First, understanding is difficult to achieve, and the obstacles to its attainment are formidable. Second, possessing different kinds of minds, individuals represent information and knowledge in idiosyncratic ways. In the future, if education is to achieve greater success with more individuals, it ought to affirm and build upon these two considerations.

In the central discussion of this book, I have directly addressed the issue of how students can gain deeper understanding of significant themes and topics. I seek to make individual differences into allies of our education, rather than encumbrances to it. If we spend time on important topics, we can approach them through several entry points; we can draw a variety of analogies; and we can even capture the core ideas of such topics in a number of model languages. The result of such a multipronged education should be that most students have attained deep—or at least deeper—understanding. And, what is equally important, they will have a sense of what it means—of how it *feels*—to understand consequential topics. They will have at least a taste of a disciplined mind.

Such insight represents a crucial milestone. From that point on, students can apply the litmus test of understanding to other issues and themes from their own culture and others as well. And perhaps, having tasted the sweet fruit of understanding, students will be motivated to remain "pursuers of knowledge"—perhaps even "creators of knowledge"—for the remainder of their lives.

This is my vision of education—the education that I would like for all humans. I believe that such an education would yield individuals who feel a commitment to their community and to the larger world. Perhaps in a small and relatively homogeneous community, we could gain consensus on an education elaborated precisely along the lines that I have sketched in the book.

But life is short, and individuals disagree deeply about these issues. Not without reluctance, I have concluded that it makes sense to offer different educational pathways to each particular community, country, and culture. Students, teachers, families, community members, and policy-makers can sort themselves according to the pathway that they favor. Each pathway needs to demonstrate its legitimacy. It must help students to become citizens of their country (and their world); provide a means of assessing whether standards worth meeting have been achieved; and be prepared to reinvent itself should such standards not be met. It is my firm belief that this enterprise should be handled by the public sector and not by private interests. Businesses can be wonderfully helpful in improving the quality of education, but they should not substitute themselves for the individuals and institutions authorized to operate schools.

I recognize that a multiplicity of pathways can pose a dilemma. Say that, as a parent, I was given a choice between two schools. I disagree with the philosophy of the pathway in School 1, but its teachers and the rest of the community agree on the merits of the philosophy and how it should be carried out. As for School 2, I endorse the philosophy of its pathway, but the staff is in disarray and the community fails to support the school. I would unhesitatingly choose to send my children to the first school. In my view, coherence and common vision win out over ideological congeniality.

There are two riders on this perhaps surprising confession. First, as a parent, I would be able to provide experiences that complement ones in the school. For example, if the school to which I sent my children elimi-nated the arts, or had everyone read a single canon, I would provide some artistic experiences "on the side" and also make sure that my chil-dren were exposed to books and films that had eluded canonization. Second of all, there are some pathways I would reject. My trio of topics serves as a convenient point of reference. I could not accept a school that denies the importance of evolution or the occurrence of the Holocaust. And as for the music of Mozart, I would certainly think twice about a school where works of classical music were rejected, or where postmodern sentiments were regnant. I cannot accept that all artistic works are equally meritorious or equally deserving of study.

A World Worth Striving For

Our world has changed enormously in this century. But what of the future? Conservatively speaking, we could say that changes of a technological sort are taking place four times as fast as they did a century ago. (Indeed, if someone were to say that they were occurring forty or four thousand times as fast, I would not contest the estimate.) Think about the meaning of those figures. By 2025 we will see changes as vast as the ones that took place between 1900 and 2000. And if we choose a less cautious estimate, then the world will look much different even two years from now. For those of us who had never heard of the Internet, the World Wide Web, or cloning a few years ago, or who expected to die with the Iron Curtain still in place or polio still rampant, the prospect of future quantum changes comes as no surprise.

Two considerations seem beyond dispute. The first is that everyone must become as comfortable as possible with change. We may not like it; we might wish that things would remain the same; but we must accept that change is the order of the day. More so than in the decades past, we have to monitor what is going on in the world—and, in particular, the new trends in economy, culture, and technology. Some will do this by reading; some by surfing; some by paying close attention to what is happening at their places of work, play, and continuing education.

The second consideration may appear to conflict with the first but is actually complementary and synergistic. One must remain ever conscious of the constants in human experiences—the things that do not change, either because they cannot or because we do not want them to. Many truths will change, but some will not: We grow old, more or less gracefully, and we eventually die; human beings and cultures are subject to the laws of evolution. Many beauties will change but some will not: the artifacts of Greece, Egypt, Angkor Wat, and pre-Columbian society remain as compelling as they did in past centuries.

In morality, with respect to a sense of goodness and evil, the constants are robust. I do not think that we (as a species) have transcended the commandments of Moses, the teachings of Jesus, the wisdom encoded in Confucianism, Buddhism, and Islam (not that I agree with every facet of these doctrines). Perhaps there is progress in this domain, but it is agonizingly slow. We no longer accept slavery and almost no one exalts the most flagrant examples of racism, sexism, torture, xenophobia, and other violations of universal human rights. But there is also regression in this domain. Our weapons kill more people, with little personal travail on the part of those who launch them; the fraying of ties of family and community may produce callousness and inhumanity that would have been difficult to envisage at an earlier, more intimate time.

Assume that an individual today has been raised in a moral way, thanks to parents, schools, and a circle of friends (and despite the often amoral messages of the media and the consumer society). Threats to this moral sense need to be identified. First of all, people are far more mobile today than ever before, and we often find ourselves in settings where no one is familiar. It is more difficult to keep one's moral bearings under those conditions. Then, too, the situation at the workplace changes with enormous rapidity; the norm of mutual loyalty—employer to employee, employee to employer, employee to employee or to "the firm"—seems less plausible at times of downsizing, reengineering, and opportunistic searching for better positions or more affluent merger partners.

Particularly at a time of rapid change, and at a time when the identity of "good guys" and "bad guys" is no longer so evident, many are searching for models of humaneness. This hunger has fueled recent efforts to craft a broader definition of intelligence. Traditionally, "intelligence" meant aptitude for school subjects and school skills. Those of us who seek a fuller view—who speak of personal intelligence, emotional intelligence, moral intelligence, wisdom—are all declaring that skill in the literacies and facility at a certain kind of problem-solving are not enough. We seek individuals who not only can analyze but also will do the right thing; individuals who will be admirable not only as thinkers or creators but also as human beings. We endorse Emerson's aphorism: "Character is higher than intellect."

Such a search would have been familiar to individuals in earlier times. The Greeks saw all human virtues as part of a single balanced whole; Confucians saw no distinction between beauty and goodness; Keats equated truth and beauty. It does not suffice, however, simply to endorse these earlier models of human accomplishment uncritically. We have lost our innocence. Studies in psychology and brain science confirm that the human mind treats each of these realms as separate, and that, indeed, there are multiple forms of intelligence, skill, creativity, morality. Studies in anthropology demonstrate the overwhelming number of ways in which cultures can combine—or fail to combine—different virtues and vices, even in blends that are mutually incomprehensible. I expect that further studies will find even greater neurological specialization in each human mind and even greater differences among cultures.

We must accept the harsh reality that one can be intelligent without being moral; creative without being ethical; sensitive to emotions without using that sensitivity in the service of others. We must accept the reality that one may be aware of what is true, while blind to what is beautiful or good. Similarly one may appreciate what is ethical without showing any tendency to pursue the good in one's own life.

Connecting

However, we need not resign ourselves to this "disjoined" state of affairs. The key to resolving the difficulty lies in E. M. Forster's famous formula "Only connect." It may be a fact that creativity and goodness are not necessarily linked; but as human beings in a culture we can strive to connect these virtues. We may fail in the effort, but that is no reason not to try.

Mihaly Csikszentmihalyi, William Damon, and I have been asking the following question: How does one maintain a sense of responsibility, civility, and morality in a world in which cutting-edge work and constant mobility have come to characterize every domain? At such a time the traditional checks placed on behavior by religious values and legal sanctions seem inadequate to provide guidance and, when needed, counterweights. Who among us has been prepared to make thoughtful decisions about what content (personal, pornographic) should be permitted on the Internet; how to protect privacy at a time when information flows so freely; the possibility of altering our genes and those of our descendants, of cloning ourselves, or of extending life indefinitely? To what extent can traditional moral values and religious or legal canons guide us in these and so many other equally uncharted territories?

It is necessary, we believe, for each individual working in a domain or discipline to develop a righting mechanism—a sense of what is proper and what is not, independent of the signals being telegraphed in the wider society. Such a righting mechanism may derive from a variety of sources. One is the norms and values that one absorbs in one's youth. Sometimes these prove capacious enough to sustain one throughout life. A second is a sense of connection to the rest of the community and even to all of humanity—a Golden Rule that keeps one grounded and oriented. A third is loyalty to one's own discipline or profession—a sense that one would betray one's calling if one were to behave in certain ways or avoid accountability for one's professional actions. Support from ethical peers may also help to establish and maintain a sense of "rightness," particularly in the face of seductive counterpressures.

A few brilliant or saintly individuals may figure out and construct such righting mechanisms on their own. Most of the rest of us are aided by contact, at strategic points in our life, with people who themselves embody such virtues, such as a sense of what to do and what not to do, even when temptation yanks one sharply in a certain direction. Such a mentoring role has been assumed in the recent past by scientists like Niels Bohr, musicians like Pablo Casals, political leaders like Mohandas Gandhi and Nelson Mandela, writers like Rachel Carson and George Orwell. We need to help young professionals-in-training have personal relationships with (or, at the very least, regular exposure to) such "orienting figures." This is one reason I cherish people who "walk the ethical talk"—people like political organizer Ernesto Cortes, cancer biologist George Klein, performance artist Anna Deavere Smith, social entrepreneur William Drayton, and educational reformers Patricia Bolanos, James Comer, Deborah Meier, and Ted Sizer. And it is the reason that I have continued to seek out and write about individuals of extraordinary abilities and accomplishment.

This line of thinking has implications for education, for how we teach and how we assess. It does not suffice simply to hope that students admire and seek to embody virtues like truthfulness and goodness and beauty. We must relate these to one another, whenever possible; equally, we need to help students proceed from recognition to admiration, and from admiration to the enduring desire to pursue truth, beauty, and goodness in their own lives. To be sure, when assessing students and their work, we cannot simply conflate these virtues. And yet we can give special recognition—privately and publicly—to those individuals who succeed in connecting the true, the beautiful, and the good.

I am convinced that much of the dis-ease felt in our society, at a time when it appears in some ways to be as "successful" as it has ever been, comes from these troubling disjunctions. We observe daily that only one kind of talent—say, technological creativity—is being rewarded, and only one measure—say, profit in the marketplace—is being recognized. Yet we know in our bones that these indices are insufficient, that other parts of the human spirit ought to command recognition, respect, veneration. A person can succeed on Wall Street or in Washington and yet fail as a human being. To be sure, it will be more difficult, more controversial to agree on who embodies these "soft" virtues and these "connections." And yet, as a society, we will not feel legitimate unless we make the effort to do so. The Czech playwright and political leader Václav

Havel has said it eloquently:

> Regardless of where I begin my thinking about the problems facing our civilization, I always return to the theme of human responsibility, which seems incapable of keeping pace with civilization and preventing it from turning against the human race. It's as though the world has simply become too much for us to deal with. The main task for the coming era is something else: a radical renewal of our sense of responsibility. Our conscience must catch up to our reason; otherwise we are lost.

We are born as little creatures and for years we feel relatively helpless. And of course, a feeling of insignificance is appropriately part of the human condition. We live for but an instant, and even during that instant, there are billions of other equally worthy human beings on the face of this tiny planet.

During our moment, however, we should try to make the most of our vantage point. Education can equip us to make a difference, and perhaps it can orient us toward making a positive one. We must be humble in the face of the biological limitations under which we operate. We must be equally humble with reference to the constraints and opportunities afforded by the culture in which we happen to be born and those to which we are exposed by our schooling, our travel, our media, and our personal contacts.

Our contributions depend on our rootedness in visions of the true, the beautiful, and the good; our willingness to act upon these visions, individually and synergistically; our understanding of the changes as well as the constants in the world; and the accident of our location in a particular domain, institution, or problem space at a particular historical moment. (Pity those individuals who find themselves living in a society headed by a ruthless tyrant; envy those who live in a society where individual independence is respected and service to the local and the wider community is esteemed.) We do not have control of these contingencies—but we are not at their mercy, either. The educational vision put forth here should better equip human beings to make the most of the opportunities within their grasp and to help to create new ones for those who come later.

Appendix:
"The Trio of Colliding Agendas"

Adapted with permission from W. A. Mozart, *The Marriage of Figaro (Le Nozze di Figaro)* (Mineola, N.Y.: Dover Publications, 1979), pp. 80–91.

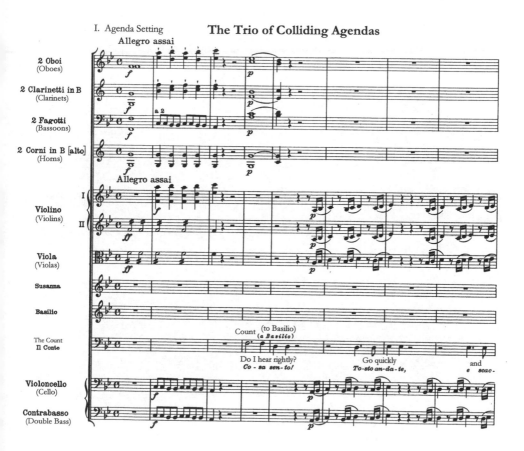

V. Back to the Page

VII. What Did Cherubino Do?

References

Chapter 1

On evolution, see S. Blakeslee, "Computer 'Life Form' Mutates in an Evolution Experiment," *The New York Times,* November 25, 1997; G. Kolata, *Clone: The Road to Dolly and the Path Ahead* (New York: Morrow, 1998); G. Taubes, "Community Design Meets Darwin," *Science,* no. 277, September 26, 1997, pp. 1931–32.
On the evolutionary approach to the understanding of cognitive and social phenomena, see S. Pinker, *How the Mind Works* (New York: Norton, 1997), and E. O. Wilson, *Sociobiology: The New Synthesis* (Cambridge: Mass.: Harvard University Press, 1975), and *Consilience* (New York: Knopf, 1998).

18   On ignorance about evolution, see C. Yoon, "Evolutionary Biology Begins Tackling Public Doubts," *New York Times,* July 9, 1998. See also R. Zacks, "What Are They Thinking: Students' Reasons for Rejecting Evolution Go Beyond the Bible," *Scientific American,* October 1997.

18   Carl Sagan: quoted in E. M. Gaffney, "How the Scopes Trial Frames the Modern Debate over Science and Religions," *Los Angeles Times,* July 12, 1998.

18   American ignorance of the Holocaust: news report on Cable News Network, April 12, 1998.

18   Robert Simon is cited in J. Leo, "Absolutophobia," *The Responsive Community,* winter 1997–1998, pp. 4–6.

21   On the attainment of understanding, see Howard Gardner, *The Unschooled Mind: How Children Think and How Schools Should Teach* (New York: Basic Books, 1991). On multiple intelligences, see Howard Gardner, *Frames of Mind: The Theory of Multiple Intelligences* (New York: Basic Books, 1983; rev. ed. 1993) and *Multiple Intelligences: The Theory in Practice* (New York: Basic Books, 1993).

23 "The organized subject matter": John Dewey, *Experience and Education* (New York: Macmillan, 1938), p. 103.

24 sustained dialectic: See E. D. Hirsch, *Cultural Literacy* (Boston: Houghton Mifflin, 1987) and *The Schools We Need and Why We Don't Have Them* (New York: Doubleday, 1996).

Chapter 2

33 The ancient Greeks evolved a sense: See H. D. F. Kitto, *The Greeks* (London: Penguin, 1965), and W. Jaeger, *Paideia: The Ideals of Greek Culture,* 3 vols. (Cambridge, Mass.: Harvard University Press, 1943–1945).

33 In the Confucian view: See B. Schwartz, *The World of Thought in Ancient China* (Cambridge, Mass.: Harvard University Press, 1985), and Jonathan Spence, "What Confucius Said," *New York Review of Books,* April 10, 1997, pp. 8–11.

36 "Let the main ideas": A. N. Whitehead, *The Aims of Education and Other Essays* (New York: Free Press, 1929), p. 2.

36 On the liberal or progressive side of education, see R. Archambault, ed., *John Dewey on Education: Selected Writings* (Chicago: University of Chicago Press, 1964).

36 On transformative traditions, see P. Jackson, *The Practice of Teaching* (New York: Teachers College Press, 1986).

36 For Cardinal Newman's view, see J. H. Cardinal Newman, *The Idea of a University* (Garden City, New York: Image Books, n.d.; first published 1873). Also see F. W. Turner, ed., *The Idea of a University* (New Haven, Conn.: Yale University Press, 1997).

Chapter 3

41 On schools as conservative institutions and the difficulties in bringing about school change, see L. Cuban, "Reforming Again, Again, and Again," *Educational Researcher,* vol. 19 (1990), pp. 2–13.

43 On new demands for an educated citizenry, see F. Trompenaars and C. Hampden Turner, *Riding the Waves of Culture* (New York: McGraw-Hill, 1998); R. Marshall and M. Tucker, *Thinking for a Living: Education and the Wealth of Nations* (New York: Basic Books, 1992); R. Murnane and F. Levy, *Teaching the New Basic Skills* (New York: Free Press, 1996); and E. Vogel, *Japan as Number One* (Cambridge, Mass.: Harvard University Press, 1979).

43 On technological and scientific breakthroughs, see M. Dertouzos, *What*

Will Be (New York: HarperCollins, 1996); R. C. Schank and C. Cleary, *Engines for Education* (Hillsdale, N.J.: Erlbaum, 1995); and D. Viadero, "Brave New Worlds: Virtual Reality Technology," *Education Week,* August 7, 1996, pp. 51–58.

44 Sim City: S. Turkle, paper presented at the World Economic Forum, Davos, Switzerland, February 1997.

45 almost everything that can be handled algorithmically: S. Zuboff, *In the Age of the Smart Machine: The Future of Work and Power* (New York: Basic Books, 1988).

47 "Wandering between two worlds": M. Arnold, "Stanzas from the Grande Chartreuse" (1855), l. 85.

48 On the new environment of globalization: R. Altman, "The Nuke of the 90s," *The New York Times Magazine,* March 1, 1998, pp. 33–34.

50 For Samuel Huntington's views, see his *The Clash of Civilizations* (New York: Simon & Schuster, 1996).

51 "ligatures": R. Dahrendorf, *Life Chances* (Chicago: University of Chicago Press, 1978).

54 Changes in the cartography of knowledge: T. Becher, "The Countercul-ture of Specialization," *European Journal of Education,* vol. 25, no. 3 (1990), pp. 333–46; J. W. Botkin, M. Elmandjra, and M. Malitza, *No Limits to Learning: Bridging the Human Gap, a Report to the Club of Rome* (Oxford, England: Pergamon Press, 1979).

55 On postmodernism, see M. H. Abrams, "The Transformation of English Studies: 1930–1995," *Daedalus,* winter 1997, pp. 105–32; Z. Bauman, *Postmodernity and Its Discontents* (Oxford, England: Polity, 1997).

55 On Sokal's fake article, see A. Sokal and J. Bricmont, *Intellectual Imposters* (London: Profile, 1998).

56 The study of beauty: Mary B. W. Tabor, "Rescuing Beauty, Then Bowing to Her Power," *The New York Times,* April 11, 1998.

57 For representative samples of Derrida, Lyotard, and Rorty, see J. Der-rida, *Writing and Difference* (Chicago: University of Chicago Press, 1978); J.-F. Lyotard, *The Postmodern Condition* (Minneapolis: University of Minnesota, 1984); and R. Rorty, *Contingency, Irony, and Solidarity* (New York: Cambridge University Press, 1989).

57 On multiculturalism and canons, see L. Levine, *The Opening of the Ameri-can Mind* (Boston: Beacon Press, 1996).

58 "to learn and propagate": M. Arnold, *Essays in Criticism: First Series, 1865. The Function of Criticism at the Present Time.*

58 multicultural curricula and approaches: E. Rothstein, "As Culture Wars Go On, Battle Lines Blur a Bit," *The New York Times,* May 27, 1997; J. Banks, "Multicultural Education: Historical Development, Dimen-

sions, and Practice." In L. Darling-Hammond, *Review of Research in Education* (Washington, D.C.: American Educational Research Association, 1993), vol. 19, pp. 3–49; M. Lefkowitz, *Not Out of Africa* (New York: Basic Books, 1996).

Chapter 4

62 "To an understanding": E. L. Thorndike, "The Contribution of Psychology to Education," *The Journal of Educational Psychology,* vol. 1 (1910), pp. 5–8.

63 Two dominant strands characterized academic psychology: See H. Gardner, *The Mind's New Science: A History of the Cognitive Revolution* (New York: Basic Books, 1985).

64 the teaching machine: B. F. Skinner, *The Technology of Teaching* (New York: Appleton Century Crofts, 1968).

64 For J. B. Watson's famous declaration, see his *Psychology from the Standpoint of a Behaviorist* (Philadelphia: Lippincott, 1919).

65 On the history of the study of intelligence, see H. Gardner, M. Kornhaber, W. Wake, *Intelligence: Multiple Perspectives* (Fort Worth, Tex.: Harcourt Brace, 1996), and R. Sternberg, *Handbook of Human Intelligence* (New York: Cambridge University Press, 1982).

65 For the debate over the mutability or fixedness of intelligence, see N. Block and G. Dworkin, eds., *The IQ Controversy: Critical Readings* (New York: Pantheon Books, 1976) (Lippmann-Terman debate); A. Jensen, "How Much Can We Boost IQ and Scholastic Achievement?" *Harvard Educational Review,* vol. 39, no. 1 (1969), pp. 1–123; R. J. Herrnstein and C. Murray, *The Bell Curve: Intelligence and Class Structure in American Life* (New York: Free Press, 1994).

67 mental representation and the cognitive revolution: See H. Gardner, *The Mind's New Science* (New York: Basic Books, 1985).

69 On Piaget, see H. Gardner, *The Quest for Mind: Piaget, Lévi-Strauss and the Structuralist Movement* (Chicago: University of Chicago Press, 1981), and J. Piaget, "Piaget's Theory." In P. Mussen, ed., *Handbook of Child Psychology,* vol. 1 (New York: Wiley, 1983), pp. 103–28.

70 Young children have distinctive moral outlooks: L. Kohlberg, *The Psychology of Moral Development* (San Francisco: Harper & Row, 1984).

70 On young children's artistic views, see H. Gardner and E. Winner, "First Intimations of Artistry." In S. Strauss, ed., *U shaped Behavioral Development* (New York: Academic Press, 1982), pp. 147–68.

70 For Chomsky's views, see his *Rules and Representations* (New York: Columbia University Press, 1980).

71 On distributed and contextualized views, see B. Rogoff, *Apprenticeship in Thinking: Cognitive Development in Social Context* (New York: Oxford University Press, 1990).

71 The argument from evolutionary psychology: See J. Barkow, L. Cosmides, and J. Tooby, *The Adapted Mind: Evolutionary Psychology and the Generation of Culture* (New York: Oxford University Press, 1993); "Matters of Life and Death: The Worldview from Evolutionary Psychology," *Demos,* no. 10 (1996); M. Ridley, *The Origins of Virtue* (New York: Viking, 1996); and R. Wright, *The Moral Animal* (New York: Vintage, 1994).

71 According to my analysis: H. Gardner, *Frames of Mind: The Theory of Multiple Intelligences* (New York: Basic Books, 1983; rev. ed., 1993).

73 youngsters develop quite powerful theories: On these early theories and misconceptions, see H. Gardner, *The Unschooled Mind: How Children Think and How Schools Should Teach* (New York: Basic Books, 1991), especially chapters 5, 8, and 9.

74 On higher cognitive functions: See J. Baron, *Rationality and Intelligence* (New York: Cambridge University Press, 1985); J. Bruer, *Schools of Thought* (Cambridge, Mass.: MIT Press, 1993); and D. Perkins, *Outsmarting IQ: The Emerging Science of Learnable Intelligence* (New York: Free Press, 1995).

76 On motivation, see T. Amabile, *The Social Psychology of Creativity* (New York: Springer Verlag, 1983).

76 "flow state": M. Csikszentmihalyi, *Flow* (New York: HarperCollins, 1990).

76 "It may be more beneficial": Quoted in P. Barrett, ed., *The Collected Papers of Charles Darwin* (Chicago: University of Chicago Press, 1977), pp. 232–33.

77 The role of emotions: A. Damasio, *Descartes' Error: Emotion, Reason, and the Human Brain* (New York: Putnam, 1994); D. Goleman, *Emotional Intelligence* (New York: Bantam, 1995); and J. LeDoux, *The Emotional Brain* (New York: Simon & Schuster, 1996).

80 For descriptions of recent research on the brain, see A. Battro, "Half a Brain Is Enough" (unpublished manuscript); J. Bruer, "Education and the Brain: A Bridge Too Far," *Educational Researcher,* vol. 26, no. 8 (1997), pp. 4–16; "The Brain," *Daedalus* (special issue), Spring 1998; G. Dawson and K. Fischer, *Human Behavior and the Developing Brain* (New York: Guilford Press, 1994); S. Dehaene, *La bosse des maths* (Paris: Odile Jacob, 1997); H. Gardner, *The Shattered Mind: The Person After Brain Damage* (New York: Vintage, 1976); W. Greenough, J. E. Black, and C. S. Wallace, "Experience and Brain Development," *Child Development*, vol. 58 (1987), pp. 539–59. E. Klima and U. Bellugi, *The Signs of Language* (Cambridge,

Mass.: Harvard University Press, 1979); F. Newman, "Brain Research Has Implications for Education," *State Education Reader,* vol. 15, no. 1 (winter 1997), pp. 1–2; D. Rumelhart and J. McClelland, *Parallel-Distributed Processing* (Cambridge, Mass.: MIT Press, 1986); and D. Schacter, *Searching for Memory* (New York: Basic Books, 1996).

82   organizing role played . . . by music: F. Rauscher, G. L. Shaw, L. J. Levine, E. L. Wright, W. R. Dennis, and R. L. Newcomb, "Music Training Causes Longterm Enhancement of Preschool Children's Spatial-temporal Reasoning," *Neurological Research,* vol. 19, no. 1 (1997), pp. 2–7.

82   genetics and heritability: T. J. Bouchard, et al., "Sources of Human Psychological Differences: The Minnesota Study of Twins Reared Apart," *Science,* no. 250 (1990), pp. 223–28; M. L. Rutter, "Nature-Nurture Integration," *American Psychologist,* vol. 52, no. 4 (April 1997), pp. 390–98. R. Plomin, *Genetics and Experience: The Interplay Between Nature and Nurture* (Thousand Oaks, Cal.: Sage Publishers, 1994).

84   going to school has steadily raised the IQs: S. Ceci, *On Intelligence: More or Less* (Cambridge, Mass.: Harvard University Press, 1996); U. Neisser, *The Rising Curve* (Washington, D.C.: American Psychological Association, 1998).

84   On the need for early stimulation of the brain, see F. Newman, "Brain Research Has Implications for Education," *State Education Reader,* vol. 15, no. 1 (winter 1997), p. 1.

Chapter 5

86   For descriptions of the Reggio Emilia preschools, see L. B. Caldwell, *Bringing Reggio Emilia Home* (New York: Teachers College Press, 1997); C. Edwards, L. Gandini, and G. Forman, eds., *The Hundred Languages of Children,* 2nd ed. (Greenwich, Conn.: Ablex Publishing Company, 1998); "The 10 Best Schools in the World and What We Can Learn From Them," *Newsweek,* December 2, 1991, pp. 50–59.

93   Serious efforts have been undertaken: A. Gambetti, personal communication, April 3, 1998.

94   My wife and I: The incident is also told in H. Gardner, *To Open Minds: Chinese Clues to the Dilemma of Contemporary Education* (New York: Basic Books, 1989).

95   my studies of creativity in the East and West: ibid.

97   many psychologists now leave the laboratory: J. S. Bruner, *Acts of Meaning* (Cambridge, Mass.: Harvard University Press, 1990).

97   Learning is now seen: On distributed and contextualized knowledge, see E. Hutchins, "The Social Organization of Distributed Cognition." In

L. B. Resnick, J. M. Levine, and D. Teasley, eds., *Perspectives in Socially Shared Cognition* (Washington, D.C.: American Psychological Association, 1991), pp. 283–307; J. Lave and E. Wenger, *Situated Learning: Legitimate Peripheral Participation* (New York: Cambridge University Press, 1991); G. Salomon, ed., *Distributed Cognitions: Psychological and Educational Considerations* (New York: Cambridge University Press, 1993); J. Stigler, R. A. Shweder, and G. Herdt, eds., *Cultural Psychology: Essays in Comparative Human Development* (New York: Cambridge University Press, 1990).

100 Kuhn's competing scientific paradigms: T. Kuhn, *The Structure of Scientific Revolutions,* 2nd ed. (Chicago: University of Chicago Press, 1970).

100 O. Sacks, *The Island of the Colorblind* (New York: Knopf, 1996), p. 68.

102 "the one best system": D. Tyack, *The One Best System: A History of American Urban Education* (Cambridge, Mass.: Harvard University Press, 1974).

103 On the Suzuki method, see H. Gardner, *Frames of Mind: The Theory of Multiple Intelligences* (New York: Basic Books, 1983; rev. ed. 1993), Chapter 14.

104 On Spectrum classrooms, see M. Krechevsky, et al., *Building on Children's Strengths: The Experience of Project Zero* (New York: Teachers College Press, 1998).

105 On Japan's primary education system, see N. D. Kristof, "Where Children Rule," *The New York Times Magazine,* August 17, 1997, pp. 40–44; C. Lewis, *Educating Hearts and Minds: Reflections on Japanese Preschool and Elementary Education* (New York: Cambridge University Press, 1994); L. Peak, *Learning to Go to School in Japan* (Berkeley: University of California Press, 1991); T. Rohlen, *Education and Training in Japan* (New York: Routledge, 1998); N. Sato, "Ethnography of Japanese Elementary Schools: Quest for Equality." Unpublished doctoral dissertation, Stanford University, 1991; H. Stevenson and J. Stigler, *The Learning Gap* (New York: Simon & Schuster, 1994); E. Vogel, *Japan as Number One: Lessons for America* (Cambridge, Mass.: Harvard University Press, 1979); M. White, *The Japanese Educational Challenge* (New York: Free Press, 1987).

105 In Chinese primary schools: H. Gardner, *To Open Minds: Chinese Clues to the Dilemma of Contemporary Education* (New York: Basic Books, 1989).

106 At the Key School: See L. Olson, "Children flourish here: Eight teachers and a theory changed a school world," *Education Week* 1988, 7(18), 1, 18–20.

107 inspired by E. D. Hirsch: For Hirsch's approach, see his *Cultural Literacy* (Boston: Houghton Mifflin, 1987) and *The Schools We Need and Why We Don't Have Them* (New York: Doubleday, 1996).

108 Much of this education follows an apprentice model: S. Hamilton, *Apprenticeship for Adulthood: Preparing Youth for the Future* (New York: Free

Press, 1990). On apprenticeships, see H. Hansen, "Caps and Gowns: Historical Reflections on the Institutions That Shaped Learning for and at Work in Germany and the United States, 1800–1945." Unpublished manuscript, Harvard University, 1998.

109 Max Weber: in *The Protestant Ethic and the Spirit of Capitalism* (London: G. Allen and Unwin, 1930).

109 Central Park East Secondary School: D. Meier, *The Power of Their Ideas* (Boston: Beacon Press, 1995).

111 International Baccalaureate: "Guide to the Middle Years Programme." Geneva: International Baccalaureate Programme, 1994.

Chapter 6

115 University of Phoenix: E. Brommer, "University of Working Adults Shatters Mold," *The New York Times,* October 15, 1997; J. Traub, "Drive Thru U," *The New Yorker,* October 20–28, 1997; C. Shea, "Visionary or Operator? Jorge Klor de Alva and His Unusual Intellectual Journey," *Chronicle of Higher Education,* July 3, 1998.

115 "The people who are our students": Traub, op. cit., p. 184.

116 "plan backward": R. Elmore, "Backward Mapping: Using Implementation Analysis to Structure Program Decisions," *Political Science Quarterly,* vol. 94 (1979–1980), pp. 606–16; J. McDonald, "Planning Backwards from Exhibitions." In J. P. McDonald et al., *Graduating by Exhibition* (Alexandria, Va.: Association for Supervision and Curriculum Development, 1993).

117 Teaching for understanding: S. Wiske, *Teaching for Understanding* (San Francisco: Jossey-Bass, 1998); see also D. K. Cohen, M. W. McLaughlin, and J. E. Talbert, eds., *Teaching for Understanding: Challenges for Policy and Practice* (San Francisco: Jossey-Bass, 1993).

120 H. Gardner, *The Unschooled Mind* (New York: Basic Books, 1991).

120 On the physics students, see P. Sadler, cited in K. Koman, "High School Physics: A Dead End?" *Harvard Magazine,* October 1997, pp. 11–12.

128 disconfirming experiences: L. Resnick, personal communication, October 13, 1997.

128 On education for understanding, see the references cited for page 117; also, *Educational Leadership,* February 1994, passim, and T. Blythe, *The Teaching for Understanding Guide* (San Francisco: Jossey-Bass, 1998).

133 As the educator Lee Shulman has insisted: in "Knowledge and Teaching: Foundations of the New Reform," *Harvard Educational Review,* vol. 57, no. 1 (1987), pp. 1–22; see also Lee Shulman, "Those Who Understand: Knowledge Growth in Teaching," *Educational Researcher,* vol. 15 (1986), pp. 4–14.

134 Deborah Meier recalls: in a talk on the occasion of the 75th anniversary of the Little Red Schoolhouse, New York, April 25, 1997.

Chapter 7

138 For general reading about Darwin and evolution, see J. Bowlby, *Charles Darwin* (London: Hutchinson, 1990); J. Browne, *Charles Darwin* (London: Jonathan Cape, 1995); C. Darwin, *On the Origin of Species* (New York: Mentor/New American Library, 1958; originally published 1859); R. Dawkins, *The Selfish Gene* (Oxford, England: Oxford University Press, 1976); D. Dennett, *Darwin's Dangerous Idea* (New York: Simon & Schuster, 1995); S. J. Gould, *Ever Since Darwin* (New York: Norton, H. Gruber, *Darwin on Man: A Psychological Study of Scientific Creativity*, 2nd ed. (Chicago: University of Chicago Press, 1981); E. Mayr, *Populations, Species, and Evolution* (Cambridge, Mass.: Harvard University Press, 1975); E. Mayr, *The Growth of Biological Thought: Diversity, Evolution, and Inheritance* (Cambridge, Mass.: Harvard University Press, 1982); C. Ralling, *The Voyage of Charles Darwin* (New York: New Mayflower Books, n.d.); M. Ridley, ed., *The Essential Darwin* (London: Unwin, 1987); J. M. Smith, *The Theory of Evolution* (Cambridge, England: Cambridge University Press, 1995); F. Sulloway, *Born to Rebel* (New York: Pantheon, 1996); and J. Weiner, *The Beak of the Finch* (New York: Vintage, 1994).

138 For a critique of evolution, see D. L. Wheeler, "A Biochemist Urges Darwinists to Acknowledge the Role Played by an Intelligent Designer," *The Chronicle of Higher Education*, November 1, 1996.

139 For general reading about Mozart and *The Marriage of Figaro*, see E. Crozier, ed., *Mozart's The Marriage of Figaro* (London: John Lane/Bodley Head, 1948); A. Einstein, *Mozart: His Character, His Work* (New York: Oxford University Press, 1945); W. Hildesheimer, *Mozart* (New York: Farrar, Straus & Giroux, 1982); R. B. Moberly, *Three Mozart Operas: Figaro, Don Giovanni, The Magic Flute* (New York: Dodd, Mead and Company, 1968); M. Solomon, *Mozart: A Life* (New York: HarperCollins, 1995); A. Steptoe, *The Mozart–Da Ponte Operas* (Oxford: Clarendon Press, 1988).

141 For general reading about the Wannsee Conference and the Holocaust, see C. Browning, *The Final Solution and the German Foreign Office* (New York: Holmes and Meier, 1978); C. Browning, *The Path to Genocide: Essays on the Launching of the Final Solution* (New York: Cambridge University Press, 1992); R. K. Chartock and J. Spencer, eds., *Can It Happen Again? Chronicles of the Holocaust* (New York: Black Dog and Leventhal, 1995); S. Friedlander, *Nazi Germany and the Jews*, vol. 1 (New York:

HarperCollins, 1997); D. J. Goldhagen, *Hitler's Willing Executioners: Ordinary Germans and the Holocaust* (New York: Vintage, 1996), pp. 3–4; P. Levi, *Survival in Auschwitz* (New York: Collier Books, 1993); C. S. Maier, *The Unmasterable Past: History, Holocaust, and German National Identity* (Cambridge, Mass.: Harvard University Press, 1988); M. Marrus, *The Holocaust in History* (Dartmouth, N.H.: University Press of New England, 1987); D. Patterson, *When Learned Men Murder* (Bloomington, Ind.: Phi Delta Kappan Educational Foundation, 1996).

145 officer named Hoffmann: Goldhagen, op. cit., pp. 3–4.

148 the insight expressed by Galileo: H. Butterfield, *The Origins of Modern Science 1300–1800* (New York: Macmillan, 1953), p. 67.

148 the most marvelous experience: G. H. Hardy, *A Mathematician's Apology* (Cambridge, England: Cambridge University Press, 1967).

155 denuded of species: See E. O. Wilson, *Naturalist* (Washington, D.C.: Island Press, 1994), chapter 13.

156 when Darwin encountered the finches: see references to page 165.

Chapter 8

161 On Darwin collecting birds, see C. Ralling, *The Voyage of Charles Darwin* (New York: New Mayflower Books, n.d.), p. 137.

161 Darwin, "each variety is constant": J. Browne, *Charles Darwin* (London: Jonathan Cape, 1995), p. 305.

161 "When I see these islands": ibid., p. 339.

162 Drawings of finches: M. Ridley, ed., *The Essential Darwin* (London: Unwin, 1987), pp. 51–52.

163 "the most curious fact": quoted in Ralling, op. cit., p. 127.

163 "One may say there is a force": quoted in Browne, op. cit., p. 388.

164 "Considering the small size": quoted in ibid., p. 467.

165 David Lack . . . It is now known: See D. Lack, *Darwin's Finches* (Cambridge, England: Cambridge University Press, 1947); E. Mayr, *Populations, Species and Evolutions* (Cambridge, Mass.: Harvard University Press, 1963); J. M. Smith, *The Theory of Evolution* (New York: Cambridge University Press, 1993); F. Sulloway, "Darwin and His Finches: The Evolution of a Legend," *Journal of History of Biology,* vol. 15, no. 1 (1982), pp. 1–43, and "Darwin and the Galapagos," *Biological Journal of the Linnaean Society,* vol. 21 (1984), pp. 29–59; J. Weiner, *The Beak of the Finch* (New York: Vintage, 1994).

166 "It is interesting to contemplate": C. Darwin, *On The Origin of Species* (New York: Mentor/New American Library, 1958; originally published 1859), p. 450.

177 "the annihilation of the Jewish race in Europe": D. J. Goldhagen, *Hitler's Willing Executioners: Ordinary Germans and the Holocaust* (New York: Vintage, 1996), p. 142.

177 "doubtless imminent final solution": quoted in C. Browning, *The Final Solution and the German Foreign Office* (New York: Holmes and Meier, 1978), p. 44.

178 "thinking of many things": quoted in C. Browning, *The Path to Genocide: Essays on the Launching of the Final Solution* (New York: Cambridge University Press, 1992), p. 25.

178 "final solution project": Goldhagen, op. cit., p. 146.

178 At some point: Browning, *The Final Solution; The Path to Genocide.*

179 eight held doctoral degrees: D. Patterson, *When Learned Men Murder* (Bloomington, Ind.: Phi Delta Kappan Educational Foundation, 1996), p. 5.

180 "natural wastage": Goldhagen, op. cit., p. 322.

180 "in our history": M. Marrus, *The Holocaust in History* (Hanover, N.H.: University Press of New England, 1987), p. 26.

181 Once these elements: Some works by the historians and other writers cited in the paragraph are R. Hilberg, *The Destruction of European Jewry* (Chicago: Quadrangle Books, 1961); T. Keneally, *Schindler's List* (New York: Random House, 1979); P. Levi, *If This Is a Man; The Truce* (New York: Vintage, 1996); T. Mason, "Intention and Explanation: A Current Controversy about the Interpretation of National Socialism," in G. Hirschfeld and L. Kettenacket, eds., *Der "Fuehrerstaat": Mythos und Realitaet* (Stuttgart: Klett Cotta, 1981); W. Styron, *Sophie's Choice* (New York: Random House, 1979); E. Wiesel, *Against Silence: The Voice and Vision of Elie Wiesel,* I. Abrahamson, ed. (New York: Holocaust Library, 1985).

Chapter 9

191 Heinz Schirk: D. Patterson, *When Learned Men Murder* (Bloomington, Ind.: Phi Delta Kappan Educational Foundation, 1996), p. 26.

191 Dolph Schluter's program: J. Weiner, *The Beak of the Finch* (New York: Vintage, 1994), pp. 155–56.

195 "In the first section": E. Mihopoulos, "Invitation to the Death Camps: Review of *Dissonance—Robin Lakes's Rough Dance,*" *Chicago Reader,* June 1990.

196 George Steiner: See his *Language and Silence* (New York: Atheneum, 1967).

197 Milgram's obedience studies: See his *Obedience to Authority* (New York: Harper & Row, 1974).

199 On powerful analogies and metaphors, see B. Holland, "Mining Music and Law for Original Meanings," *The New York Times,* April 22, 1998.

Chapter 10

216 essential questions: See T. Sizer, *Horace's Compromise* (Boston: Houghton Mifflin, 1984) and *Horace's School* (Boston: Houghton Mifflin, 1992).

217 On disciplinary and interdisciplinary study, see H. Gardner and V. Boix-Mansilla, "Teaching for Understanding in the Disciplines—and Beyond," *Teachers College Record,* vol. 96, no. 2 (1994), pp. 198–218; V. Boix-Mansilla and H. Gardner, "Of Kinds of Disciplines and Kinds of Understanding," *Phi Delta Kappan,* vol. 78, no. 5 (1997), pp. 381–86; and V. Boix-Mansilla and H. Gardner, "On Disciplinary Lenses and Disciplinary Work." In S. Wineburg and P. Grossman, eds., *Interdisciplinary Encounters: A Second Look* (New York: Oxford University Press, forthcoming).

220 On communities of learning, see V. Battistich, D. Solomon, D. Kim, Marilyn Watson, and E. Schaps, "Schools as Communities, Poverty Levels of Student Populations, and Students' Attitudes, Motives, and Performance: A Multilevel Analysis," *American Educational Research Journal,* vol. 32, no. 3 (fall 1995), pp. 627–56; M. Scardamalia and C. Bereiter, "The CSILE Project: Trying to Bring the Classroom into World 3," and A. Brown and J. Campione, "Guided Discovery in a Community of Learners." Both in K. McGilly, ed., *Classroom Lessons* (Cambridge, Mass.: MIT Press, 1994), pp. 201–28, 229–70; J. Comer, *School Power: Implications of an Intervention Project* (New York: Free Press, 1980); and E. Schaps, "A Sense of Community Is Key to Effectiveness in Fostering Character Education," *Journal of Self Development,* vol. 17, no. 2 (1966), pp. 42–47.

223 On multiple pathways, see J. Katzman and S. Hodas, *Class Action* (New York: Villard Books, 1995).

228 Effective leaders: On leadership, see H. Gardner with E. Laskin, *Leading Minds* (New York: Basic Books, 1995).

230 On the ATLAS Communities Project, see C. J. Orell, "ATLAS Communities: Authentic Teaching, Learning and Assessment for All Students," in S. Stringfield, S. Ross, and L. Smith, eds., *Bold Plans for School Restructuring: The New American Schools Designs* (Mahwah, N.J.: Erlbaum, 1996), pp. 53–74. For additional information, write to ATLAS Communities, Education Development Center, 51 Chapel Street, Newton, MA 02158.

232 On dealing with setbacks, reflecting on experiences, and developing strengths, see H. Gardner, *Extraordinary Minds* (New York: Basic Books, 1997).

232 "make new mistakes": Esther Dyson had this message as a header on her electronic mail in 1997.

233 communities of caring: L. Darling-Hammond, *The Right to Learn: A Blue-print for Creating Schools That Work* (San Francisco: Jossey-Bass, 1997), and Battistich, Solomon, et al., op. cit.

233 There now exist many schools: See R. Brown, *Schools of Thought* (San Francisco: Jossey-Bass, 1993); J. Bruer, *Schools for Thoughts: A Science of Learning in the Classroom* (Cambridge, Mass.: MIT Press, 1993); E. Fiske, *Smart Schools, Smart Kids* (New York: Simon & Schuster, 1991); D. Perkins, *Smart Schools* (New York: Free Press, 1992); and Stringfield, Ross, and Smith, op. cit.

234 On change in education, see M. Fullan, *The New Meaning of Educational Change* (New York: Teachers College Press, 1990). On "learning organizations," see P. Senge, *The Fifth Discipline: The Art and Practice of the Learning Organization* (New York: Doubleday, 1990), and D. Schon, *The Reflective Practitioner: How Professionals Think in Action* (New York: Basic Books, 1983).

234 marked by "flow": M. Csikszentmihalyi, *Flow* (New York: HarperCollins, 1990).

235 "scaling up": R. Elmore, "Getting to Scale with Good Educational Practices." In S. Fuhrman and J. A. O'Day, eds., *Rewards and Reform: Creating Educational Incentives That Work* (San Francisco: Jossey-Bass, 1996), pp. 294–329.

235 quick jags: M. Neill, "High Stakes Tests Do Not Improve Student Learning," *Fairtest,* January 1998; see also D. C. Cohen and H. C. Hill, "State Policy and Classroom Performance: Mathematics Reform in California," *Consortium for Policy Research in Education Policy Brief,* RB 23 (January 1998), pp. 1–13.

Chapter 11

242 Darwin's ideas: See F. Sulloway, *Born to Rebel: Birth Order, Family Dynamics, and Creative Lives* (New York: Pantheon, 1996).

242 Committee of Ten: See D. Ravitch, *The Schools We Deserve* (New York: Basic Books, 1985).

243 so-called Stone Age persons: See D. C. Gajdusek, "Paradoxes of Aspiration for and of Children in Primitive and Isolated Cultures," *Pediatric Research,* vol. 27, supplement 59 (1990). See also G. Klein, "Proteus 2," in his *Live Now* (New York: Prometheus Books, 1996), pp. 85–164.

244 "And they are what we know": quoted in N. Frye, *T. S. Eliot: An Introduction* (Chicago: University of Chicago Press, 1963).

251 "Regardless of where I begin my thinking": V. Havel, Commencement address, Harvard University, June 15, 1995.

Name Index

Subject Index

About the Author

Howard Gardner is John H. and Elisabeth A. Hobbs professor of cognition and education and adjunct professor of psychology at Harvard University, adjunct professor of neurology at the Boston University School of Medicine, and codirector of Harvard Project Zero. The recipient of many honors, including twelve honorary degrees and a MacArthur Prize Fellowship, Gardner is the author of eighteen books and several hundred articles. In 1990, he was the first American to receive the University of Louisville's Grawemeyer Award in education. Gardner is best known in educational circles for his theory of multiple intelligences, a critique of the notion that there exists but a single human intelligence that can be assessed by standard psychometric instruments. During the past decade, he and colleagues at Project Zero have been working on the design of performance-based assessments, education for understanding, and the use of multiple intelligences to achieve more personalized curriculum, instruction, and assessment. Most recently, Gardner has been carrying out intensive case studies of exemplary creators and leaders; he and colleagues have launched an investigation of the relationship between cutting-edge work in different domains and a sense of social responsibility for the use and implications of that work. Gardner lives in Cambridge, Massachusetts.